Online Matchmaking

Online Matchmaking

Edited by

Monica T. Whitty
Queen's University Belfast, Northern Ireland, UK

Andrea J. Baker
Ohio University, USA

and

James A. Inman
University of Tennessee, USA

First published 2007 by
PALGRAVE MACMILLAN
Houndmills, Basingstoke, Hampshire RG21 6XS and
175 Fifth Avenue, New York, N.Y. 10010
Companies and representatives throughout the world

PALGRAVE MACMILLAN is the global academic imprint of the Palgrave
Macmillan division of St. Martin's Press, LLC and of Palgrave Macmillan Ltd.
Macmillan® is a registered trademark in the United States, United Kingdom
and other countries. Palgrave is a registered trademark in the European
Union and other countries.

ISBN-13: 978–1–4039–9849–1 hardback
ISBN-10: 1–4039–9849–3 hardback

This book is printed on paper suitable for recycling and made from fully
managed and sustained forest sources.

A catalogue record for this book is available from the British Library.

Library of Congress Cataloging-in-Publication Data
Online matchmaking/edited by Monica T. Whitty, Andrea J. Baker, and
    James A. Inman.
        p.   cm.
    Includes bibliographical references and index.
    ISBN-13: 978–1–4039–9849–1 (cloth)
    ISBN-10: 1–4039–9849–3 (cloth)
    1. Online dating.   I. Whitty, Monica T., 1969–   II. Baker, Andrea J.
    III. Inman, James A.
    HQ801.82.O55 2007
    306.730285′4678—dc22   2006050193

10   9   8   7   6   5   4   3   2   1
16   15   14   13   12   11   10   09   08   07

Printed and bound in Great Britain by
Antony Rowe Ltd, Chippenham and Eastbourne

Contents

List of Tables

Preface

Try to imagine a world without the Internet. Not so easy to do despite the relative newness of the technology. So many of us use email in our everyday working and personal lives. We surf the net for pleasure and for work. We often choose to send a text rather than phone a friend. We seek out romantic and sexual relationships online. In such a relatively short time in history the way we communicate, initiate, and form relationships has dramatically changed. Yet there are few academic books available that examine online relating.

Online Matchmaking began as a research project at the University of South Florida, where James Inman and several graduate students were researching online identities, especially the way that individuals choose to represent themselves. In this research, it quickly became clear that online personals offered one of the most compelling and intriguing examples. At that time, however, while useful research had been done across the disciplines, there was no simple way of pulling together those strands. Thus James and his colleagues decided to turn their efforts to assembling a collection that would make a positive difference for everyone interested in online matchmaking, and the book project was created.

Approximately a year and a half later, Monica Whitty and Andrea Baker became co-editors. The project was reconceptualised and a contract was secured with Palgrave Macmillan. Reviewing new contributions along with the writings of authors involved from the start of the project, the editors developed the framework that provided a good fit for the book. The first chapters define online matchmaking and highlight some of the questions researchers need to consider in this field. The chapters move forward to examine how online daters present themselves to potential partners. The book then turns to consider how relationships progress in cyberspace and how they often progress to face-to-face settings. Final sections cover the darker sides of online dating and subgroups of special populations of people meeting in cyberspace.

This book includes scholars from across the globe. The editors also live in different locations (Monica an Aussie living in Northern Ireland, and Andrea and James Americans residing in the Midwest and Southeast in the USA) and most of the construction and editing of the book took place in cyberspace. Something we took for granted.

Each contributor or set of co-authors wrote an original chapter especially for this collection of readings, based upon their own research. As the authors in this book demonstrate, the topic of online relating can be approached from a number of different disciplines. It is our hope that this will encourage further cross-disciplinary work in this field.

Working with these authors has been an interesting and rewarding experience. As editors we would like to thank them for their incredibly hard work and their willingness to be involved in what we believe is an important project. Personally it has enriched our own work and we hope that it will do the same for those who read this volume.

Monica T. Whitty
Andrea J. Baker
James A. Inman

Acknowledgements

We are so grateful to all of the contributors, who through their insight, creative ideas, and good research have helped make this volume a reality. Furthermore, we would like to thank the editors and staff at Palgrave Macmillan for their expertise in supporting this project. Finally, we would like to thank our families and friends for all of their love, support, and humour throughout this project.

Monica T. Whitty
Andrea J. Baker
James A. Inman

Notes on the Contributors

Julie M. Albright is a lecturer in Sociology at the University of Southern California, USA, and is a licensed Marriage and Family Therapist. Her research interests lie in the intersection of culture and communication, marriage and family, gender, and sexuality. She is currently working on a project on body image and plastic surgery makeover shows, which will result in an article and a documentary film for which she is Associate Producer. She is also writing several journal articles based on a large-scale study of sex and relationships online for *Elle* magazine.

Andrea J. Baker is a Sociology Professor at Ohio University, USA. She is co-editor of *Online Matchmaking* and has studied online relationships and communities since 1997. She teaches sociology to students online and offline, comparing student learning in each venue. Continuing areas of research interest include where and how people become attracted online, and how people developing close relationships communicate with each other in cyberspace, particularly in their expression of emotion.

William R. Cupach is Professor of Communication at Illinois State University, USA. His research pertains to problematic interactions in interpersonal relationships, such as embarrassing predicaments, relational transgressions, interpersonal conflict, and obsessive relational pursuit. He has co-authored or co-edited ten books and is a past President of the International Association for Relationship Research.

Dànielle Nicole DeVoss is an Associate Professor and Director of Professional Writing at Michigan State University, USA. DeVoss' research interests include computer/technological literacies; feminist interpretations of and interventions in computer technologies; philosophy of technology/technoscience; and online representation and embodiment. Her work has most recently appeared in *Computers and Composition*; the *Journal of Business and Technical Communication*; *Pedagogy: Critical Approaches to Teaching Literature, Language, Composition, and Culture*; *CyberPsychology*; and *Sexuality and Culture*.

Beverly Dolinsky is a Professor of Psychology at Endicott College, USA. She received her Bachelor of Arts in Psychology from UCLA. She holds a Master of Arts in Experimental Psychology from the California State

University-Sacramento. Her doctoral work was completed in the field of Social Psychology at the State University of New York at Albany. She has published in the areas of teaching pedagogy, higher education curriculum design and assessment, intimate relationships and health psychology. She is currently involved in research on the freshman year experience, general education models in higher education, and teaching methods in psychology.

Robin Hamman has been researching and writing about the online community since 1995 when he realised that the online world he'd been experiencing for ten years was often misunderstood by those outside it. Robin, who has published articles about life online in numerous books, magazines and newspapers, now works as a Senior Producer at the British Broadcasting Corporation (BBC). Robin blogs about online community management, citizen journalism and Internet law at cybersoc.com.

Alice Horning is a Professor of Rhetoric and Linguistics at Oakland University in Rochester, Michigan, USA. She teaches courses in reading, writing, psycholinguistics, language, and literacy development and directs the writing programme.

James A. Inman is at the College of Law, University of Tennessee, USA. He teaches and researches on rhetoric, technology, and pedagogy. His previous books include *Technology and English Studies: Innovative Professional Paths* (with Beth L. Hewett), *Computers and Writing: The Cyborg Era*, and *Electronic Collaboration in the Humanities: Issues and Options* (with Cheryl Reed and Peter Sands)

Robert A. Jerin is a Professor of Law and Justice, Endicott College, USA. He has published two books, numerous articles and chapters in Victimology. He is a life member of the National Organisation for Victim Assistance, the World Society of Victimology, is a board member of the American Society of Victimology, and a member of the National Center for Victims of Crime. Dr Jerin is also a recipient of the John P. J. Dussich award from the American Society of Victimology for his contributions to the field of Victimology.

Robin M. Mathy was a pioneer in conducting Internet-mediated research. She earned her BS *summa cum laude* in Sociology from the Arizona State University Honours College, and went on to earn graduate degrees in Sociology (Indiana University, Bloomington), Clinical Social Work (University of Minnesota, Twin Cities), Evidence-Based Health

Care (Oxford University), and International Relations (Cambridge University). She is the author or editor of four books and over 50 peer-reviewed articles, and is currently a doctoral candidate at Oxford University.

Katelyn Y. A. McKenna (Yael Kaynan) is a Senior Lecturer at Ben-Gurion University and at the Interdisciplinary Center Herzliya Israel in the departments of Communication. Her research interests are in the areas of relationship cognition, the self, and social identity, particularly in terms of their applicability to Internet interactions.

Susanna Paasonen is Assistant Professor in Digital Culture at the University of Jyväskylä, Finland. Her research interests include feminist theory, popular culture, and Internet research, and she is currently investigating online pornography. She is the author of *Figures of Fantasy: Internet, Women and Cyberdiscourse* (2005) and, together with Mia Consalvo, co-editor of *Women and Everyday Uses of the Internet: Agency & Identity* (2002).

Brian H. Spitzberg, School of Communication, San Diego University, USA, is co-author of two books on interpersonal communication competence, co-author of a book on stalking and unwanted relationship pursuit, and co-editor of three books on the dark side of communication and personal relationships, as well as numerous scholarly book chapters and articles on communication competence, conflict, jealousy, aggression, and stalking.

Jennifer Thalken received her BS in Sociology from the University of Nebraska at Kearney, in 2003. She obtained her MA in Sociology from California State University, Fullerton, in 2005. She is currently working on her Special Education Teaching Credential at National University, California, USA.

Monica T. Whitty was born and bred in Sydney, Australia and obtained her PhD in psychology from Macquarie University. She now resides in sunny Northern Ireland and is a lecturer in psychology at Queen's University Belfast. She is well-known for her research on Internet Relationships, and has co-written a book on the topic titled, *Cyberspace Romance: The psychology of online relationships*. Her current research interests include: online dating, Internet infidelity, identity, misrepresentation of the self online, cyber-ethics, and Internet and email surveillance in the workplace.

Diane Kholos Wysocki is a Professor of Sociology at the University of Nebraska at Kearney, USA. She has written a number of articles on Internet behaviour. Her areas of interest include sex, gender, sexuality, medical sociology, the Internet, and methodology.

1
Introduction

Monica T. Whitty

The courting process has taken on many different forms throughout history and across cultures. Sometimes romantic matches have been arranged, and at other times individuals have been free to choose their own match. Sometimes matches are based on reason, and at other times more on 'love'. One of the most significant changes in current times is the range of places individuals can potentially meet romantic partners.

In postmodern times individuals have a plethora of methods available to them to find their 'perfect match'. No longer are individuals limited to face-to-face chance meetings, such as the local pub, night clubs, and social gatherings. There are also more options available for those who prefer a more 'scientific' approach (e.g., video-dating), or a self-advertising approach (e.g., personal ads). We have the Internet to thank for many of these new opportunities to find romantic partners. The Internet has become a very popular place for singles to meet, so much so that Madden and Lenhart (2006) report that 74 per cent of single Americans searching for partners have used the Internet to facilitate their romantic pursuits.

Although the Internet has not been around for a long time, it is difficult to believe that the Web and the Internet were not originally created to link people. In the 1960s when the ARPANET was created (an earlier from of the Internet) the intention was to link computers to preserve data in the event of a military strike against a single geographic location. However, people quickly found a way to use such a system to also link individuals. As most readers would be aware, we have Tim Berners-Lee to thank for the World Wide Web. In 1993 we saw the first release of a commercial web browser and from that time onwards individuals 'began to embrace the technology as a means of communication as well as a way to initiate and develop relationships' (Whitty & Carr, 2006, p. 3).

So how do singles meet other singles online? Whitty and Carr (2006) in their book *Cyberspace romance: The psychology of online relationships* clearly point out that cyberspace is not one generic space and that there is an assortment of ways for singles to find romance on the Internet. How these relationships begin and progress vary depending on which space online we are referring to. So let us pause to consider some of these online matchmaking methods.

One of the earlier popular ways for singles to meet potential romantic partners online was through MUDs and MOOs. These were originally spaces where interactive role-playing games could be played. MUDS and MOOs are 'very similar to Dungeons and Dragons ... Participants appear as characters and communicate with other characters online. Many MUDs have hundreds of players logged in at the same time' (Whitty & Carr, 2006, p. 4). These places were set up purely as a way to play – but soon many of the players were playing another game – the game of love! Sonja Utz (2000), for example, found that 77 per cent of the MUD users in her study reported forming a relationship online that developed offline. Of these 25 per cent stated this was a romantic relationship.

Other places not originally designed for romantic matchmaking include chat rooms and newsgroups. A newsgroup is 'a continuous public discussion about a particular topic' (Whitty & Carr, 2006, p. 3) and is a form of asynchronous communication. The discussions can range from serious academic discussions, to discussions about people's hobbies and interests, fan discussions, or even discussions about people's favourite fetishes. No matter the type of discussion, relationships often form in these arenas, and again many of these turn into romantic relationships. Parks and Floyd (1996), for instance, found in their research on newsgroups that almost two-thirds of their sample (61 per cent) admitted to forming a personal relationship with someone they had met for the first time in a newsgroup. Of these, 8 per cent stated that this was a romantic relationship.

Chat rooms provide a space for individuals to engage in more synchronous communication. Moreover, when one types a message in this space, the message is typically visible to all other individuals in the chat room at the time. In addition, there are ways that individuals can communicate one-on-one or with select groups within the chat room. 'Most chat rooms have a particular theme, although this is not necessary. IRC (Internet Relay Chat) and ICQ (I seek you) are examples of chat systems' (Whitty & Carr, 2006, p. 3). Of course, friendships and romantic relationships form in these places too (Baker, 2002; Whitty & Gavin, 2001).

Places, such as MUDs and MOOs, newsgroups, and chat rooms, share something in common – much of the time, individuals are anonymous (i.e., they are unknown to one another face-to-face). Moreover, often these individuals are unaware of what others in the same space 'actually' physically look like. This obviously alters the dynamics of the relationship and how the relationship progresses. Researchers such as McKenna and Bargh have argued that given that physical appearance is often absent in spaces such as newsgroups and chat rooms, the way individuals 'get to know' one another within this space is a bit different to the way individuals 'get to know' each other face-to-face (Bargh, McKenna, & Fitzsimons, 2002; McKenna & Bargh, 2000; McKenna, Green, & Gleason, 2002). Individuals are more likely to open up in such spaces about very intimate and private aspects of their lives (Joinson, 2001; McKenna, this volume). Whitty (2003a, 2004a) contends that cyberspace can provide a safe space to 'play at love' and cyberflirt. She argues that although one might be able to actually see the physical body in some places online, the body still does matter. Individuals can potentially be more playful in cyberspace and can play with reconstitutions of the body, potentially inhabiting any body they desire. Whitty (2003a, Whitty & Carr, 2003, 2006) suggests that in cyberspace shy individuals might build up confidence to flirt and can potentially take these new-found skills offline.

There are, of course, other spaces online where individuals are often visually represented, for example, on websites, blogs, Friendster, Myspace, and online dating sites. Singles are clearly flocking to online dating sites and it would appear that there is much less of a stigma associated with those who use such sites than there was in the past. Yahoo.com claims almost 380 million visitors per month to their online dating site (Pasha, 2005), and FriendFinder.com claims to currently have over 2.6 million active members (Dating Sites Reviews.com, n.d.). Having visual information about someone online (as with face-to-face) can affect the judgements we make about someone and can play a deciding role in whether individuals want to get to know one another (Walther, Slovacek, & Tidwell, 2001; Whitty, 2003a; Whitty & Carr, 2006). Individuals on online dating sites, for instance, will often bypass a profile with a photo that they find physically unattractive (Whitty & Carr, 2006, Whitty, this volume).

This chapter began with making the claim that the Internet provides individuals with more 'scientific' ways to find their perfect match. Online dating sites are continuing to work on refining tools to match the most suitable people together. They do so by asking their clients to complete personality tests, as well as surveys on their interests and what aspects they are looking for in a partner. From there matches are often given compatibility ratings. Sometimes individuals seek out matches on the sites themselves and are given a compatibility rating with their choice; at other times the site plucks out a compatible profile from their database for individuals to consider. The question of course needs to be asked: Is there a real science to matchmaking? Many academics, and of course, online dating sites, hold hope that matchmaking can become more accurate. However, some would argue to do so the matchmaking tools need to consider both similarity and complementarity when it comes to finding the 'perfect' match (Houran, Lange, Rentfrow, & Brukner, 2004).

In addition to the general online dating sites that exist, such as, e-Harmony, True.com, Match.com, and so forth, there are also more specialised online dating sites which gather like-minded individuals together. For example, there are sites designed specifically for Christians, Jews, Vegans, Goths, or Spiritual people. Such sites are similar to social groups which one might join in the hope to find another that shares the same values or interests. Moreover, it potentially cuts out some of the work with the search for the perfect other.

Online matchmaking is not just about finding 'love', but is also about finding sexual partners to hook up with – either online or offline. Cyberspace allows individuals to locate others with similar sexual interests or fetishes. For example, sadomasochist sites abound on the Internet. There are also places online for those with more quirky fetishes to seek out others. Who will forget the self-confessed cannibal who managed to find a volunteer online to kill for his own sexual gratification? Cyberspace is also used by many to find available sexual partners in one's locality. This might be through bulletin boards, chat sites, or even some online dating sites. Gaydar, for example, has been embraced by the gay population in numerous countries as a means to finding either long-term romantic relationships or one-night stands.

Outline of our book

There is a gamut of pop psychology books on the market that attempt to explain the art of online matchmaking and the best strategies required to find one's perfect match online. There are now also a number of good academic books which have explored the phenomenon of cyberspace romance. This book adds to the academic field by considering online matchmaking through an interdisciplinary lens. The authors in this book are from a number of disciplines, including Communications,

Cultural studies, English, Health, Journalism, Psychology, Rhetoric, and Sociology. They present here their theories and empirical data on their examinations of romantic and sexual encounters in cyberspace.

This book has been divided up into a number of sections. In the first section, the authors define online matchmaking, and also provide a brief historical account of online matchmaking. This is followed by a section that considers how the self is presented in cyberspace to attract lovers. As a natural progression, we then consider how relationships develop online and move to the offline world. While of course cyberspace is potentially a safer and more playful space to play at love (Whitty, 2003a; Whitty & Carr 2003, 2006), the darker aspects of online dating cannot be ignored. Hence, we also consider the unique problems individuals might encounter while initiating and forming romantic relationships in cyberspace. Finally, we consider some sub-groups online and how these groups' dating strategies compare with more mainstream matchmaking methods.

Part 1: Defining online matchmaking

This book begins with a chapter written by Dànielle DeVoss. In Chapter 2 Devoss takes a big step back in the history of cyberspace, and examines online matchmaking on Bulletin Board Systems (BBS). The Bulletin Board System was one of the most popular spaces in cyberspace in the late 1980s to about the mid 1990s. They were a precursor to the modern form of the World Wide Web. Through some enlightening anecdotes, DeVoss provides accounts of how men and women interacted in this space. Unique to this space is the use of text to initiate a romantic match. How individuals play with text in this space to pursue or attract others is of interest. DeVoss, like others before her (e.g., Danet, 1998; Turkle, 1995), considers gender play in cyberspace. In line with previous theorists, she concurs that while there were (and obviously still are) many opportunities to play with gender online, that nonetheless, individuals still often re-enacted the same gender roles in cyberspace as they played out face-to-face. For example, women on BBS were more likely to talk about their personal relationships. In contrast, men on BBS, similar to the offline world, were more likely to be the pursuers of relationships and sex. BBS is not just unique in its structure but also in the types of people who inhabited this space. DeVoss is quick to point out that it was mostly men who interacted in this space. Through some interesting examples, she demonstrates how an imbalance of the genders sometimes gives rise to dysfunctional interactions.

Ever since the Internet has been in existence, researchers have been curious about the types of online sexual activities that take place in this space (e.g., Lipton, 1996). In Chapter 3 Hamman points out that cybersex is a very media friendly topic. One of the pioneering researchers in this field is, of course, the late Al Cooper. Cooper and his colleagues have examined the benefits and costs of engaging in sexual activities in cyberspace (e.g., Cooper, Delmonico, & Burg, 2000; Cooper, McLoughlin, & Campbell, 2000). They also found out what types of people are more likely to engage in online sexual activities (e.g., Cooper, Morahan-Martin, Mathy, & Maheu, 2002). In this chapter, Hamman adds to this growing field by presenting anecdotal stories of his own experiences and observations online during the early days of the Internet.

In Chapter 4 Susanna Paasonen considers women's experiences of using the Internet to find romance. Paasonen presents findings of her analysis of fictions, guidebooks, self-help, and advisory literature on online dating. She points out that these books are typically targeted at a female readership. This chapter addresses the ways in which these books define and frame the experience and function of women's Internet use, and the shape and form of the Internet as a medium. Similar to advice books on traditional offline dating, books on online dating encourage women to be passive and not too eager. They instruct women as to how they ought to communicate. For example, they suggest how long a woman ought to wait to reply to an email from a potential mate and what the content of their email should consist of. The literature Paasonen examines goes as far as telling women how to best write a cybersex dialogue, and how to essentially 'fake' it online.

Part 2: Presentation of self to attract lovers

The next section of our book considers presentation of self on the Internet to attract lovers. When it comes to online presentation of self, researchers have been interested in which types of selves are more likely to be presented in cyberspace (e.g., Bargh, McKenna, & Fitzsimons, 2002), and whether individuals are honest about who they really are in this space (e.g., Whitty, 2002). If the presentation of self online is inauthentic, then can 'real' relationships initiate or develop from there?

In Chapter 5, Monica Whitty outlines her '*BAR approach theory*'. She presents data from a telephone interview study that she conducted with 60 online daters. In agreement with other theorists (e.g., Bargh et al.,

2002), Whitty argues that cyberspace presents individuals with unique opportunities to present different aspects of themselves. Moreover, individuals can be very strategic in which self they elect to present (e.g., Walther, 1996). However, Whitty contends that which self is more likely to be presented, and which self is more likely to successfully attract an ideal romantic partner can vary depending on the space one is referring to. When it comes to online dating, Whitty shows that individuals are very aware of the need to construct a profile that not only attracts others, but will also attract their 'ideal' romantic partner. Her 'BAR approach theory' argues that a more successful profile is one that is able to create a nice balance between an 'attractive' and a 'real' self; that is, a self that they can live up to in the flesh and also one that is not too clichéd. Whitty warns us that savvy online daters are wary of profiles that claim to be charming romantics who enjoy strolls on the beach and sipping red wine.

Alice Horning, in Chapter 6, continues with the theme of presentation of self online. Horning makes some interesting comparisons between personal ads and job ads. She argues that a personal profile is in many ways similar to a résumé. According to Horning, although personal ads are typically longer than job ads, they both use some of the 'major rhetorical topoi or modes' described by rhetoricians. However, online personal ads and job ads are obviously different in many ways. For example, Horning argues that unlike job ads, online dating ads appeal to the emotions. Although not considered by Horning, one might also argue that in some ways personal ads can be quite similar to any other ad, in the way that they appeal to the emotions, making us feel that we must acquire the desired object – for example, an ad for an mp3 player, a car, or a house. Perhaps constructing a personal ad is like selling anything else? Horning suggests that job ads are more honest than personal ads. She also posits that despite their honest nature, some people who are clearly not qualified for the job will still apply. This could be equally applied to personal ads. As Whitty (2004b, Whitty & Carr, 2006) has found in her work – some online daters complain that despite their immense efforts to describe the exact date they are seeking out, the wrong candidates often still respond to their ads.

The final chapter in this section considers the maintenance of multiple simultaneous intimate relationships online. Offline, maintaining 50 romantic relationships at once would seem quite a feat; however, Julie Albright, in her chapter, explains the ease with which individuals are able to do this online. Albright's qualitative data presents clearly how individuals are prone to trusting others online, and the sometimes cunning ways individuals have deceived others in this space. In agreement with researchers like Walther (1996), Albright contends that individuals are very strategic in the ways they present themselves online and that these strategies potentially woo over more romantic partners than a person could potentially do face-to-face. She points out that the Internet provides individuals with a greater pool of others to form relationships with and that it is easy to co-ordinate online relationships. For example, a number of the men in her research admitted to using the 'cut and paste' method – that is, copying the same romantic message to multiple women. Of course the question that needs to be asked here is: Are online relationships 'real' relationships and if so is forming attachments online a 'real' act of infidelity if one is already in a relationship offline? Previous research suggests that acts, such as cybersex and falling in love online are considered by many to be real acts of betrayal if one is in an offline relationship (Whitty, 2003b, 2005). So while maintaining over 50 relationships online might appear to be just playing around in this space – this can potentially be considered as a 'real' relationship transgression that might indeed hurt one's offline partner.

Part 3: Online dating progression to face-to-face: Success or failure?

Part 3 of our book considers how relationships that initiate online progress offline. Is it possible for such relationships to move successfully offline? The research over the last decade or so suggests they can, but that some relationships do work better if they remain online (Whitty & Gavin, 2001). Perhaps this has something to do with what individuals self-disclose to one another online, the pace at which they do so, and individuals' expectations of each other when they first meet offline.

Andrea Baker, in Chapter 8, considers how people impart their emotions and feelings online. Social scientists are yet to come to any agreement as to how we should formally define an emotion. Do emotions have a cognitive and behavioural component? Are there basic emotions and are they universal? Ekman and his colleagues, for example, are well known for their work on the universality of emotions and have found high agreement across cultures in selecting emotion terms that fit facial expressions (Ekman, 1992, 1993; Ekman, Levenson, & Friesen, 1983). These researchers also contend that there are basic emotions, such as joy, sadness, and fear. Given the lack of facial expressions online are such emotions as easily recognisable in text? The emotions, as defined by Baker, that are focused on in this chapter include affection, support, longing, and apologies. From her analysis of emails between 14 couples she found that affection is often expressed through the use of nicknames and symbols, such as, x (kiss) and o (hug). Baker notes that couples often mirror each others' gestures in their emails to one another. Interestingly, Baker notes here, as others have before her (e.g., Levine, 2000; Whitty & Carr, 2006; Whitty & Gavin, 2001), the importance of writing style when it comes to attracting others online. Baker's results, in addition to those of other researchers in the field, seem to suggest that a different set of communication competence skills are required online in order to successfully woo another and to develop and maintain online romantic relationships.

Katelyn McKenna is well known for her important work on possible selves and online interactions. In Chapter 9, McKenna presents her views on how relationships initiate online and progress offline. In this chapter McKenna reminds us how previous theorists have drawn from Thibaut and Kelley's (1959) formulation of the 'stranger on the train' phenomenon to explain how individuals often communicate online. Thibaut and Kelley theorised that individuals are more likely to self-disclose intimate details about themselves to those whom they never expect to meet again (e.g., people like passengers on trains or taxi drivers). In a similar way, Parks and Roberts (1998) have argued that individuals self-disclose very personal details about themselves online to others they do not envisage meeting face-to-face. It is noteworthy that McKenna points out that even when people use their real names online and provide photographs of themselves, they still feel relatively anonymous or non-identifiable (e.g., in blogs). How people communicate online can be very different to the ways individuals might communicate face-to-face or on the telephone. McKenna contends that individuals have greater control in what they decide to present about themselves online compared to face-to-face interactions. This is because individuals have time to plan what they want to communicate and have time to edit their responses. Given these opportunities, individuals can be more strategic in which self they elect to present in cyberspace, and McKenna argues that in some spaces online individuals are better able to express their 'real self'. She reminds us of her previous research which found that individuals who expressed more of the 'real me' in newsgroups were more likely to form close friendships and romantic relationships with others online and successfully take this to the offline world. McKenna, akin to other researchers (e.g., Whitty, this volume; 2004b; Whitty & Carr, 2006) argues that this result may not hold when it comes to interactions between individuals in online dating sites.

Part 4: Darker sides of online dating

Of course a realistic picture of online matchmaking is not necessarily the utopian dream of finding your perfect partner and walking off into the sunset together. Part 2 of our book touched upon the problems with deception in cyberspace. Part 4 of our book considers the dark side of online relating in more depth.

Electronic communication can be used to harass people in both similar and new ways to offline traditional harassment. One of these more severe forms of harassment is cyberstalking. In Chapter 10 Brian Spitzberg and William Cupach discuss this darker side of online relating. Although a number of definitions have been offered for cyberstalking, perhaps the most comprehensive comes from Bocij (2004), who defines it as:

> A group of behaviors in which an individual, group of individuals, or organization uses information and communications technology to harasses another individual, group of individuals, or organization. Such behaviors may include, but are not limited to, the transmission of threats and false accusations, identity theft, damage to data or equipment, computer monitoring, solicitation of minors for sexual purposes, and any form of aggression. Harassment is defined as a course of actions that a reasonable person, in possession of the same information, would think causes another reasonable person to suffer emotional distress. (p. 14)

In this chapter, Spitzberg and Cupach summarise evidence from previous studies that have examined the number of people who have been harassed and stalked online, and how they were harassed and stalked. They report that some of the most common types of cyber-stalking tactics are sending exaggerated messages and tokens of affection in cyberspace, and counter-allegations of stalking.

Chapter 11 of our book, written by Robert Jerin and Beverly Dolinsky, focuses on perceived and actual victimisation risks found as result of a survey of women who have used online dating services. Akin to previous researchers, these authors argue that forms of cyber-victimisation include threatening email, unsolicited obscene email, receiving a multitude of junk e-mail (spamming), verbal online abuse (flaming), leaving improper messages on message boards, receiving electronic viruses, and being the subject of electronic identity theft. Of interest here is their finding that women who had been using an online dating service for longer than one year were more likely to experience verbal threats online. Many online dating sites try to educate their clients on how to safely use their service (e.g., by not giving out their home address, place of work, or home or work phone numbers). Jerin and Dolinsky report that it was the women who used online dating services for more than one year who were more likely to employ such safety measures.

Part 5: Online dating sub-groups

No book on online matchmaking would be complete without considering the various sub-groups that exist online. The cyber-world is not a generic space that everyone experiences the same way. Nor are the individuals who inhabit this space a homogeneous group. As mentioned earlier in this chapter, in addition to the mainstream online dating sites, there are online dating sites which target sub-groups of society, such as Christians, Vegans, Goths, and so forth. This final section of our book considers variations in online sexual activities by sexual identity and sexual orientation, as well as spaces where people with sadomasochistic fetishes interact.

Robin Mathy in Chapter 12 provides some descriptive statistics about heterosexual, homosexual, and bi-sexuals' online and offline sexual activity. Some interesting results emerged from her analysis of 6423 US participants' responses to a short survey. For instance, she found that gay and bisexual men spent more time online engaging in sexual activities compared to heterosexual men. Gay men were more likely than bisexual men to use the Internet to meet dates or arrange meetings for sex. Bisexual men were more likely than gay men to use the Internet to explore sexual fantasies. Lesbians and bisexual women were also more likely to engage in online sexual activities more than heterosexual women. Mathy believes that further research is needed to understand how individuals of different sexual orientations and identity use the Internet for online sexual activities and matchmaking.

As is argued in a number of the chapters in this book, in many ways cyberspace can be a safer space to play at love and sexuality. In our final chapter, Diane Wysocki and Jennifer Thalken consider sexual behaviours of sadomasochists on the Internet. These researchers analysed the desires and characteristics of individuals who have placed advertisements on an alternative adult personals web page. In their analysis they describe the different types of sadomasochistic behaviours that individuals engage in. For instance, they found that about a third of individuals on the site were interested in role playing (e.g., role playing nurses/doctors, rape scenes, and nun/priest play). Wysocki and Thalken report that more women than men preferred the submissive role and more men than women were willing to switch between being dominant and submissive. They argue that the most common reason people gave for using the site was to meet people who had the same specific fantasies and desires, but that the ultimate goal was to live these fantasies out with others from the site face-to-face.

Collectively, the chapters in this book represent a showcase of that which is currently internationally known about online matchmaking. We all come from different academic disciplines; however, we would all concur that just as with the offline world there are both joys and disappointments when it comes to online relationships.

References

Baker, A. J. (2002). What makes an online relationship successful? Clues from couples who met in cyberspace. *CyberPsychology & Behavior, 5* (4), 363–75.

Bargh, J. A., McKenna, K. Y. A., & Fitzsimons, G. M. (2002). Can you see the real me? Activation and expression of the 'true self' on the internet. *Journal of Social Issues, 58* (1), 33–48.

Bocij, P. (2004). *Cyberstalking: Harassment in the internet age and how to protect your family*. Westport, CT: Praeger.

Cooper, A., Delmonico, D. L., & Burg, R. (2000). Cybersex users, abusers, and compulsives: New findings and implications. *Sexual addiction and compulsivity, 7*(2), 5–29.

Cooper, A., McLoughlin, I. P., & Campbell, K. M. (2000). Sexuality in cyberspace: Update for the 21st century. *CyberPsychology & Behavior, 3* (4), 521–36.

Cooper, A., Morahan-Martin, J., Mathy, R. M., & Maheu, M. (2002). Toward an increased understanding of user demographics in online sexual activities. *Journal of Sex Marital Therapy, 28* (2), 105–29.

Danet, B. (1998). Text as mask: Gender, play and performance on the internet. In S. G. Jones (ed.), *Cybersociety 2.0: Revisiting computer-mediated communication and community* (pp. 129–58). Thousand Oaks, CA: Sage.

Dating Sites Reviews.com (n.d.). Retrieved 13 April 2006, from: http://www.datingsitesreviews.com/staticpages/index.php?page=2010000100-Friend Finder

Ekman, P. (1992). An argument for basic emotions. *Cognition & Emotion, 6*, 169–200.

Ekman, P. (1993). Facial expression and emotion. *American Psychologist, 48* (4), 384–92.

Ekman, P., Levensen, R. W., & Friesen, W. V. (1983). Autonomic nervous system activity distinguishes between emotions. *Science, 221*, 1208–10.

Houran, J., Lange, R., Rentfrow, P. J., & Bruckner, K. H. (2004). Do online matchmaking tests work? An assessment of preliminary evidence for a publicized 'predictive model of marital success'. *North American Journal of Psychology, 6*, 507–26.

Joinson, A. N. (2001). Self-disclosure in computer-mediated communication: The role of self-awareness and visual anonymity. *European Journal of Social Psychology, 31,* 177–92.

Levine, D. (2000). Virtual attraction: What rocks your boat. *CyberPsychology & Behavior, 3,* 565–73.

Lipton, M. (1996). Forgetting the body: Cybersex and identity. In L. Strate, R. Jacobson & S. Gibson (eds), *Communication and cyberspace: Social interaction in an electronic environment* (pp. 105–20). Cresskill, NJ: Hampton Press.

Madden, M., & Lenhart, A. (2006, March). *Online dating.* (Pew Internet & American Life Project). Retrieved 22 March 2006, from: http://www. pewinternet.org/pdfs/PIP_Online_Dating.pdf

McKenna, K. Y. A., & Bargh, J. A. (2000). Plan 9 from cyberspace: The implications of the internet for personality and social psychology. *Journal of Personality and Social Psychology, 4,* 57–75.

McKenna, K. Y. A., Green, A. S., & Gleason, M. E. J. (2002). Relationship formation on the Internet: What's the big attraction? *Journal of Social Issues, 58,* 9–31.

Parks, M. R., & Floyd, K. (1996). Making friends in cyberspace. *Journal of Communication, 46* (1), 80–97.

Parks, M. R., & Roberts, L. D. (1998). 'Making MOOsic': The development of personal relationships online and a comparison to their off-line counterparts. *Journal of Social and Personal Relationships, 15,* 517–37.

Pasha, S. (2005, August). Online dating feeling less attractive. *CNN/Money,* 18 August 2005, Retrieved 13 April 2006 from: http://money.cnn.com/ 2005/08/18/technology/online_dating/index.htm

Thibaut, J., & Kelley, H. (1959). *The social psychology of groups.* New York: Wiley.

Turkle, S. (1995). *Life on the screen: Identity in the age of the Internet.* London: Weidenfeld & Nicolson.

Utz, S. (2000). Social information processing in MUDs: The development of friendships in virtual worlds. *Journal of Online Behavior, 1* (1), Retrieved 7 February 2005 from: http://www.behavior.net/JOB/v1n1/utz.html

Walther, J. B. (1996). Computer-mediated communication: Impersonal, interpersonal and hyperpersonal interaction. *Communication Research, 23,* 3–43.

Walther, J. B., Slovacek, C., & Tidwell, L. (2001). Is a picture worth a thousand words? Photographic images in long-term and short-term computer-mediated communication. *Communication Research, 28,* 105–34.

Whitty, M. T. (2002). Liar, Liar! An examination of how open, supportive and honest people are in Chat Rooms. *Computers in Human Behavior, 18* (4), 343–52.

Whitty, M. T. (2003a). Cyber-flirting: Playing at love on the Internet. *Theory and Psychology, 13* (3), 339–57.

Whitty, M. T. (2003b). Pushing the wrong buttons: Men's and women's attitudes towards online and offline infidelity. *CyberPsychology & Behavior, 6* (6), 569–79.

Whitty, M. T. (2004a). Cyber-flirting: An examination of men's and women's flirting behaviour both offline and on the Internet. *Behaviour Change, 21* (2), 115–26.

Whitty, M. T. (2004b). Shopping for love on the Internet: Men and women's experiences of using an Australian Internet dating site. *Communication Research in the Public Interest*: ICA, New Orleans, USA, 27–31 May 2004.

Whitty, M. T. (2005). The 'Realness' of Cyber-cheating: Men and women's representations of unfaithful Internet relationships. *Social Science Computer Review, 23* (1), 57–67.

Whitty, M. T. & Carr, A. N. (2003). Cyberspace as potential space: Considering the web as a playground to cyber-flirt. *Human Relations, 56* (7), 861–91.

Whitty, M. T. & Carr, A. N. (2006). *Cyberspace romance: The psychology of online relationships.* Basingstoke: Palgrave Macmillan.

Whitty, M. & Gavin, J. (2001). Age/Sex/Location: Uncovering the social cues in the development of online relationships. *CyberPsychology and Behaviour, 4* (5), 623–30.

Part 1

Defining Online Matchmaking

2
From the BBS to the Web: Tracing the Spaces of Online Romance

Dànielle Nicole DeVoss

There are three assumptions I would like to start with: First, the Internet and its big sister, the Web, have affected and altered the shape and pace of modern society and the everyday lives of many. Second, previous technologies leave traces behind – traces of the social, cultural, and historical worlds out of which they emerged. Third, the larger cultural trajectory in which the Web exists is the postmodern condition of contemporary life.

First, that the Internet has altered the course of modern life is a given. The Internet poses murky legal questions (related, for instance, to personal privacy, intellectual property issues, and much more), emerging and evolving social mores, and revolutions in literacies and skills. Second, and further contextualising this chapter, is the fact that the past emerges in the present. In visible and invisible ways, the past emerges within the technology itself – within interfaces, across online documents, and embedded deep inside of web pages. Crucial to understanding the development of the Web is understanding the technologies remediated within and upon it. The Web evolved as a part of the Internet, and the Internet bears traces of similar and earlier communication technologies. One particular technology that ran tandem with and affected the ecology of the Internet is the computer bulletin board system. Third, emerging technologies, rapidly changing global conditions, and the seemingly paradoxical but real shrinking *and* expansion of the world has altered the shape of our lives. The conditions of our lives have been locally and globally altered by changes in economic structures, trends in globalisation, and transformations of information and communication technologies (Castells, 1997; Mann, 1994). These interconnected and interarticulated conditions have encouraged many of us to resituate our social and romantic interactions; our desires and romantic relationships have been digitally dispersed – no longer are they reliant upon nor do they emerge within geographical proximity.

Whereas the conditions of modernism and the 18th- and 19th-century world typified the self as individual, stable, unified, and inherently understandable, changes in economy, globalisation, the rapid spread of technological change, and a variety of other interconnected and interarticulated forces have required us to shift our understandings of the self (Castells, 1998; Mann, 1994). Cooper (1999) associated this shift in our approaches to subjectivity with 'the changed circumstances of our lives ... and our adaptations to these circumstances' (p. 142). These changed circumstances include the (at least partial) dissolution of many of the networks that previously provided a sense of identity and meaning for us (such as, family and church) and the rise of different networks, such as the Web, for which we only have partial intellectual, cultural, emotional, and rhetorical tools at our disposal to navigate.

Out of this political, social, and cultural landscape, new understandings of and approaches to subjectivity arise. Theories of the self that allow us to better understand identity, subjectivity, and agency recognise the self as complex, sometimes contradictory, and shifting. This more complicated notion of self is better suited to the complications of our postmodern world. Our subjectivity and identities shift as we enter into and negotiate different social spaces, both physical and digital. Across and within these spaces, we are multiply and contradictorily constituted at any given moment, with emergent and competing values, desires, and responsibilities. Further, as scholars like Bakhtin (1993) and Cooper (1999) pointed out, these new forms of identity are formed dynamically and constantly in dialectical exchanges with multiply constituted others.

Combine these three initial assumptions and it is obvious that we must develop a more complex and complete picture of how individuals have adjusted – and continue to adjust, especially in terms of the everyday issues and activities that, unfortunately, are often contextualised as 'mundane,' including instant messaging, blogging, using digital dating sites, creating and updating personal web spaces, and so forth. Although these paths and traces are complex, we *can* – and, indeed, should – better understand the history of virtual spaces, how this history may shape user experiences, and how this history affects user representations of their identities, subjectivities, sexualities, and agencies.

Fortunately, recent scholarship has exploded notions of the everyday, and rhetorics and research of everyday practices are beginning to flourish (e.g., de Certeau, 1988; Grabill, 2003; Johnson, 1998; Nystrand & Duffy, 2003; Suchman, 1987). One crucial everyday practice is, of course, the development and sustenance of romantic relationships. Here, I focus on the interconnected and interarticulated conditions of the Web and postmodernity, and how our desires and romantic relationships have been digitally dispersed – no longer are they reliant upon nor do they emerge within geographical proximity or at traditional sites of affiliation (e.g., church).

Specifically, I explore how user profiles at a specific digital site rhetorically reproduce *and* rupture historical conventions of romance, sexuality, and identity, and offer a picture of postmodern love dispersed in, across, and through digital contexts. The analyses offered here allow for a discussion of how, when, why, and where these sites both reproduce and rupture conventions of romance, sexuality, and identity and how, when, why, and where these sites allow users a space to rhetorically and digitally construct *alternate* romantic and sexual identities.

Bulletin board systems as historical context

A brief overview of bulletin board systems

'Culture is a slingshot moved by the force of its past.'

(Kingsolver, 1990, p. 528)

'Simulation and fantasy merge with "reality" as BBS generated personas with disembodied anonymity join dreams, create mutual adventures, share secrets, lies, personal disclosures, and act on each other in cyberspace.'

(Wiley, 1999, p. 135)

Remarkably little work has been done on bulletin board systems (BBS) and the culture surrounding them. BBSs are, in today's terms, an archaic communication technology, but a technology that held great power in certain technological and social circles in the 1980s and early 1990s. Some large-scale Internet service provider systems began primarily as BBSs (e.g., America Online and Prodigy), although all have long since either disappeared or become more than anything else interfaces for and portals to the larger Internet and the Web.

BBSs allowed direct access from one computer to another computer, typically via single-line systems: Only one user could be online at a time. Users would post messages in forums areas (some moderated by a systems operator, others unmoderated), then would return later to read responses. Software configured on the SysOp's computer provided a very-basic, text-only interface. Users could leave messages in private or public message forums. The private message forums were much like the email systems of today, but with no global addressing. Instead, messages left on a BBS remained stationary on that system and users had to dial in directly to that system to access their messages. Public message forum areas were typically organised by the SysOp into themes or topics, such as, general, political issues, personal rants, adult topics, movies and music, and so forth. Users dialled in, connected, and could scan and reply to new and existing messages. They would then logoff, disconnect, and the next user could connect. Certainly, these spaces – even bearing in mind user attempts to push at the text-only conventions – looked and felt very different from the robust digital-visual spaces of the web today.

Primarily the realms of young, white men, females were often flamed (see Brown 1996; Chapman, 1995; Minerd, 2000; Schwartz, 1994; Sproull & Kiesler, 1991; Tamosaitis, 1994; Welch, 1997) or even kicked off BBSs if they did not conform to expected norms. At the same time that virtually mouthy women were quickly verbally attacked and, at other times, entirely ignored, they were also sexually pursued. 'Helpful' male users would virtually pursue women, offering support and guidance to those who seemed lost in the system or confused. Male users would often become angry when the women they were helping did not reciprocate in sexual or romantic ways online. Michele Le Doueff (1990) argued that 'the less need we have for this kind of support ... the more intensively we find this tutelage being pressed on us' (p. 199). The result was that women often spent their virtual time declining offers of help (often rooted in the assumption that female users can't possibly know what they are doing) or declining sexual advances.

The evolution of a digital-social realm

The social world of BBSs drastically changed in the early 1990s, when smaller systems began to disappear as more and more users moved onto the Internet (especially into Internet Relay Chat or IRC). Those BBSs that survived the radical shift to the Internet and then later to the Web survived, typically, only if they offered more than one-line access. With multiple lines, teleconferencing or synchronous chatting became the norm – rather than the earlier norm of asynchronous message boarding. Previous to the multi-line systems, male users had little to gain performing virtual drag on most BBSs, as women's status was relatively low in this realm. However, as systems grew and BBSs became larger and supported more phone lines and synchronous chat spaces, many systems converted to use-for-pay systems. Previously, few of the one-line, local BBSs required any sort of payment – most could be accessed and used for free; the BBS software used was typically shareware or freeware, and the only cost was that of a phone line. Installing more modems, expanding hard drives, and purchasing commercially produced BBS software, however, came with a sizable cost, cost that translated to user fees. Users who purchased online time typically purchased chunks of time referred to as 'credits'. Importantly, credits could be transferred to other users. Because women were so rare – a study I conducted on a local BBS in 1993 revealed that of the 800 users, 96 per cent were male – so valued (at least sexually), and so aggressively pursued in this realm, male users would often create pseudonymous accounts and pose as female users in order to manipulate male users to transfer credits to them (DeVoss, 1993). They would then transfer those credits from their fake female accounts into their main, male-identified accounts.

What is particularly interesting on BBSs is the lengths that men would go to online to 'prove' themselves as women and to obtain credits. Sexually explicit chatting and email between male users and male users *representing as* females was a normal online occurrence. Surprisingly, there is little scholarly evidence or discussion of men masquerading as women online and creating elaborate relationships within this space (although Turkle, 1995, provided some examples of this, and Ross, Månsson, Daneback, & Tikkanen, 2005, report on sexual activity).

The most stunning instance of a BBS user being publicly outed that I can recall was an instance of a female user. Her handle was Princess and within four months of her initial login, several male users had broken off relationships with girlfriends, one had asked for a divorce from his wife, and countless others had fallen deeply in love with Princess' online persona. Her registry claimed that she was 5'1", a 'curvaceous' 102 pounds, had deep brown eyes, and waist-length black hair. She flirted online, and male users would virtually fight to enter her private chat room. As online time passed, the men she was so eloquently seducing in cyberspace desperately wanted to meet her and made louder and more frequent demands indicating their desire for a face-to-face meeting. Over and over again, she resisted their efforts to entice her off the BBS and into physical public space. She wrapped herself in an elaborate story – that she was hiding from a violent ex-husband who was involved in organised crime, and although the FBI and local authorities would allow her to chat with a pseudonym online, she wasn't allowed to give out her real name, phone number, address, or to actually meet anyone.

Somehow, however, one of the more aggressive male users (one who had broken up with his girlfriend to virtually court Princess), found out where she lived. He encouraged another online admirer of Princess to come to her house with him to confront her, and they both knocked on her door one night, only to find her the exact opposite of her online identity, as the heart-broken and bitter men later described her in teleconference. They reported her to be phenomenally hefty, incredibly ugly, partially toothless, and surrounded by a gaggle of children – the stereotypical antithesis of the online persona she had created.

Digital gender play

Some theorists have suggested that online gender play offers virtual inhabitants access to becoming Other. For example, gender choices in MUD/MOO systems often offer such options as neuter, male, female, either, Spivak, plural, and so forth. Enacting another gender online might allow a user to explore what it 'feels like' to be something other (McRae, 1996). But adopting a different gender does little to change the actual gendered representations and realities of everyday life; as Kendall (1999) argued, 'choosing a gender, even a neutral gender, doesn't free people from standard gender expectations' (p. 218). In fact, men exploiting the BBS systems and attempting to convince other men to transfer credits to them commonly chose to represent themselves as stereotypical bombshells. The physicality of the 'real' body does not escape any online user; Turkle referred to this as a 'curiously irrational preoccupation of attempting to orient oneself by figuring out others' genders' (p. 211). Rather than freeing us from gender codes, gender play often further solidifies gender, and reproduces gender codes by dramatisng our attachment to them. This is part of the gender trouble we experience in online spaces.

I tell these stories and cite these theorists not to make any grand claims about gender performance online, but instead to make two points: First, I tell these stories to paint a picture. This brief overview of BBSs and discussion of gender play creates a sketch of online life at a particular time – a time certainly easy to forget as we zoom forward in terms of technology. Second, although I agree with Stone, McRae, and other theorists who explore and sometimes celebrate gender play online and the representation and enactment of multiple identities, I do so with hesitation. Wiley (1999) romanticised online bulletin board systems in one of the few academic pieces about them, noting that 'newly generated personas – faceless, voiceless, bodiless – displace history with a timeless present and multiple selves easily co-exist with the flick of a finger' (p. 135). Clearly, although we can celebrate gender play and freedom from the trappings of gender in online space, we can never leave our material bodies behind – just as we can never entirely leave behind the traces of earlier technologies and our uses of earlier technologies.

Romance in digital, postmodern spaces

Sexuality and conditions of romance have always been porous, negoti-ated, and culturally scripted. Digital spaces – the Web being the most dominant today – make up a progressive geography in which to view some of the contemporary negotiations and related transformations of romance, sexuality, and identity.

Both Castells (1997) and Giddens (1992) noted the process of sexual autonomisation occurring within the postmodern context. This process includes the delinking of sexuality with heterosexuality, marriage, and the activities associated to the roles women historically have been resigned to within various social institutions. In becoming sexually autonomous and in asserting control over sexuality, sexual activities, and reproductive possibilities,

> feminists and sexual identity movements affirm the control of their most immediate spaces, their bodies, over their disembodiment in the space of flows, influenced by patriarchalism, where recon-structed images of the woman, and fetishes of sexuality, dissolve their humanity and deny their identity. (Castells, p. 358)

The spaces of sexual autonomisation further de-link sexuality – from physical trappings, geographical barriers, and other constraints of face-to-face romance. Online, men and women are free to rewrite the scripts of conventional, traditional relationships.

Research in online romance

Research has explored a variety of aspects of digital romance. Merkle and Richardson (2000), for instance, analysed psychological factors influencing relationship formation and dissolution, and suggested that the 'developmental and behavioral sequence of online relationships is different from that of face-to-face relationships' (p. 188). The research of

Whitty and Gavin (2001), however, reported on interviews with subjects regarding their online relationships, and concluded with the general suggestion that the same ideals valued in face-to-face relationships are valued in online relationships (e.g., trust, honesty, commitment). These researchers responded specifically to earlier research indicating that online relationships are shallow and meaningless because they lack the bandwidth of face-to-face, 'real' relationships (Slouka, 1995). The earlier research conducted in the late 1980s and early 1990s by researchers, such as, Slouka (1995), however, is marked by the fact that it was conducted on the pre-visual, text-only Internet; whereas, the research conducted later by Whitty and Gavin (2001) reported on relationship dynamics that took place in the robust visual, multimedia space of the World Wide Web. Part of the relationship 'bandwidth' is certainly access to a variety of multimodal means of communication, and with the Web, individuals can share pictures, videochat, and so forth.

Research has also focused on the larger context and dynamics within which digital romance unfolds; Cornwell and Lundgren (2001), for instance, found that involvement (commitment and seriousness) tended to be lower in cyberspace, whereas misrepresentation (age and physical) tended to be higher. Other researchers have studied the relationship formation of youth and young adults (Bonebrake, 2002; Wolak, Mitchell, & Finkelhor, 2002, 2003). Other studies have addressed a range of factors related to online relationship formation (see, for instance, Anderson, 2005; Baker, 1998; Donn & Sherman, 2002; Ward & Terence, 2004; Wildermuth, 2001).

Identity formation and affiliation on bulletin board systems

I want to return to the BBSs of the past to read users' registry entries and to suggest that many of the women users were constructing alternate representations of themselves – identities that ruptured the ways in which they were more conventionally seen within technological systems. This analysis of registry entries provides an admittedly technologically dated but rich read of how we might approach and read the user entries on online dating sites and within other contemporary web-based romance spaces.

On one of the large-scale, multi-line BBS systems I used, approximately 1,000 users had public registry entries. The registry area is a public information space, where users have the option of completing a profile of themselves for other users to read. As the introductory screen to the registry area of Cyberspace BBS stated, 'the Registry of Users helps you get to know other users of this system. And, you can describe your-self, so that others can get to know YOU' (Anonymous, Cyberspace Bulletin Board System, n.d). This, of course, is an interesting claim in a space where virtual representations can be constructed to contradict with physical/real representations.

Users could not manipulate the categories within the public registry database; they did have some freedom, however, in how they chose to complete the categories. 'Categories are: Name, Sex, Age, Aliases, City/State, Voice #, Physical Discription [*sic*], BBS Run, BBS #, Computer owned, Favorites (Movie, Food, Music, Drink, TV Show, Sport), Hobbies, General Info, and Summary' (Anonymous, Cyberspace Bulletin Board System, n.d). Manipulation of responses occurred most often seen in the Sex category, where users disrupted the expected options (M or F) to include entries ranging from A, C, N, Q, S, T, -, *, !, ., ~, and the ever popular 'Y.' Entries in the age category include OO, ??, 2*, um, 4X, », Gr, ol, and so forth. (Most of these can be read as humorous or resistant responses to listing actual age or designating either M or F.)

In reviewing the archived registry entries of the 245 female users on Cyberspace BBS, several trends emerge. Overwhelmingly more than the men, the women often described themselves in the 'Physical Discription [*sic*], Hobbies, General Info and Summaries section' (Anonymous, Cyber-space Bulletin Board System, n.d), in relation to their roles as wives and mothers. Although several male users did note their marital or parent status in their registry entries, far fewer did than women. Examples of male users doing so include:

Broken Glass (M, -9), Summary: i love Jessica
Crazy Bill (M, 30), General Info: I'M GOIG TO MARRY THE MOST BEAUTIFUL LADY!!!!!!!; Summary: IM HERS AND I LOVE IT!!!
Prospero (M, 33), General Info: My kid is great and my wife is too. So There!
(Anonymous, Cyberspace Bulletin Board System, n.d).

Women much more frequently report their relationships in registry entries, some defining themselves in relationship to apparently failed romantic relationships. Squeaky (F, 20), noted in her registry Summary that her 'ex-fiancé sucks'. Sweetheart (F, 19) included in her Phys-ical Discription [*sic*] 'guess not good enough your with someone else =('(Anonymous, Cyberspace Bulletin Board System, n.d). AnneRKey (F, 22), constructed a morbid poem out of her registry entry, which read (pieced together from each section entry):

so many times they play with
my mind. I cried for daysweek
months Telling me
they loved me
Maybe it would have been simpler just to hear five simple words 'I
just want to f**k' then maybe I could hav
blacked out let
them desecrate my
body and feel
.... nothing afterward
.... to stop the pain
.... tears
.... blackness
.... I felt when they loved me
.. Ciao
(Anonymous, Cyberspace Bulletin Board System, n.d)

Certainly, there are a variety of possible reasons for women defining and describing themselves in relation to their partners.

It's particularly interesting, though, that the women often include this description in the 'Physical Discription [sic]' (Anonymous, Cyberspace Bulletin Board System, n.d) category. First, the women might have found that reporting their marital or relationship status in their registry entries kept overzealous men from barraging them with virtual come-ons (incredibly common on BBSs and in online chat spaces). Mazzy Star's (F, 18) General Info statement attested to this: 'Yes I have a boyfriend, No I don't wanna go out on a date' (Anonymous, Cyberspace Bulletin Board System, n.d). Tiger Lily (F, 19) also noted 'I have a Boyfriend' (Anonymous, Cyberspace Bulletin Board System, n.d). Skittles (F, 43) took another approach and noted in her 'Physical Discription [sic]' (Anonymous, Cyberspace Bulletin Board System, n.d) section 'Old & Fat...don't bother' (Anonymous, Cyberspace Bulletin Board System, n.d). Second, women are socialised to put their relationships first and often themselves and their interests second. In this context, it's not surprising that women define themselves in relation to their sexual others, putting them first. Le Doueff (1989) described this as 'the loss of self implied in the female condition' (p. 183). Furthermore, more traditional women might define themselves much more strictly based on their relationships to their boyfriend or husband.

Some women define themselves not in terms of their current romantic relationships – those that often reveal their path to computers via their sexual partners – but instead noted their single – and looking – status:

> Black Cat (F, 24), Physical Discription: Sweet Kind And Looking for a nice guy
> BlueBird (F, 24), General Info: i like to have a good time, and am looking for a good man
> Rainbow (F, 28), General Info: I'm a single person.
> Scissors (f, **), Physical Discription: Single
> Teen Angel (F, 15), General Info: Just a girl that's new to town and looking for
> some guys and something to do
> (Anonymous, Cyberspace Bulletin Board System, n.d)

Some registry entries reveal women who had broken out of the roles women were virtually relegated to; Bogam (F, 19) noted in her General Info summary that 'a person defines themself. By thoughts, words, actions' (Anonymous, Cyberspace Bulletin Board System, n.d). Akasha (F, 21) joked in her General Info section: 'a guy walks into a bar with a chicken under his arm…' (Anonymous, Cyberspace Bulletin Board System, n.d), and also noted in the Summary line that 'someone once told me I was the devil' (Anonymous, Cyberspace Bulletin Board System, n.d). Fourteen-year-old Amity (F) listed her Hobbies as 'reading, cyber, writing, and ummm i dunno yet' and noted in her 'General Info' section that she has 'been online for 2 years now' (Anonymous, Cyberspace Bulletin Board System, n.d). Angel (F, 23) suggested in her Computer owned section 'a piece of crap'(Anonymous, Cyberspace Bulletin Board System, n.d), and Angelfire (F, 21) notes that her Computer owned is 'mine' (Anonymous, Cyberspace Bulletin Board System, n.d). Maynerd (F, 00) declared that she's a 'happy, fiesty harley riding kind of gal (Anonymous, Cyberspace Bulletin Board System, n.d) in her 'Physical Discription section' (Anonymous, Cyberspace Bulletin Board System, n.d), and summarised herself as 'goin for it :)' (Anonymous, Cyberspace Bulletin Board System, n.d).

Shifting dynamics of online romance: some implications

> 'The things we call "technologies" are ways of building order in our world.'
> (Winner, 1999, p. 32)

Because of the ways in which relationship development has changed shape, and because of the explosion of online dating sites and other romance-related spaces accessible via the Internet and the Web, and because the conditions of our lives have evolved, it is crucial that we deeply interrogate contemporary technologies and also look to past technologies to best anticipate the changes that new technologies will bring.

To do so, no one method of data is enough – we need narratives and stories, quantitative and qualitative research. Also, and not surprisingly, we need more long-term data. The Internet has been in popular use for a relatively short time, and the Web has only existed since 1992, and been a popular medium since approximately 1995. We often piece apart technologies in fairly unsophisticated and simplistic ways. For instance, we choose a space and study that particular space without considering related dynamics – studying a dating-based website without paying attention to how users also connect using instant messaging or even cell phones with cameras built-in. Studying the larger context of communications technologies will, admittedly, expand the focus and complexity of research, but will allow for a larger window through which we can observe and better understand how it is people establish, build, and sustain relationships. Our research frames are often constrained in that we bring a lens developed for the study of face-to-face, traditional interactions modes to cyberspace. We have not yet fully explored the multiple, rich, multimodal ways people create cues, sustain interaction, and develop intimacy in digital and electronic spaces. Tending to these core questions will provide for rich and productive research in the years that come, within the digital spaces that emerge.

References

Anderson, T. L. (2005). Relationships among Internet attitudes, Internet use, romantic beliefs, and perceptions of online romantic relationships. *CyberPsychology & Behavior, 8* (6), 521–31.

Baker, A. (1998, July). Cyberspace couples finding romance online then meeting for the first time in real life. *CMC Magazine*. Available: http://www.december.com/cmc/mag/1998/jul/baker.html

Bakhtin, M. M. (1993). *Toward a philosophy of the act* (Vadim Liapunov, trans., Vadim Liapunov & Michael Holquist, eds). Austin: University of Texas Press.

Bonebrake, K. (2002). College students' Internet use, relationship formation, and personality correlates. *CyberPsychology & Behavior, 5*, 551–7.

Brown, A. (1996). Flaming Nora! *New Statesman, 128*(4467), 112–13.

Castells, M. (1997). *The power of identity.* Oxford: Blackwell.

Castells, M. (1998). *End of millennium.* Oxford: Blackwell.

Chapman, G. (1995). Flamers: Cranks, fetishists and monomaniacs. *The New Republic, 212*(15), 13.

Cooper, M. (1999). Postmodern pedagogy in electronic conversations. In G. E. Hawisher & C. L. Selfe (eds), *Passions, pedagogies and 21st century technologies* (pp. 140–60). Logan, UT: Utah State University Press.

Cornwell, B., & Lundgren, D. C. (2001). Love on the Internet: Involvement and misrepresentation in romantic relationships in cyberspace vs. realspace. *Computers in Human Behavior, 17*, 197–211.

Cyberspace Bulletin Board System: BBS (n.d.). Registry entry introduction text. Retrieved 1 January 1997.

de Certeau, M. (1988). *The practice of everyday life.* Berkeley: University of California Press.

DeVoss, D. N. (1993). *Gender dynamics on Bulletin Board Systems: A review and research report.* Unpublished manuscript.

Donn, J., & Sherman, R. (2002). Attitudes and practices regarding the formation of romantic relationships on the Internet. *CyberPsychology & Behavior, 5*, 107–23.

Giddens, A. (1992). *The transformation of intimacy: Sexuality, love, and eroticism in modern societies.* Stanford: Stanford University Press.

Grabill, J. T. (2003). On divides and interfaces: Access, class, and computers. *Computers and Composition, 20*(4), 455–72.

Johnson, R. R. (1998). *User-centered technology: A rhetorical theory for computers and other mundane artifacts.* Albany: State University of New York Press.

Kendall, L. (1996). 'MUDder? I hardly know 'er!' Adventures of a feminist MUDder. In L. Cherny & E. R. Weise (eds), *wired_women: Gender and new realities in cyberspace* (pp. 207–23). Seattle: Seal Press.

Kingsolver, B. (1990). *The poisonwood bible.* New York: HarperPerennial.

Le Doueff, M. (1989). *Philosophical imaginary.* Palo Alto: Stanford University Press.

Mann, P. (1994). *Micro-politics: Agency in a postfeminist era.* Minneapolis: University of Minnesota Press.

McRae, S. (1996). Coming apart at the seams: Sex, text, and the virtual body. In L. Cherny & E. R. Weise (eds), *wired_women: Gender and new realities in cyberspace* (pp. 242–64). Seattle: Seal Press.

Merkle, E. R., & Richardson, R. A. (2000). Digital dating and virtual relating: Conceptualizing computer mediated romantic relationships. *Family Relations, 49*(2), 187–92.

Minerd, J. (2000). The rise of cyber civility. *The Futurist, 34*(1), 6.

Nystrand, M., & Duffy, J. (eds). (2003). *Towards a rhetoric of everyday life: New directions in research on writing, text, and discourse.* Madison: University of Wisconsin Press.

Ross, M. W., Månsson, S., Daneback, K., & Tikkanen, R. (2005). Characteristics of men who have sex with men on the Internet but identify as heterosexual, compared with heterosexually identified men who have sex with women. *CyberPsychology & Behavior, 8* (2), 131–39.

Schwartz, G. (1994). Flame off Internazis! *Computer Life, 1*(2), 38.

Slouka, M. (1995). *War of the worlds: Cyberspace and the high-tech assault on reality.* New York: Basic Books.

Sproull, L., & Kiesler, S. (1991). *Connections: New ways of working in the networked organization*. Cambridge, MA: MIT Press.

Stone, A. R. (1995). *The war of desire and technology at the close of the mechanical age*. Cambridge: MIT Press.

Suchman, L. (1987). *Plans and situated actions: The problem of human/machine communication*. Cambridge: Cambridge University Press.

Tamosaitis, N. (1994). Getting flamed isn't funny: Online insults leave targets feeling singed. *Computer Life, 1* (3), 207.

Turkle, S. (1995). *Life on the screen: Identity in the age of the Internet*. New York: Touchstone.

Ward, C. C., & Terence, J. G. T. (2004). Relation of shyness with aspects of online relationship involvement. *Journal of Social and Personal Relationships, 21*(5), 611–23.

Welch, J. (1997, 12 June). Electronic menaces are a flaming liability. *People Management, 3*, 14.

Wildermuth, S. M. (2001). Love on the line: Participants' descriptions of computer-mediated close relationships. *Communication Quarterly, 49*(2), 89–96.

Whitty, M., & Gavin, J. (2001). Age/sex/location: Uncovering the social cues in the development of online relationships. *CyberPsychology & Behavior, 4*(5), 623–30.

Wiley, J. (1999). NO BODY is 'doing it': Cybersexuality. In J. Price & M. Shildrick (eds), *Feminist theory and the body* (pp. 134–40). London: Routledge.

Winner, L. (1999). Do artifacts have politics? In Donald MacKenzie & Judy Wacjman (eds), *The social shaping of technology* (2nd edn). Buckingham: Open University Press.

Wolak, J., Mitchell, K., & Finkelhor, D. (2002). Close online relationships in a national sample of adolescents. *Adolescences, 37*, 441–55.

Wolak, J., Mitchell, K. J., & Finkelhor, D. (2003). Escaping or connecting? Characteristics of youth who form close online relationships. *Journal of Adolescence, 26*(1), 105–19.

3
Cyborgasms: Ten Years On and Not Enough Learned

Robin Hamman

In 1996 I completed the first in-depth ethnographic study of cybersex chat and published it online as 'Cyborgasms: Cybersex Amongst Multiple-Selves and Cyborgs in the Narrow-Bandwidth Space of America Online Chat Rooms'. Since that day, the page has received over a million visits and I have received hundreds, perhaps thousands, of emails from readers in response. The paper made a huge splash at the time and I continue to be regularly contacted by journalists, researchers, students, and cybersex participants who have found the study online and want to know more. 'Cyborgasms' wasn't about pornography, nor was it about sexual exploitation or sexual abuse, but about digitally mediated consensual sexual experiences. At the time I wrote 'Cyborgasms', the study was groundbreaking, and not just because it had a catchy title and was about an emerging form of sexual practice. It was also a direct challenge to 'the media myth' of the time, later noted by Howard Rheingold, that to others, 'people who used computers to communicate ... were pencil-necked nerds, totally lacking in social skills, whose online communications are robotic and unemotional' (Rheingold, 1998).

Despite the phenomenal rise and acceptance of the Internet as a communications tool since 'Cyborgasms' was written in 1996, little more is known today about what is likely to be an activity that millions have participated in. Recent changes in the technologies, software, and devices used to enable digitally mediated communication mean that more people have access from more places to consensual participatory sexual experiences than ever before.

Sexuality is, of course, a highly charged subject and 'Cyborgasms' not only acknowledged the existence of sex online but used it to demonstrate that people could and were having undeniably powerful communal experiences online. It showed that, while many of the

31

approximately 40 respondents who took part in online interviews and answered email questionnaires were indeed people who had recently become socially isolated after moving home, starting a new job, or graduating from university, their sexual experiences online were almost all positive, reaffirming and pleasurable. The demographics of the participants in the study, and the fact that many of them were socially isolated individuals, at least offline, did make me worry that if it were not for their computers and their access to the Internet, some of these individuals would feel lost. That is that there was a danger they had become so dependent upon the Internet for aspects of their lives that they were becoming cyborgs. I did not mean, of course, that they were actually becoming machines like in a scene out of a science fiction novel, but that they would be unable to experience their entire selves were it not for the interplay between their psyche and the Internet. Science fiction author William Gibson coined the term cyberspace to explain the 'consensual hallucination' that occurs when people extend their bodies and minds into computer created space (Gibson, 1984, p. 51).

Citing field research in cyberspace was not without controversy at the time. Sherry Turkle, one of the leading Internet researchers at the time, warned that 'virtual reality poses a new methodological challenge for the researcher: what to make of online interviews and indeed, whether and how to use them' (Turkle, 1995, p. 324). Sandy Stone, on the other side of the fence, suggested that there were very real benefits to conducting Internet based research, when she wrote 'The floppy disk has become the cyber-anthropologist's field notebook; in virtual social environments nothing escapes its panoptic gaze' (Stone, 1995a, p. 190).

Since the mid-1990s, more and more social scientists have turned their attention towards the Internet and the social structures that emerge there. The website of the Association of Internet Researchers, an 'academic association dedicated to the advancement of the cross-disciplinary field of Internet studies,' now claims to have 1000 members of its email list and my own cybersociology announcement list has just under 2000 members. Indeed, as the number of Internet users has grown exponentially, so too has the number of people actively involved in the research of life online which has led to great leaps in our understanding of the social aspects of Internet use.

Through the many studies that have been published, as well as our own personal experiences, we mainly take it for granted, these days, that people can and do build real friendships and communities online. But back in 1996, when I began researching and writing about life online, the idea that people could use the Internet to make real friends and build communities was still quite novel. The handful of social scientists and theorists looking at the Internet feared it would have a disruptive influence, making its users socially isolated and potentially harming existing communities (Hamman, 1996). Ten years on, many of us have become even more dependent upon the Internet for our daily tasks, an increasing number of which can in fact only be accomplished online. Although there are people worrying about the digital divide, that those who are not online will be left behind by those who are, there are few, if any, who would now suggest that using the Internet is isolating or damaging to one's social network. The anecdotal evidence, as well as landmark studies such as those conducted as part of the ongoing Pew Internet and American Life Project, overwhelmingly demonstrate the opposite: that families use digital communications to increase their level of connectedness, that work colleagues arrange drinks after work via email, and that many people at least know of someone who met their current partner online. Perhaps we should still worry about our increasing dependence upon our computers and the Internet, if only to remind ourselves to back up our contacts database, emails and passwords from time to time.

Thus, we have learned, over the years, that the Internet can and does allow people to make new connections or maintain existing ones. Social scientists have also learned to use the Internet as a research and publishing tool as well as a site for field research in its own right. As Internet use has grown to near ubiquity in western countries, many individual members of the public have become more dependent upon the Internet to facilitate various daily tasks ranging from contacting a friend, applying for a job, finding government information, or even purchasing groceries. There are more people online, and more social scientists researching what they do there, yet today we know little more about people's consensual participatory sexual experiences online than we did ten years ago.

Defining cybersex

One of the first things I noticed, when I began conducting research as a participant observer in the chat rooms where I'd decided to site my research, was that although the names of dozens of users appeared listed in the chat room, very few people actually seemed to be chatting publicly or, if they were, they usually only did so for a few minutes soon after they arrived. As soon as I realised that there was a hidden world online, one where hundreds, and probably thousands, of people experimented with aspects of their sexuality and engaged in new forms of sexual activity, I began the task of researching and describing that world at depth for the first time. I did this by starting with a definition that was specific enough to exclude pornography, various forms of sexual exploitation and sexual abuse from the scope of the study. I wrote:

> There are two forms of cybersex that originate in online chat rooms. The first form is computer mediated interactive masturbation in real time. In this form of cybersex, users type instructions and descriptions of what they are 'doing' to each other and to themselves while masturbating. They often type using one hand while masturbating with the other. The second form of cybersex identified here is the computer mediated telling of interactive sexual stories (in real time) with the intent of arousal. (Hamman, 1996)

Today, if I were asked to define it again, I would say that cybersex is any consensual, computer mediated, participatory sexual experience involving two or more individuals. This definition, it should be said, is only a different, perhaps more sophisticated, way of saying the same thing as before.

Although this was, as far as I am aware, the earliest attempt at defining cybersex, I certainly was not the first social scientist to note that people were engaging in sexual behaviour in social environments online. A year earlier, cyber-theorist Sandy Stone had alluded to the hidden world of cybersex when she wrote 'Work there, play there, love there – but if you have sex in cyberspace, be sure to always use a modem' (Stone, 1995b, p. 405). A short time before I published 'Cyborgasms' online, Nguyen and Alexander wrote that '50,000 now engage in daily cybersex using up to 700 real-time chat lines [chat rooms]' and that such activity was often satisfying enough to 'evoke physical orgasm' (1996, p. 116). By the time I wrote 'Cyborgasms,' journalists too were starting to notice that something sexual was going on online. In an article titled 'Trail of Cyber-sex, Lies and Floppy Disks Ends in Divorce Suit', Ian Katz, writing for the *Guardian*, wrote that online services 'have become the singles bars of the 1990's' (Katz, 1996).

Cybersex: form and function

In 1996 the format for cybersex, as shown in the study, was fairly straightforward. Participants met in one of the public spaces of the Internet, most often a chat room, and after a bit of public conversation they 'went private'. They'd often exchange photos and chat privately before initiating a sexual experience, most often referred to as 'cyber'. The experience itself would usually involve creating a shared, imaginary setting, placing the participants there together as if characters in a novel, or would be based on a real place as described by one of the participants.

It is important to note that, outside of exchanging digital photos of themselves, the actions leading up to and culminating in cybersex were, in 1996, almost exclusively limited to text. This was because the use of audio and video over the Internet wasn't yet reliable or widespread and most users had insufficient Internet bandwidth to cope with more than text and a few low resolution images. In 'Cyborgasms,' much importance had to be placed on explaining how these limitations affected the participants, their actions, and their perception of their actions:

Stone makes an important distinction between face-to-face communication and computer-mediated communication. Stone explains that

> Reality is wide-bandwidth, because people who communicate face to face in real time use multiple modes simultaneously – speech, gestures, facial expression, the entire gamut of semiotics ... Computer conferencing is narrow-bandwidth, because communication is restricted to lines of text on a screen. (Stone, 1995a, p. 93)

In narrow-bandwidth computer-mediated communications, important information is missing.

Because interactions online took place in what Stone called 'narrow-bandwidth,' users frequently misinterpreted one another. Emoticons, now commonly referred to as 'smileys,' developed to help avoid misinterpretations caused by the limitations of text only communication. Quoting Reid (1991), I wrote (Hamman, 1996):

> Reid explains the need for users of online technologies to create new ways of transmitting this important information, 'Smiles, Frowns, tones of voice, posture and dress – Geertz's 'significant symbols' – tell us more about the social contexts we are placed in than do the statements of the people we socialise with ... Communication and cultural context must be expressed through new channels, and new systems of meaning must be forged by virtual denizens who wish to make sense of and to one another.'

There were also positive aspects of narrow-bandwidth text based communication, particularly that it that it afforded users an anonymous distance from each other, enabling them to experiment with aspects of their identity, creativity, and sexuality that they wouldn't normally feel comfortable expressing in situations where they were more readily identifiable. Several respondents in 'Cyborgasms' explained that anonymity had helped them to overcome deeply rooted sexual fears and anxieties. One was able to experience positive sexual behaviour for the first time following her sexual abuse as a child, another long after a painful divorce destroyed her confidence. It is undeniable that, in these and circumstances like them, exploring and experiencing sexual feelings within the safety net of anonymity is beneficial, and perhaps life changing. I also came across the use of anonymity for negative purposes – a man who would pretend to be a woman while engaging in cybersex with other men. His goal and purpose was, by revealing that he was a man just before or at the moment of orgasm, to cause his victims to question their sexuality. To him it was like being in a videogame but, far from being just a bit of mischief, his behaviour may very well have caused some of his victims to feel uneasy about their sexuality, potentially having life-long implications.

Cybersex engages participants' interpretive creativity. As Stone suggested, and the participants in my study confirmed, the effect of narrow bandwidth communication is often to 'engage more of the participants' interpretive facilities [enabling] ... client and provider to mobilize erotic tension by taking advantage of lack – filling in missing information with idealized information' (Stone, 1995a, pp. 92–5).

This enhanced engagement of interpretative facilities is important both at the beginning of the cybersex act, where participants often imagine themselves within a scene of their creation, as later in the act, where most participants imagine themselves and their partner being with and touching each other physically. It adds to their enjoyment of their time together, and for many is essential to the sexual act itself. The creation of an idealised other, some aspects real, the others coming from one's desires and fantasies, is one reason why people who meet online then meet offline sometimes find it difficult to match the two – something some of the other chapters in this collection address.

The (slightly) changing face of cybersex

Ten years on, the development of new features offered by websites has changed some aspects of the typical format for cybersex. These days, the initial contact is much more likely than in the past to be made on a dating website or one of the social networking websites that have recently become so popular, particularly Myspace and Facebook. Internet market research from Comscore Media Matrix showed that between February 2005 and February 2006, the fastest growing sectors of the Internet were social networking and blogging sites. Myspace increased its traffic by 318 per cent over that time, turning it into one of the Internet's busiest websites (Walker, 2006). The format is, however, still pretty much the same: they might approach the other participant by posting a public comment on their profile, move on to private messages, email, or instant messenger, then have cybersex. For a time in the late 1990s I managed the UK's first anonymous SMS chat service. The pattern of meeting in a public room then moving on to a private conversation was immediately recognisable – all that had changed was the device being used to send and receive messages. Even more recently, footballer David Beckham was reported to have had 'text sex' with Rebecca Loos. What's interesting about this is that when various tabloids in the UK broke the story, they didn't feel it necessary to provide much, if any, explanation as to what text sex actually entails. I suspect the editors assumed it was a term that had entered the public consciousness, if not the vocabulary, and thus didn't warrant much by way of explanation. Ordinary people now have at least a vague understanding of what cybersex is.

As technology has advanced, the number of platforms enabling cybersex has also increased and, today, some participants use text messages, camera phone images and video, webcams, voice over IP (VOIP) and other technologies.

Both in 1996, as today, cybersex needn't always involve masturbation but it frequently does. Cybersex, like any consensual sexual activity, or solitary masturbation, often ends with an orgasm. That said, not all orgasms are equal and although Rebecca, one of the respondents to 'Cyborgasms' reported that she preferred cybersex to solitary masturbation, she also explained that 'physical sex is beyond a doubt 100 percent better, more pleasing and more satisfying'.

Moving forward

Because cybersex often does involve masturbation, there was in 1996, and remains today, a social stigma attached both to its discussion and exploration within the Internet research community. I have to admit that, ten years on, I am sometimes forced into a blush when someone points out the topic of my most widely read research or when a journalist asks if I have ever had cybersex myself. It is a shame that most of us, including the vast majority of social scientists, are unable or unwilling to openly discuss and learn about sexual behaviour – but what we're missing out on is much more than just knowledge about sex. Cybersex is, as 'Cyborgasms' demonstrated, an excellent vehicle for the investigation of identity, of gender as a social construct, and of desire and pleasure in a mediated environment. Cybersex is a tool that social scientists and theorists have yet to capitalise upon in creating a greater understanding of not just life online, but of our social structures and who we are as humans.

Another compelling reason for social scientists to begin working towards a greater understanding of cybersex is that it is likely that ever increasing numbers of teenagers and young people will have their first sexual experiences, the ones that will shape their sex lives forever, online. To understand so little about something so formative is potentially dangerous.

For the increasing numbers of participants, cybersex is about using the Internet to come together intimately online and explore, with another, issues of identity, gender, sexuality, desire, fantasy, and pleasure. Likewise for social scientists, the investigation of cybersex provides an excellent, and perhaps unique, opportunity to explore these very issues yet, as in 1996, cybersex remains today mostly hidden from view and misunderstood.

References

Gibson, W. (1984). *Neuromancer*. New York: Bantam.

Hamman, R. (1996). *Cyborgasms: Cybersex amongst multiple-selves and cyborgs in the narrow-bandwidth space of America Online chat rooms*. MA Thesis, University of Essex. Retrieved 15 April 2006, from: http://www.cybersoc.com.

Katz, I. (1996, 3 February). Trail of cyber-sex, lies and floppy disks ends in divorce suit. The *Guardian*.

Nguyen, D. T., & Alexander, J. (1996). The coming of cyberspacetime and the end of the polity. In Rob Shields (ed.), *Cultures of Internet: Virtual spaces, real histories, living bodies* (pp. 99–124). London: Sage.

Reid, E. M. (1991). *Electropolis: Communication and community on Internet relay chat*. Honours Thesis, University of Melbourne (au). Retrieved 15 April 2006 from: http://www.ee. mu.oz.au/papers/emr/electropolis.html.

Rheingold, H. (1998, 26 Oct.). Misunderstanding new media. *Feed Magazine*. Retrieved 15 April 2006, from: http://www.feedmag.com/essay/es102lofi.html.

Stone, A. R. (1995a). *The war of desire and technology at the close of the mechanical age*. London: MIT Press.

Stone, A. R. (1995b). Split subjects, not atoms, or how I fell in love with my prosthesis. *The cyborg handbook*. Ed. Gray, et al. London: Routledge. 393–406.

Turkle, S. (1995). *Life on the screen: Identity in the age of the Internet*. New York: Simon and Schuster.

Walker, L. (2006, 4 April). New trends in online traffic: Visits to sites for blogging, local information and social networks drive web growth. *Washington Post*, p. D01.

4
Scripting the Rules for Mars and Venus: Advice Literature and Online Dating

Susanna Paasonen

An Amazon.com search for 'guide to online dating' produces tens of hits ranging from *Online Dating for Dummies* and *Complete Idiot's Guide to Online Dating and Relating* to titles targeted at Christians, teens, seniors, lesbian, gay, bisexual, and straight users, and people in recovery. This plethora of advice literature – in addition to novels, films, TV programmes, and articles on the topic – corresponds to the multitude of online dating services developed during the past decade. The books outline basic principles of online dating, available solutions, and netiquette. In addition, they provide guides in self-improvement in the tradition of self-help literature, which according to Lichterman (1992) is 'as old as the American republic' (p. 421). Combining popular psychology with technical advice, real-life stories of online dating, and pairing, these titles describe the differences and benefits of online dating compared to more traditional personal ads or singles clubs.

Matchmaking sites are relatively novel arena for dating practices that have been historically intertwined with consumerism. In addition to entertainment (films, dinners, dances, and tourism), consumerist ties of dating have included the market for guidebooks and thera-peutic discourses advising partners in desirable behaviour and self-management (Illouz, 1997). Advice books on online dating are part of this continuum, but they are equally guides on Internet usage: different safety precautions, interaction styles, tactics of self-representation, the potential dangers and possibilities of cybersex, and real-life encounters (see Paasonen, 2005 for a longer discussion).

This chapter focuses on advice books on online dating that, like rela-tionships advice literature in general, are targeted primarily at a female readership, and especially to women over 30 years (Miller & McHoul, 1998; Potts, 2002). The titles addressed include advice books, such as,

Bank's (1996) *Love online*, Fein and Schneider's (2002) *The rules for online dating*, Rabin's (1999) *Cyberflirt*, and Sabol's (1999) *You've got male.* Guidebooks are also considered, such as Blackstone's (1998) *Virtual strangers*, Lynn's (2005) *The sexual revolution*, Semans and Winks' (1999) *The woman's guide to sex on the web*, and Skriloff and Gould's (1997) *Men are from cyberspace.* In addition, narratives written in an autobiographical or diary form are considered, such as Fletcher's (1997) *E-mail, a love story*, Purnell's (1998) *Dating.com*, and Singer's (2000) *Diary of an Internet junkie.* Published from 1996 to 2005, the books span a decade during which the available online dating services have undergone radical transformations and expansion, yet there is consistency in their rhetoric and themes. My interests lie especially in ways that these titles negotiate the contradictions between self-management and the scripts of romance.

The title of this chapter refers to two influential series of self-help titles of the last decade, namely John Gray's Mars and Venus books (starting with *Men are from Mars, women are from Venus*, 1992, his series includes seven other volumes) and Ellen Fein and Sherrie Schneider's *Rules* books (in addition to *The Rules*, 1995, these include three other titles). I do not argue that similar reductionism would be the norm in advice literature discussed here, but that these titles have considerable influence on the scripts employed for making sense of romance and relationships. Like the *Mars and Venus* and *Rules* books, the advice books have been published in the United States. Although distributed and translated internationally, they are embedded in culturally specific discourses on gender and dating.

Therapy and romantic advice

Romance is one of the central themes, or even constituents, of contemporary popular culture and personal narratives or 'life stories'. Romance involves culturally available scripts concerning romantic situations, moments and expressions of emotion (Langford, 1999; Duncombe and Marsden, 1995). Jackson (1995) points to this, arguing that '[w]e create for ourselves a sense of what our emotions are, of what being in love is, through positioning ourselves within a discourse, constructing narratives of self, drawing from whatever cultural resources are available to us' (p. 58). This chapter considers advice books as cultural resources that provide scripts for narrating and making sense of online encounters and emotional investments. In what follows, I investigate their employment of discourses of therapy and personality management, as well as their ways of balancing romance and sexuality.

The authors of the books in my sample generally take the role of an educator, describing dilemmas of online dating and advising their readers in a manner of relationships experts. Hence, they follow the general position of advice books authors as 'emotional investment counsellors' who tell different exemplary or cautionary stories based on their own experiences or those of interviewees (Hochschild, 1994). Sabol (1999) writes of having dated 67 men via the Internet within two years, while the books in diary form list these encounters as logs (Purnell, 1998; Singer, 2000). Lynn (2005) also assures her readers that she knows whereof she speaks: 'Cybersex, online dating, connecting with lovers across the country – I've sampled them all' (p. 3). Radner (1995, p. 37) identifies the use of 'the voice of private and personal experience' as a criterion of validity widely employed in the self-help genre and its vocabulary. Authors' experiences of online dating, relationships, and self-discovery authorise them as people who are able to advise others.

The advice literature tends to be connected by a therapeutic ethos of self-help articulated as inner growth, 'healing', and self-discovery that cuts across the genre boundaries of fiction, self-help, and guidebook literature. Several of the items address personal problems, such as, addictive behaviour or marital crisis. In *You've got male*, Sabol (1999) describes her process of overcoming an abusive marriage, divorce, eating disorders, and low self-esteem with the aid of online dating. The Internet – with its dating, relationship, and romance possibilities – becomes a way out from a dissatisfactory life.

Advice books on online dating border on self-help, especially when addressing addiction (Fletcher, 1997; Sabol, 1999; Singer, 2000). Online dating is depicted simultaneously as a means of overcoming personality disorders and as a potential addiction in itself. Sabol (1999) provides twelve reasons to stop overeating and advices in healthier eating, while Singer (2000) depicts recovery from overeating, engagement in twelve step programmes, sponsoring others online and addiction to online dating. Katherine, the protagonist of Stephanie Fletcher's (1997) novel *E-mail: A love story*, is a housewife and married to a career-oriented husband whom she rarely sees. She struggles with a history of eating disorders, low self-esteem, and an acute sense of loneliness. In order to overcome these, she joins an adult bulletin board service and establishes intimate exchange of email, photographs, and erotic stories with screen names Buck and John. The gallery of characters also includes Carol, who is able to overcome her violent marriage thanks to an increased self-esteem found from an online relationship, and William Ramsay, the online counsellor who helps Katherine to solve her personal problems.

After Katherine's graphic exchanges are revealed to her husband, she decides to recommit herself to her marriage, enter couple therapy, and let her user account expire. In her goodbyes to her online friends Katherine explains that as her healing has begun, she no longer needs her online community membership:

> I have used my sexuality and I have used you, John, to try to fill the gaping hole inflicted by my self-loathing... My addiction relieved me from the misery of my depression. What I really needed was to simply let go of the idea I am not lovable, and it was much easier than I thought to do that. (Fletcher, 1997, p. 246)

Online affairs help Kathleen to lose weight, find inner balance and even rediscover desire in her marriage. After these achievements, there is no need to participate in online communities. Similarly, an interviewee in Blackstone's (1998) *Virtual strangers* describes her extra-marital cyber-affair as 'healing of my soul, a completing of my heart' (p. 181). In both these examples, the self is improved, 'healed', and found through online romance. Online dating partners are cast in a somewhat instrumental role in a process of managing the – ultimately damaged, vulnerable and fragile – self.

Banks (1996) describes discovering her suppressed spiritual, emotional, and sexual needs while looking for a partner online and suggests that successful romancing necessitates introspection. While this idea of self-knowledge as precondition for finding love has also been widely circulated in romantic fiction (Neale, 1992), I would argue that this emphasis draws from the terminology and logic of therapeutic culture, as analysed by Furedi (2004). Therapeutic rhetoric postulates a self at risk, in need of emotional expression and professional advice. The genre of online dating books makes full use of the rhetoric, describing damaged individuals in need of therapy and positioning authors as people able to help. In the books, relationship problems are sorted out in counselling and couple therapy; addictions and eating disorders are tackled with; staple reference is made to twelve step programmes; self-knowledge is gained through introspection; and the question of self-esteem – the preoccupation with which Furedi (2004, p. 153) identifies as 'the single most powerful illustration of the impact of therapeutic culture on everyday life' – resurfaces in one title after another.

According to Furedi (2004), love remains a cultural ideal and a source of self-fulfilment but is paradoxically seen as potentially addictive and harmful to the self. In the examples discussed above, online dating enables maintaining distance and instrumental interaction with romantic partners: while these may disturb the process of self-management, they are not able to disrupt it. Advice books emphasise the centrality of emotions for self-development and dating, yet provide highly rationalised and mechanical solutions to these emotional needs. Tyler (2004) notes that similar 'Taylorist' logic is widely employed in self-help books and lifestyle journalism that advice their readers in more effective, controlled, or efficient management of relationships.

The terminology of efficiency, rationality, and effortlessness is central in comparisons made between online dating and face-to-face methods: online, there is an abundance of available men merely a click away (Skriloff & Gould, 1997); online interaction is easy to control; it enables trying out different interaction tactics (Rabin, 1999), and focusing on mutual values and interest rather than signifiers of wealth (Banks, 1996); online dating is 'easy, affordable and fun' (Sabol, 1999), 'effective, easy, inexpensive, and at your fingertips 24 hours a day' (Fein & Schneider, 2002, p. 6). Readers are advised in managing their online dating partners, to avoid excessive, insecure, and therefore unwise emotional invest-ments before the time is ripe. Do this and the male partner will express signs of commitment.

The compulsive game of Mars and Venus

The books firmly promote belief in true love online. Although roman-cing may be depicted as troubled and failing to culminate in a happy ending, this does not curb enthusiasm over the possibilities of online dating. Narrative trajectories often lead from initial excitement to addiction and disillusionment after numerous encounters with more or less disappointing male partners. This framing of online dating as compulsive goes against the unquestioned imperative of finding a partner that is nevertheless the central theme of the books (and appar-ently also a key motivation for purchasing them). This gap makes evident the difference between the ideal of romantic love and romancing as social practice and cultural convention. While the former implies an ideal of emotional authenticity, deep emotions, and even transcendent experiences, the latter concerns mundane practices of self-management and social negotiation. The authors make use of the romantic script of fulfilment, spontaneity, and passion, whereas the process of acquiring a partner is depicted as a rational, calculated, and rehearsed series of acts in which spontaneity risks making oneself vulnerable to harm. In fact, the majority of cautionary stories provided by the authors depict the risks of spontaneity, lack of reflection and planning that inevitably leads to regrets.

Search for 'the Right One' may be frequently narrated as a tragicomedy, but the search itself is far from playful, since it involves the very sense of the self, social acceptability, and desirability. Singer's (2000) protagonist is addicted to reading, replying to and setting up personal ads, emailing and phoning potential candidates, as well as dating them. Male partner after male partner turns out to be other than imagined, yet within a page she finds herself on yet another date, full of renewed faith in her romantic possibilities. The character is under the compulsion to repeat the rites of dating and romance, to find a partner and to regain a sense of heterosexual desirability. Divorced and approaching 50, her search is serious and optimised in its efficiency. This leads her to consider other available alternatives:

It is now 7 months later since I began looking and searching for 'Mr. Right', via cyber city. I was beginning to feel as though I should become celibate or a lesbian or something outrageous. Where would I find another human being I could confide in, with confidence and trust. (Singer, 2000, p. 23)

In this rhetorical turn, celibacy and lesbianism become outrageous alternatives to finding 'another human being' – implying that lesbian identifications function as an outlet for frustrated heterosexual desire and failures on the marriage market, but also that a lesbian partner does not quite match to the criteria of the 'human'. Patricia McDaniel points out that the unspoken possibilities of spinsterhood and lesbianism lurked in advice books on dating already in the 1950s. Spinsterhood was associated with 'lifelong unhappiness', while lesbianism stood for 'deviance and immaturity' (McDaniel, 2001, p. 550.) There seems to be considerable consistency in casting alternatives to heterosexual relationships as failures due to 'their estrangement or opposition to the normative kinship configurations by which "the human" becomes recognizable' (Butler, 1997, p. 17). As the categories of human, celibate, and lesbian are cast in an uneasy connection in online romancing, the underlying heteronormativity of romantic scripts becomes difficult to miss (Pearce & Wisker, 1998; Berlant & Warner, 2000).

Heteronormative tendencies become explicit also in discussions on male and female desire. According to advice book authors, 'Ladies need different things than men do', ... men 'are of a different species than women', ... and are 'basically from Mars' – while women, assumedly, are from Venus (Singer, 2000, pp. 38–58). Singer (2002), Banks (1996), and Skriloff and Gould (1997) all make references to John Gray's best-selling *Mars and Venus* titles. According to Banks (1996), Gray helps readers to understand that 'the way we communicate, our needs, how we approach intimacy and handle stress often make women and men act like they're from different planets' (p. 92). She even sees the model of Mars and Venus as applying to lesbian and gay relationships as an assumedly 'universal' relationship dynamic (Banks, 1996, p. 97). The model of Mars and Venus works to articulate gender differences as drastic and permanent, since men and women are basically representative of different species (Potts, 2002). This model can be understood as a regulatory fiction (Braidotti, 1994) that renders women and men as generic representatives of 'their kind' (p. 157). Consequently, readers are encouraged to follow appropriate gender scripts: the male must take the leading role in all online communication, and the female must not be too active or too readily available (Banks, 1996).

These tips resonate the better-known dating manual published the previous year, namely *The Rules* (1995) by Fein and Schneider (that emphasises the importance of male initiative and female evasiveness for successful dating). In their 2002 spin-off title, *The rules for online dating*, Fein and Schneider proceed to make rules for proper female (and, less so, male) conduct: women should wait 24 hours before replying to emails; women should not reply to any emails on Friday or Saturday nights in order to appear more popular and desirable; women should refuse attempts at instant messaging, keep their replies brief and light, never reply to men's ads and decline all sexual advances in the early stages of relationship. This practice of apparent female passivity and male pursuit is guaranteed to give rise to mystery and romance culminating in marriage.

Like the Mars and Venus books, *The Rules* books have become part of popular imagination both as successful gender and relationship discourses and as objects of controversy (McDaniel, 2001). Advice books on online dating provide fertile ground for cultivating clear-cut behavioural guidelines, since they also provide other concrete guides for online communication. The result is a highly choreographed game:

> Once a man has intercourse with a woman, his goal is reached, along with his desire for romance. . . . I know this is old-fashioned and gamey, but men have never – nor will they ever – changed for the game of love. . . .

Make a man desire you and beg. It will make you feel respected and desirable and build your self-esteem. (Sabol, 1999, pp. 160–1)

Played well, the game of Mars and Venus results in increased female self-esteem and marriage. A failure to follow the rules, again, leads to the unwise path of casual sex, one-night stands and solitude without romance.

Sex scripts

As a term, online dating includes a wide range of communication practices from relationships that remain textual (chat and email based) to relationships resulting in physical encounters, from romantic courtship to cybersex and fleshy offline encounters. Sex is a key feature of online dating even to the degree that sex and romance become conflated. Nevertheless, most advice books set these two clearly apart. Explicit sexual practices are described as a possible direction to take in online communication, but as one highly problematic in terms of romance.

Of the eleven books in my sample, only two explicitly promote female sexual exploration and initiative – and these are both guides on online sex (Semans & Winks, 1999; Lynn, 2005). Lynn (2005, p. 107) argues that 'online, the rules change' as women can express sexual activeness generally considered a male prerogative and she goes on to question the norms of monogamy and matrimony (and hence the attraction of the discourses of both *Mars and Venus* and *The Rules*). Such departures are exceptional. In general, cybersex is celebrated as liberating and gratifying since anonymity enables a safe way of exploring one's sexual desires and fantasies (Banks, 1996; Lynn, 2005; Sabol, 1999; Semans & Winks, 1999; Skriloff & Gould, 1997). However, it is also recurrently marked as 'off limits,' as improper and unfit for romancing.

Advice books do not articulate any unified discourse on representations of sex and desire, although – given their genre – they do share a certain enthusiasm towards the possibilities of online encounters, sexual, or other. Another uniting theme concerns women and men's assumed desires and needs and the possibilities of communicating with 'the opposite sex'. In *The woman's guide to sex on the web* Semans and Winks (1999) argue for the radical possibilities for female sexual expression online:

Both men and women appreciate authentic (rather than scripted) expressions of women's sexuality.... As one of our male respondents points out, 'Women's viewpoints aren't represented enough. I'd like to know more about women, sex, and what really turns them on without male sexual fantasies interfering'. (p. 54)

Quite unlike Semans and Winks (1999) who separate between scripted (narrated, represented, already-made) sexual fantasies, and assumedly direct, authentic expressions of sexuality and desire, Skriloff and Gould (1997), in *Men are from cyberspace* (1997), advise their female readers on male preferences with literally scripted representations of sexuality:

If you need some ideas about what men want women to say or do to them, read a few Penthouse letters, or watch an X-rated video. Pretend to *be* that woman in the centerfold or porn flick.... Most women (if they're honest about it) have faked an orgasm or two. Just fake it on the screen. (Skriloff & Gould, 1997, p. 70)

For Skriloff and Gould, text-based sexual encounters are not expressions of authentic desire inasmuch as a mirroring of fantasies. Partners perform on the basis of each other's assumed desires but women are left with the task of masquerading as objects of male fantasy. The contents of this (apparently unified and identifiable) male fantasy can be deciphered from mass-marketed representations, such as, centrefolds, erotic stories and porn films, and the authors encourage their readers to simulate these in an imitation of sexual gratification. Cybersex enables arousing male desire through a certain 'cultural capital' concerning the codes and clichés of erotica and porn. Female sexual gratification seems less of an issue.

   Although these two examples are arguing opposite things – expressing female sexual desire versus mimicking pin up models and porn actresses – they both evoke the fiction of Mars and Venus as a regulatory fiction of binary gender. In hetero-cybersex one apparently encounters an otherness whose desires, wants, and needs are something of a mystery, even more so because the other's body cannot be seen or felt. One basically communicates with a fantasy character, an interpretation that is also a projection. Available cultural scripts fill in potential gaps in communication. This is not to say that the needs and desires of 'desired others' (Shalom, 1997) *could* be known but that desires seldom fall in a neatly binary model. Richardson (1996) notes that desire is conventionally articulated as attraction to difference and differently gendered individuals are seen to 'complement each other, right down to their bodies and body parts fitting together' (p. 7). Interestingly enough, this complementation of desire does not really apply in the examples quoted above. Partners are left to imagine each other's supposedly alien wishes and to articulate them in familiar figures of written erotica and porn. Complementation, then, appears to be a product of learning, practice, and effort, rather than 'natural connection'. As in Potts' (2002) analysis of Gray's Mars and Venus books, the 'ostensibly natural attributes of each gender actually break down into a series of learned body movements and gestures that must be repeatedly rehearsed so as not to be forgotten' (p. 58).

Gray provides lists of 'turn on phrases' recommended to be used during (hetero)sex to increase female enjoyment, while the female partner is recommended not to use complete sentences in order to express absorbedness with the bodily act (Potts, 2002). As Potts (2002, p. 67) points out, this produces sex 'as a series of pre-scripted parts and performances' that need to be rehearsed in order to become second nature. In cybersex exchanges, female incoherence or silence is obviously less recommendable as this would lead to lack of communication. A different kind of script is needed, as demonstrated by Skiroloff and Gould (1997) in an example cybersex dialogue. The dialogue progresses from describing one's clothing (e.g., one's blouse and panties) to kissing (e.g., 'Your soft, sweet tongue parts my lips...mmmm...I kiss you deeply...I loooove kissing'), groping (e.g., 'seeing your taut nipples excites me'), petting ('My hand finds your hot mound under your lacy panties'), oral sex ('I love watching my thick cock sliding between your full, sexy lips'), and male ejaculation ('I'M GONNA CUMMM') (Skriloff & Gould, 1997, pp. 71–4).

Even with the possibilities for play and experimentation in forums like erotic chats, there is not necessarily all that much innovation and play involved in what counts as erotic, stimulating, or 'sexy' (Lynn, 2005).

With onomatopoetic expressions of seduction, pleasure, arousal, and orgasm – 'mmmm...Oh Goddd...Give me...,' (Skriloff & Gould, 1997, pp. 72–4) – private chats make evident how desire is narrated through various scripts. Their descriptions of bodies, sexual acts, and sensations are obviously scripted since they are textual representations typed on the screen and borrowing from the conventions of erotica and porn. Yet, as proposed above, scripting should also be understood as a fundamental way in which representations of intimacy tie into cultural norms and institutions of gender and sexuality. Romance, erotica, and porn all function here as influential reservoirs of scripts.

Advice authors promote cybersex as liberating and exciting when it is anonymous and detached from physical encounters: after all, explorations of and experimentation in textual sexuality may be part of identity work and self-discovery. However, the lines of proper behaviour are drawn differently in the context of romantic relationships. Women should not be too readily available for sexual encounters online any more than offline, since female sexual activity translates as 'loose' and 'unfeminine' behaviour. Rabin (1999) reminds her readers 'never ever' to allow private chats turning into cybersex as this will derail possibilities of romantic offline encounters. Sabol (1999, p. 53) makes a similar point, arguing that women have to prolong 'the chase', make the man beg and perform romantic acts, both online and offline. Finally, Fein and Schneider (2002) provide online dating with a total choreography – or jurisdiction – featuring carefully scripted, rehearsed and performed lines, gestures and feedback. Online, women should not write anything about sex (Fein & Schneider, 2002). Performing by the rules necessitates self-control, self-management, and considerable planning. Far from spontaneous attraction and socialising, online dating (like dating in general) is explicitly a scripted and teleological pursuit.

Following the rules

The oldest advice book in my sample was written a decade ago, during a time when the Internet and the WWW were only becoming familiar concepts to a wider audience. Online dating manuals have been since published in dozens, commercial dating services have attracted millions of users and romantic relationships originating online are hardly longer exotic. Books on online dating have been primarily addressed at women who remained in the minority as Internet users until the 2000s. As relationships advice authors have begun to tackle online communications, they have worked to reiterate an understanding of women as experts of relationship management also in the context of the Internet.

The genre of therapeutic, lifestyle, and sex guidebooks was popular throughout the 20th century. Books advising women in flirting, dating, and sex outside marriage were introduced in the 1960s and they often operated on a simplified model of gender difference and sexual desire (Miller & McHoul, 1998). This is also the context for most advice books on online romancing. Self-help and advice books have contributed to therapeutic culture that, according to Furedi (2004), provides a script for making emotional deficits part of cultural vernacular and tools for making sense of everyday life. Self-help and advice books have contributed to therapeutic culture, which 'provides a script through which individuals develop a distinct understanding of their selves and their relationship with others' (Furedi, 2004, p. 23). According to Furedi, therapeutic culture renders emotional deficits part of cultural vernacular, while also providing tools for making sense of everyday life. It affects people's self-perception and ways of dealing with emotions and moments of crisis (p. 21). According to Furedi (2004), therapy was mainstreamed as a cultural script during the last decade – roughly the same period as covered by the titles addressed in this chapter. The books may be part of the mainstreaming of therapy discourse, but in the vibrant tradition of manuals, guidebooks, self-help, and advisory texts their discourse is definitely more than a decade old.

Advice books on online dating divide the process of meeting people, getting to know them and developing relationships into neatly separated stages – and each of these comes with guidelines, inspirational, as well as, cautionary tales. The books postulate general, and distinctly gendered scripts for individual experience and suggest that one is foolish not to take these into consideration. The titles celebrate romantic love and rela-tionships while depicting the journey towards such emotional culmin-ation as one of calculation and perfection through practice. Combined with semi-technical advice on setting up a computer and a personals account, these depictions can indeed be seen as commercialisation and technologisation of the individual (Miller & McHoul, 1998).

In advice literature, the Internet is rhetorically made into being as a dimension of female self-exploration and romancing. Combined with therapeutic discourse and ample references to self-help, these rhetorical tools figure the Internet as a romance machine, which, with the correct amount of scripting, will be transformed into a portal towards fuller self-discovery and better life.

References

Banks, L. (1996). *Love online*. Franklin Lakes, WI: Career Press.
Berlant, L., & Warner, M. (2000). Sex in public. In L. Berlant (ed.), *Intimacy* (pp. 311–30). Chicago, IL: University of Chicago Press.
Blackstone, E. (1998). *Virtual strangers: A woman's guide to love and sex on the Internet*. Bellingham, WA: Prospector Press.
Braidotti, R. (1994). *Nomadic subjects: Embodiment and sexual difference in contem-porary feminist thought*. New York, NY: Columbia University Press.
Butler, J. (1997). Against proper objects. In E. Weed and N. Schor (eds), *Feminism meets queer theory* (pp. 1–30). Bloomington, IN: Indiana University Press.

Duncombe, J., & Marsden, D. (1995). 'Can men love?' 'Reading', 'staging' and 'resisting' the romance. In L. Pearce & J. Stacey (eds), *Romance revisited* (pp. 238–50). London: Lawrence & Wishart.

Fein, E., & Schneider, S. (1995). *The rules: Time-tested secrets for capturing the heart of Mr. Right.* New York, NY: Warner Books.

Fein, E., & Schneider, S. (2002). *The rules for online dating: Capturing the heart of Mr. Right in cyberspace.* New York, NY: Pocket Books.

Fletcher, S. D. (1997). *E-mail: A love story.* New York, NY: Donald I. Fine Books.

Furedi, F. (2004). *Therapy culture: Cultivating vulnerability in an uncertain age.* London: Routledge.

Gray, J. (1992). *Men are from Mars, women are from Venus: A practical guide for improving communication and getting what you want in your relationships.* New York, NY: HarperCollins.

Hochschild, A. R. (1994). The commercial spirit of intimate life and the abduction of feminism: Signs from women's advice books. *Theory, Culture & Society, 11,* 1–24.

Illouz, E. (1997). *Consuming the romantic utopia: Love and the cultural contradictions of capitalism.* Berkeley, CA: University of California Press.

Jackson, S. (1995). Women and heterosexual love: Complicity, resistance and change. In L. Pearce and J. Stacey (eds), *Romance revisited* (pp. 49–62). London: Lawrence & Wishart.

Langford, W. (1999). *Revolutions of the heart: Gender, power and the delusions of love.* London: Routledge.

Lichterman, P. (1992). Self-help reading as thin culture. *Media, Culture and Society, 14,* 421–47.

Lynn, R. (2005). *The sexual revolution 2.0: Getting connected, upgrading your sex life and finding true love – or at least a dinner date – in the Internet age.* Berkeley, CA: Ulysses Press.

McDaniel, P. (2001). Shrinking violets and caspar milquetoasts: Shyness and heterosexuality from the roles of the fifties to the rules of the nineties. *Journal of Social History, 34,* 547–68.

Miller, T., & McHoul, A. (1998). *Popular culture and everyday life.* London: Sage.

Neale, S. (1992). The big romance or something wild? Romantic comedy today. *Screen, 33,* 284–99.

Paasonen, S. (2005). *Figures of fantasy: Internet, women, and cyberdiscourse.* New York, NY: Peter Lang.

Pearce, L., & Wisker, G. (1998). Rescripting romance: An introduction. In L. Pearce and G. Wisker (eds), *Fatal attractions: Rescripting romance in contemporary literature and film* (pp. 1–19). London: Pluto Press.

Potts, A. (2002). *The science/fiction of sex: Feminist deconstruction and the vocabularies of heterosex.* London: Routledge.

Purnell, K. (1998). *Dating.com: Diary of an Internet romance.* Bryn Mawr, PA: Buy Books on the Web.

Rabin, S. (1999). *Cyberflirt: How to attract anyone, anywhere on the World Wide Web.* New York, NY: Plume.

Radner, H. (1995). *Shopping around: Feminine culture and the pursuit of pleasure.* New York, NY: Routledge.

Richardson, D. (1996). Heterosexuality and social theory. In D. Richardson (ed.), *Theorising heterosexuality: Telling it straight* (pp. 1–20). Buckingham, UK: Open University Press.

Sabol, M. (1999). *You've got male: The Internet dating game.* Denver, CO: Write Way Publishing.

Semans, A., & Winks, C. (1999). *The woman's guide to sex on the web.* San Francisco, CA: HarperCollins.

Shalom, C. (1997). That great supermarket of desire: Attributes of the desired other in personal advertisements. In K. Harvey and C. Shalom (eds), *Language and desire: Encoding sex, romance and intimacy* (pp. 186–203). London: Routledge.

Singer, S. (2000). *Diary of an Internet junkie.* Orlando, FL: Firstpublish.

Skriloff, L., & Gould, J. (1997). *Men are from cyberspace: The single woman's guide to flirting, dating, and finding love on-line.* New York, NY: St. Martin's Griffin.

Tyler, M. (2004). Managing between the sheets: Lifestyle magazines and the management of sexuality in everyday life. *Sexualities, 7,* 81–106.

Part 2
Presentation of Self to Attract Lovers

5

The Art of Selling One's 'Self' on an Online Dating Site: The BAR Approach

Monica T. Whitty

Singles have many places and spaces available to them to find a romantic partner. How one creates a 'first impression' in each of these spaces can vary. This chapter argues that some of these spaces allow individuals to gradually get to know one another, while other spaces expect individuals to reveal a wealth of information about themselves prior to any one-on-one communication with potential dates. An online dating site is an example of the latter. Given that details about one's 'self' are presented differently on an online dating site compared to other dating arenas, it is argued here that unique skills and strategies are required to successfully sell oneself on an online dating site. In other words, there is an art to selling oneself on an online dating site. This chapter will outline my BAR approach theory, which contends that if individuals are to successfully develop a romantic relationship from an online dating site, they need to present a balance between an 'attractive' and a 'real' self on their online profiles.

Theories on the development of online relationships

Researchers have found that people meet and develop romantic relationships in a range of places in cyberspace. Parks and Floyd (1996) found that 7.9 per cent of newsgroup users had formed a romantic relationship with someone they had met in a newsgroup. In a similar study, Parks and Roberts (1998) found that 26.3 per cent of the MOOs users they sampled had formed a romantic relationship. These researchers remarked that 'the formation of personal relationships on MOOs can be seen as the norm rather than the exception' (p. 529). Similarly, Utz (2000) found that 24.5 per cent of the MUDders she surveyed began a romantic relationship in this online space. Whitty and Gavin (2001) also found ample evidence for the initiation of romantic relationships via chat rooms. Moreover, some of their participants reported that some of these romantic relationships worked better online than in face-to-face. Although there are several obstacles that make it difficult to initiate and maintain online relationships (e.g., lack of social presence, and non-verbal and paralinguistic cues) individuals can overcome these to develop satisfying online relationships that often move successfully offline (Baker, 2002; Walther, 1995; Whitty, 2003; Whitty & Carr, 2003; 2006; Whitty & Gavin, 2001). Researchers have explained how these obstacles can be overcome. For example, Whitty (2003; 2004a) has argued that the nonverbal cues individuals typically display when they flirt can be represented online in text, as well as through the use of emoticons and acronyms. Walther (1995) suggests that with time, and longer and more frequent communication, individuals can form close relationships in cyberspace. Whitty and Gavin (2001) propose that relationships online are developed through increments of trust. These levels of trust are represented by the modes of communication individuals select to use. In their study where they interviewed 60 chat room users aged 19–51 years, it was found that allowing someone to know your email, then your phone number, and finally your address, represented increasing levels of trust in the relationship and in one's online partner.

Which self to present?

Individuals can be very strategic when it comes to presenting themselves in cyberspace (Walther, Slovacek, & Tidwell, 2001; Whitty, 2003; Whitty & Carr, 2006). Walther and his colleagues believe that in CMC (computer mediated communication) impression management is more controllable and fluid. They claim that 'online communicators may exploit the capabilities of text-based, nonvisual interaction to form levels of affinity that would be unexpected in parallel offline interactions' (Walther et al., 2001, p. 110). Bargh, McKenna, and Fitzsimons (2002) and McKenna, Green, and Gleason (2002) have drawn from work on the *'true self'* by Rogers (1951) and work on possible selves by Higgins (1987) to consider which traits individuals typically present in newsgroups, and which presentation of self in newsgroups will more likely lead to long lasting relationships that can move successfully offline. In their research they found that those who present their 'true self' (i.e., traits or characteristics that individuals possess and would like to express, but are usually unable to demonstrate to others) online were more likely to develop close Internet relationships and bring these relationships into their 'real' lives. People can also be strategic in their visual presentations of self online. For example, Whitty (2003) has argued that individuals can be considerably experimental when describing how they look in cyberspace. Walther et al. (2001) found that the presence of a photograph prior to and during CMC had a positive effect on intimacy/affection and social attractiveness for short-term CMC partners. However, CMC partners who met online felt less intimacy/affection and social attraction once a photograph was introduced compared to individuals with long-term CMC partners who never saw each other's picture. Interestingly, Walther et al. (2001) also found a negative relationship between physical attractiveness and self-presentation online, as they describe:

It appears that when partners' photographs are shown, the less physically attractive they are, the more they engage in successful self-presentation, perhaps in a compensatory manner. Or, the more physically attractive partners are, the less successful they believe their impression management efforts are. (Or, they are wrong about their perceived success at self-presentation, and they more successfully they believe they self-presented, the less physically attractive they were rated.) (pp. 123–4)

McKenna et al. (2002) have proposed that forming a friendship online:

based initially upon mutual self-disclosure and common interests, rather than superficial features such as physical attractiveness, provides a more stable and durable basis for the relationship and enables it to survive and flourish once those 'gates' do come into operation when the partners meet in person. (pp. 23–4)

Although the above studies tell us some fascinating details about the way individuals present themselves in cyberspace, it is noteworthy that cyberspace is not a generic space that everyone experiences the same way (Whitty & Carr, 2003; 2006). It is argued here that the sequence with which information is revealed about the self online can vary depending on which space one is interacting in. As will be made clear in this chapter, online daters disclose information about themselves in a very different way to other spaces online.

Personal ads and video dating

Personal ads and video dating are probably the closest equivalents to online dating. Personal ads can be found in a range of newspapers and magazines and are written to attract a potential romantic and/or sexual partner. For a small cost, individuals can compose an ad, where in a few lines they describe themselves and what they are looking for in a partner. Advertisers can remain anonymous in their ads and provide either a personal phone number or a number where individuals can leave a message if they are interested in meeting this person. In contrast, video daters are presented with written information and video clips of their potential dates. The video dating service typically selects potential partners they consider might be a good match for their client. The client is next presented with demographic information, self-descriptions, and photographs of prospective dates followed by a videotaped interview. The client then decides which of these potential dates they are interested in. The individuals they select are then contacted to decide, if in turn, they might be interested in meeting this individual.

Similar to those who advertise themselves in personal ads and video dating, online daters are required to write a self-description, and can write about the sort of partner they are seeking. Online daters can display more information than in a personal ad, and akin to video dating can represent themselves in photographs and video. Unlike personal ads and video dating, initial contact on online dating sites typically occurs through the site or email, rather than phone, which is generally the next step (see Whitty & Carr, 2006). Given that contact is made initially in cyberspace, individuals might feel safer to cyberflirt and experiment with presentations of their identity (Whitty, 2003). Moreover, individuals are presented with more and cheaper opportunities than with video dating and personal ads to rewrite their profiles on an online dating site.

Numerous studies on personal ads and video dating have elucidated that men and women choose to present themselves in gender-defined ways (e.g., Bolig, Stein, & McHenry, 1984; Cameron, Oskamp, & Sparks, 1977; Cicerello & Sheehan, 1995; Green, Buchanan, & Heuer, 1984; Smith, Waldorf, & Trembath, 1990). Men are more likely to write or talk about their physical characteristics, occupation, and offer financial security, while women are more likely to offer attractiveness (Cameron et al., 1977; Cicerello & Sheehan, 1995). In their ads, men are more likely to request an attractive, thin partner, while women are more likely to specify a desired occupation, personality qualities, and financial security (Cameron et al., 1977; Cicerello & Sheehan, 1995; Green et al., 1984; Smith et al., 1990).

Some researchers have examined which advertisers and video daters are more successful at obtaining responses (e.g., Rajecki, Bledsoe, & Rasmussen, 1991). Rajecki et al. (1991) found that the most successful women's ads received an average of 55.3 replies, while the more unsuccessful ads received an average of 4.1 responses. These researchers argued that the more successful women's ads were written by younger women (an average age of 35 years), were longer, and consisted of more persuasive vocabulary. In contrast, the more successful men's ads received an average of 39.1 replies and the unsuccessful one's received an average of 2.0 replies. As was found with the women's personal ads, the more successful men's ads were longer; however, in contrast to the women they were written by older men (an average of 43.9 years). Woll and Young (1989) made the observation that video daters hoped that by presenting a realistic picture of themselves they will, in turn, be successful in attracting the ideal partner they were looking for. Despite this apparent sensible strategy, Woll and Young (1989) point out that these same video daters are dissatisfied with the people who have been selecting them, perceiving a discrepancy between their ideal partner and the person who is realistically interested in their profile.

Research on online dating

Given the claim made here that online dating best compares to newspaper personal ads and video dating, what have studies revealed about online dating? How important is a visual image? Are the same gender differences evident on online dating sites?

One of the first studies on online dating was conducted by Scharlott and Christ (1995). In August 1990 they recruited 102 registered users of an online matchmaking site. Similar to Rajecki et al.'s (1991) study, men sent more messages to women than women sent to men. This was also found in Whitty's study on online daters, where some men revealed they played the 'the numbers game' (Whitty, 2004b; Whitty & Carr, 2006). They claimed to play this game with the hope to increase the probability of receiving a response.

When it comes to physical appearance online, the site Scharlott and Christ (1995) studied did not give participants the opportunity to present a photograph or video of themselves. This is possibly due to the capabilities of the Internet in those days. In current times individuals are able to present photos, videos, and voice files on the online dating sites. Whitty's research has revealed the importance of displaying a photograph on online dating sites (Whitty 2004b; Whitty & Carr, 2006).

In her study, where she interviewed 60 online daters (30 men and 30 women), she found that well over half of the participants (65 per cent) decided to put a photograph of themselves on their profiles. Women (87 per cent) were more likely to put a photo up compared to men (66 per cent). Moreover, only women (8 per cent) reported displaying a glamour photograph (i.e., one that was professionally taken). Many of the online daters claimed they would skip a profile if it did not display a photograph, as explained by Kath (name changed for confidentiality):

I   *What about photographs?*
K   *A must.*
I   *So, you wouldn't waste your time with anyone if they didn't have a photograph?*
K   *I have and I have been extremely disappointed a couple of times. And even with photographs, they tend to be misleading. I know myself, I take a photograph, I take a horrendous photo and people just always say to me, 'you don't look anything like it'. I have met guys who look at me and go 'oh my God'. You can see it is them in the photos but it's not really but people without photos I tend to stay away from.*
(Kath)

Online daters might also elect to display a photograph that depicts an important aspect of their identity. For example, in Scott's (2002) study on a Mormon online dating site he found that many of the men on the site selected photographs of themselves with a white shirt and tie image. He argued that 'these men are making it clear to others that they have fulfilled their obligation to serve Mormon missions' (Scott, 2002, p. 208). Scott (2002) also found that more of the women (almost one quarter) submitted professional photographs of themselves. Perhaps this was to ensure they looked their best. However, a professional photograph also demonstrates a pride in one's appearance – arguably a trait men look for in a woman.

The same gender differences found in studies on personal ads and video dating are apparent on online dating sites. Scharlott and Christ (1995) found that those women who rated themselves as having an appearance that was above average or very good were much more likely to be contacted by men on the site than those who reported themselves as average (note: none of the participants ticked the below average box). This result was not evident for the men. In Whitty's (2004b; Whitty & Carr, 2006) research it was found that women (46.7 per cent) were more likely to misrepresent their looks (typically by using a photo a few years out of date) than men were (6.7 per cent). They were motivated to do this to attract more potential dates. The studies mentioned above on personal ads and video dating found that women were attracted to men with higher socio economic status. However, Whitty's (2004b; Whitty & Carr, 2006) research on online daters found no gender differences for desiring someone with higher financial or professional status. She argues that the reason for this lack of difference is because of the numerous perceived choices available to individuals. Online daters are adding more to their 'wish list' and are setting the hurdle higher when it comes to online dating.

Comparing online dating with other online relationships

It would seem that how a romantic relationship begins and progresses may vary online depending on which space one is referring to. The work by Bargh et al. (2002) and McKenna et al. (2002) on newsgroups found that relationships develop gradually online. They found that participants felt comfortable to self-disclose aspects of themselves they might not feel as comfortable with self-disclosing in the 'real' world. In contrast, Whitty's (2004b; Whitty & Carr, 2006) research revealed that on online dating sites participants felt they had learnt enough about their potential mate on their profile and that they typically met within a couple of weeks of first contact on the online dating site. They stated this was important to check the information on the site and to establish physical chemistry. This is explained by Jenny (name changed for confidentiality):

> J   *I had learnt from a few very early test runs that too many emails and phone calls before actually meeting over coffee or whatever can be a big mistake. Well at least for me, because although you start to develop a sort of friendship and a certain intimacy if there is no chemistry and you don't want to retain them as a friend it feels very awkward. So I make it a rule that ... I don't sort of become emotionally close to someone I don't actually, I haven't seen in the flesh, because it is disappointing for both parties and it can feel quite strange.*
> (Jenny)

Unlike other spaces online physical appearance plays a very important role in determining whether people will meet up face-to-face when first introduced through an online dating site. Scharlott and Christ's (1995) study found that the men often chose to meet women who were physically attractive. Additionally, Whitty's (2004b; Whitty & Carr, 2006) study found that most participants stressed that good looks was an important quality in a potential date and more women went to great efforts to ensure their physical looks left a good impression.

The BAR approach

As has been demonstrated in this chapter, there are some important differences between how people meet and present themselves on an online dating site compared to other places online; however, this does not mean that people are not strategic in their presentation of selves on online dating sites. In Whitty's (2004b; Whitty & Carr, 2006) interview study it was found that people spent much time constructing and reconstructing their profiles. This is explained by Lynn (name changed for confidentiality):

> I   *OK, looking at your own profile, how did you decide what information to include about yourself?*
>
> L   *After many hours and trial and error, I changed it a few times, ... I did want to describe myself in a way that would give a bit of a cross section of me and depending on what sort of results that I got... with each profile I would then sort of go and revise that. Having said that, I have only revised it I think three times.*
>
> I   *But you feel like you got different responses accordingly to different profiles?*
>
> L   *Yeah a little bit.*
>
> (Lynn)

In addition to specific sought-out characteristics (described later in this chapter), such as, physical attractiveness, interests, values, and socio economic status individuals stated they were looking for authentic/genuine people. They singled out profiles that seemed fake or clichéd, for example, profiles that described perfect dates of sipping wine by fireplaces, or going for long romantic strolls on the beach. This is nicely highlighted by another participant in Whitty's (2004b; Whitty & Carr, 2006) research:

> T   *I tend to stay away from those people with sort of cliché stuff. I think it appears in a lot of profiles ...*
>
> I   *What would be some of the clichés that you would be turned off by?*
>
> T   *With some, on some profiles it has a very sexual overtone, which puts me off totally. Sometimes it is like a passage of clichés, walks on the beach, romantic evenings, romantic getaways, a bottle of wine, and*

nice crackling fire. It just doesn't ring true, it just sounds like a, it doesn't seem very real
(Teresa, name changed for confidentiality).

In addition to ruling out clichéd profiles, Whitty's (2004b; Whitty & Carr, 2006) online daters attempted to read between the lines to ensure they identified honest profiles. Kevin (name changed for confidentiality), for example, talked about the profiles he looked for:

K *Usually if they sounded really down to earth and family orientated. You know somebody with standards and values. Somebody who didn't seem to be playing the game, somebody that seems to be totally genuine.*
(Kevin)

The online daters in Whitty's study (2004b; Whitty & Carr, 2006) were often extremely disappointed when their date did not match up to their profile. Although seemingly pedantic, online daters were put off by misrepresentations of any sort; for example, inaccurate descriptions of height (sometimes even an inch or two out), age (sometimes only a couple of year's difference), weight, interests, and personality. To give some examples:

B *I find that 6 foot 2 is a lot shorter these days than it used to be.*
I *So men lie a little bit about the height?*
B *Yes I think height tends to be one area that has been a little bit of a mislead.*
(Bronwyn, name changed for confidentiality)

J *I think we are all optimistic when we look, it's like real estate, you imagine your dream home and anything they don't mention isn't there in general so you do have to take off the rose coloured glasses. There is obvious things, like men will tell you they are 5 foot 10 when they are sort of 5 foot 6 and you are sort of going to figure out that one anyway.*
(Jenny, name changed for confidentiality)

I *Was there any information that people exaggerate or distort?*
S *Oh I think people, there are individuals who clearly have a high opinion of themselves and it's not warranted ... the other thing is that they are actually much better looking [on their profiles] than they ... actually are ... and they misjudge ... size ... people lie about their age.*
(Shane, name changed for confidentiality)

Consequently, honest profiles were sought out. Individuals who matched up to their profiles were given greater credence. Online daters often described their first date experiences with people from the site as positive and successful if the date matched their profile. This is described by both Tom and Kevin (names changed for confidentiality):

T   *Some I found that told a whole lot of dribble, let's face it, the people who tell the truth you want to be the ones you want to be interested in. So, like there is so many, what I have found that I have meet women there, they have put their age on there and when you actually meet them they have actually been 2 to 5 years older than what they have said on there.*
(Tom)

K   *First of all, that person did not portray to be anybody different in their profile than they were in real life, even though I made the mistake of reading more into it but that's my own shortcoming. Because it turned into a relationship, actually a quite close relationship for a short while, that's why I would classify that as reasonably successful.*
(Kevin)

At the same time as seeking out authentic and genuine profiles, individuals were also looking for the more attractive and appealing profiles. That is, they were searching for profiles of individuals that not only looked good, but also profiles that delineated many of the other qualities on their wish list, as another of the participants in Whitty's (2004b; Whitty & Carr, 2006) explains:

A   *Characteristics that I'm looking for in a person. They have to have a photo and that had to be attractive, they had to be into fitness, reasonably intelligent, show that they were independent, just the qualities I'm looking for.*
(Andrew, name changed for confidentiality)

As detailed in my previous work, online daters are acutely aware that the best strategy for developing a 'successful' profile (i.e., one that will attract a desirable potential partner) is to create a balance between an 'attractive' and a 'real' self. (Whitty, 2004b; Whitty & Carr, 2006). This I have named the 'BAR' approach. This is a little different to what theorists, such as, Bargh et al. (2002) and McKenna et al. (2002) contend (as highlighted earlier in this chapter). However, these theorists were considering relationship development in newsgroups. In the spaces they investigated individuals were not necessarily or at least obviously seeking out a romantic partner, nor do they typically display photographs or videos of themselves. This is very different to a profile on an online dating site, which contains all the information an individual needs to make a decision about face-to-face contact.

Online daters were also very aware that they needed to re-write their profiles if they were attracting either people they did not desire, or if their date appeared disappointed with them when they meet face-to-face (given that they did not live out to their profile). For example, Christopher (name changed for confidentiality) described the changes that he made to his profile:

I *How did you decide what to include on your profile and how accurate was the information that you presented?*

C *Well I believe it has always been mostly accurate, there was a time there, you see because I have boys, 3 little kids, I know that puts a lot of people off so there was a time when I didn't include the fact that I had children on there but I would tell people as soon as I started emailing them because I found that I got better results that way. Now I just, whatever it is, the fact that I have children on there and that doesn't seem to be a bother for me now, but at one stage I felt as if I was being judged on the fact. But generally I would say that the information about me is quite accurate, I have a bunch of friends I have met through ... [the online dating site] and you know they all know what my profile is, I get them to check it if I update it.*
(Christopher)

In getting the profile 'real' as described by Christopher, online daters had others check their profiles. Hence, many understood that who they 'ideally' see themselves as is not necessarily the self they typically present to others. To successfully attract one's perfect match, individuals needed to present a profile that matched up with how others see them.

Conclusions

The way to one's heart can be a different path online than it is offline. Although cyberspace allows unique opportunities for relationship development, how the relationship proceeds varies depending on which space individuals originally meet. Like personal ads and video dating, online daters present a wealth of information about themselves prior to any one-on-one communication with one's potential date. Dissimilar to personal ads and video dating, the kind of information individuals are able to present about themselves on an online dating site varies. Moreover, there are more opportunities for online daters to reconstruct their presentations of self. The self one elects to present on an online dating site determines the success of attracting an ideal match. Arguably, that self needs to be a balance between an 'attractive' self and a 'real' self.

References

Baker, A. J. (2002). What makes an online relationship successful? Clues from couples who met in cyberspace. *CyberPsychology & Behavior, 5* (4), 363–75.

Bargh, J. A., McKenna, K. Y. A., & Fitzsimons, G. M. (2002). Can you see the real me? Activation and expression of the 'true self' on the internet. *Journal of Social Issues, 58* (1), 33–48.

Bolig, R., Stein, P. J., & McHenry, P. C. (1984). The self-advertisement approach to dating: Male–female difference. *Family Relations, 33* (4), 587–92.

Cameron, C., Oskamp, S., & Sparks, W. (1977). Courtship American style: Newspaper ads. *Family Coordinator, 26* (1), 27–30.

Cicerello, A., & Sheehan, E. P. (1995). Personal advertisements: A content analysis. *Journal of Social Behavior and Personality, 10* (4), 751–6.

Green, S. K., Buchanan, D., & Heuer, S. (1984). Winners, losers, and choosers: A field investigation of dating initiation. *Personality and Social Psychology Bulletin, 10* (4), 502–11.

Higgins, E. T. (1987). Self-discrepancy theory. *Psychological Review, 94* (3), 1120–34.

McKenna, K. Y. A., Green, A. S., & Gleason, M. E. J. (2002). Relationship formation on the Internet: What's the big attraction? *Journal of Social Issues, 58* (1), 9–31.

Parks, M. R., & Floyd, K. (1996). Making friends in cyberspace. *Journal of Communication, 46* (1), 80–97.

Parks, M. R., & Roberts, L. D. (1998). 'Making MOOsic': The development of personal relationships online and a comparison to their off-line counterparts. *Journal of Social and Personal Relationships, 15* (4), 517–37.

Rajecki, D. W., Bledsoe, S. B., & Rasmussen, J. L. (1991). Successful personal ads: Gender differences and similarities in offers, stipulations, and outcomes. *Basic and Applied Social Psychology, 12* (4), 457–69.

Rogers, C. (1951). *Client-centered therapy.* Boston: Houghton-Mifflin.

Scharlott, B. W., & Christ, W. G. (1995). Overcoming relationship-initiation barriers: The impact of a computer-dating system on sex role, shyness, and appearance inhibitions. *Computers in Human Behavior, 11* (2), 191–204.

Scott, D. W. (2002). Matchmaker, matchmaker, find me a mate: A cultural examination of a virtual community of single Mormons. *Journal of Media and Religion, 1*(4), 201–16.

Smith, J. E., Waldorf, V. A., & Trembath, D. L. (1990). 'Single white male looking for thin, very attractive...' *Sex Roles, 23* (11/12), 675–85.

Utz, S. (2000). Social information processing in MUDs: The development of friendships in virtual worlds. *Journal of Online Behavior, 1* (1), Retrieved 7 February 2005 from: http://www.behavior.net/JOB/v1n1/utz.html

Walther, J. B. (1995). Relational aspects of computer-mediated communication: Experimental observations over time. *Organizational Science, 6* (2), 186–203.

Walther, J. B., Slovacek, C., & Tidwell, L. (2001). Is a picture worth a thousand words? Photographic images in long-term and short-term computer-mediated communication. *Communication Research, 28* (1), 105–34.

Whitty, M. T. (2003). Cyber-flirting: Playing at love on the internet. *Theory and Psychology, 13* (3), 339–57.

Whitty, M. T. (2004a). Cyber-flirting: An examination of men's and women's flirting behaviour both offline and on the Internet. *Behaviour Change, 21* (2), 115–26.

Whitty, M. T. (2004b). Shopping for love on the Internet: Men and women's experiences of using an Australian Internet dating site. *Communication Research in the Public Interest:* ICA, New Orleans, USA, 27–31 May 2004.

Whitty, M. T. & Carr, A. N. (2003). Cyberspace as potential space: Considering the web as a playground to cyber-flirt. *Human Relations, 56* (7), 861–91.

Whitty, M. T. & Carr, A. N. (2006). *Cyberspace romance: The psychology of online relationships.* Basingstoke: Palgrave Macmillan.

Whitty, M., & Gavin, J. (2001). Age/sex/location: Uncovering the social cues in the development of online relationships. *CyberPsychology & Behaviour, 4* (5), 623–30.

Woll, S. B., & Young, P. (1989). Looking for Mr. or Ms. Right: Self-presentation in videodating. *Journal of Marriage and the Family, 51* (2), 483–8.

6
Examining Personal Ads and Job Ads

Alice Horning

In both love and work, people are making increasing use of the Internet to reach others. The rhetorical analysis of online advertisements for love (personal ads) and work (job ads) in this chapter will show that these genres draw on the well-worn rhetorical modes to facilitate connections. In both cases, if the ads work as they are intended to, successful love or work relationships develop as a by-product of careful, thoughtful writing. Writers of online personal ads and job ads use approaches similar to print ads and to each other in several ways: both use basic rhetorical modes, both share a need for large numbers of responses to make the right connections, both connect sometimes in shared meeting places, and both make use of credentials to establish a preliminary match. However, the two kinds of ads differ from each other and from print ads in terms of the Aristotelian principles of truth value (ethos), emotional appeal (pathos), and specific factual argument (logos). This chapter explores the rhetorical principles used and abused by writers of online personals and employment ads, and helps account for both success and failure to connect in love and work.

Modes, goals, sites, and credentials: Some similarities

While personals can be somewhat longer than job ads, both types of online ads, like their print analogues, draw on classical rhetorical topoi like narration, description, definition, comparison/contrast, and so on, to attract readers. More specifically, both kinds of ads use some of the major rhetorical topoi or modes as described by rhetoricians Crowley and Hawhee (2004) intended to be used for the purposes of creating an argument on any issue: description, narration, and exposition, including within these the sub-types of definition, contrast, exemplification, classification, and process. Crowley and Hawhee (2004) point out that these modes derive originally from Aristotle's *Rhetoric* as well as the work of other ancient rhetoricians. The goal in both cases is to create an argument for candidates to apply for a date or job.

The connection between dating and job hunting has been widely recognised and in some places, online dating is increasingly combined with job hunting on the Internet and in person around the country, as reported by Ellin (2003) in the *New York Times* Business section. Ellin (2003) notes that both romance experts and career experts say that seekers must actively look for opportunities, but that both goals can be served in a single step. 'Increasing numbers of event planners are offering parties geared for both love and career matchmaking' (Ellin, 2003, p. 10). These events are designed to help young adults both personally and professionally:

> Netparties in Manhattan take place every two weeks at a bar or club. People wear color-coded name tags defined by industry (fuchsia for media and entertainment, green for finance, gray for technology) and hold color-coordinated cocktail glasses. The entrance fee, $15, usually includes drinks and hors d'oeuvres. (Ellin, 2003, p. 10)

The parties provide more structure and organisation than there is in online dating, and allow participants to look for jobs and love at the same time.

Gatherings like these also occur online in various locations around the country, putting the search for love and work together. One such online analogue is Ryze.com, which is a networking site where members can share résumés, as well as personal information. The site says it 'helps people make connections and grow their networks. You can network to grow your business, build your career and life, find a job and make sales. Or just keep in touch with friends' (Ryze.com). Just as the business relationship groups see the personal side, so too, do the dating sites. In both arenas, the goal is the same, and that is to make contacts and connections. If the job hunting surveys are right, then both love seekers and work seekers must make a very large number of contacts in order to reach their goals, whether online or in person.

In the current difficult job hunting climate, applicants are using every available strategy. Feldman and Klaas (2002) report that job seekers use the Internet particularly when they are looking outside their immediate geographic area, seeking big salary increases, and wanting to consider a wide range of options. They may try posting résumés online, using email to follow up with employers, and engaging in other very persistent contact strategies. In addition, since some organisations require departments or divisions to demonstrate that the pool of candidates is diverse, employers collect applicant data information confidentially to establish the characteristics of the candidate pool. Employers may now send out optional applicant demographic data forms for candidates to complete and return electronically or by regular mail to create a clear picture of their candidate pool.

The commonalities of love and work hunting have been noticed by both groups of seekers. The first step of online dating, the personal profile, is like sending out a résumé, though it includes a good deal of information not normally found in a résumé, and the goal, of course, is a date/relationship, instead of an interview/job. Just as job hunters are told to mail or email their résumés, post them to online job sites and so on, love hunters must post their personal profiles to the dating sites.

To evaluate the pool of candidates for work, advertisers review their credentials. Applicants for love also present their qualifications, in the form of the personal profile required on nearly all online dating sites. The profile is one feature that distinguishes online dating from print ads; nearly all sites require members to post a profile. The profile on most online dating sites typically asks daters to provide facts about themselves such as height, eye colour, and so on, as well as basic features of those they seek. There is also typically a narrative section for written descriptions of the dater and his or her desired date. Online job hunting sites work in a similar way: job hunters have the opportunity to present facts about themselves in the form of their résumé. Some sites allow job seekers to paste in a previously prepared résumé, but one alternative is to build a résumé on the site, putting in information in key categories like work experience, education, and the type of job being sought.

Posting a résumé to an Internet job search site works in a similar way to the profiles on dating sites. In applying for work, particularly since the goal is to create the greatest number of possible contacts, having résumés online enhances the possibility that employers will see them and offer applicants the chance to apply and/or interview for open positions. Like dating sites, there is the possibility of fraud and misrepresentation on job sites. For this reason, it is possible to post a résumé anonymously just as it is conventional to post a dating profile using a screen name. For candidates for love and work, the essential process of posting qualifications but protecting one's identity is the same. In the same way that job seekers present their very best qualifications to potential employers, date seekers present their very best personal qualities to potential partners.

Truth value, style shifting, specifics: Some differences

Although the processes by which date seekers and job seekers make contact and move toward relationships are similar in some key ways, they also differ in ways that are essentially rhetorical in nature. The differences hinge on the ways in which writers of online personals draw on Aristotle's classic ethos (argument by appeal to character), pathos (argument by appeal to emotions), and logos (argument by appeal to logic) (Aristotle as cited in Kennedy, 1991) to create an artistic argument for their appeal to potential partners; these rhetorical features work very differently in employment advertisements.

Aristotle's strategies for argument provide a useful structure for the analysis of these differences between personal ads and job ads. In both kinds of ads, the writers are trying to make a case for themselves (either individually or as part of an organisational structure). The goal of the ad is to persuade readers to be interested in and respond to the advertiser. Artistic arguments classically rely for proof on three types of pisteis: ethos, logos, and pathos. Aristotle makes these clear:

> Of the *pisteis* provided through speech there are three species: for some are in the character [*ethos*] of the speaker and some in disposing the listener in some way, and some in the argument [*logos*] itself, by showing or seeming to show something. [There is persuasion] through character whenever the speech is spoken in such a way as to make the speaker worthy of credence. ... [There is persuasion] through the hearers when they are led to feel emotion [*pathos*] by the speech; for we do not give the same judgment when grieved and rejoicing or when being friendly and hostile. ... Persuasion occurs through the arguments [*logoi*] when we show the truth or the apparent truth from whatever is persuasive in each case. (Aristotle as cited in Kennedy, 1991, pp. 37–9)

These three classical bases for arguments work somewhat differently for love seekers than they do for job seekers.

The level of truth-telling in online environments is a topic that has been studied in various ways by scholars. While these studies do not always focus specifically on dating ads in contrast to job ads, they do give a general idea of the level of truth-telling to be found in personal relationships online. For example, Hardey (2002) looked specifically at honesty in online dating sites and found that despite anonymity, online dating sites provide 'a foundation for the building of trust and establishing real world relationships' (p. 583). However, when studies look directly at using online dating to find a mate, lying is clearly identified as a problem and leads subjects to say they prefer to meet potential partners in person rather than online (Knox, Daniels, Sturdivant, & Zusman, 2001). The popular literature reports similar problems (e.g., Harmon, 2003; Lee, 2002; Lehmann-Haupt, 2006; Nussbaum, 2002; Williams 2004).

Online dating ads appeal shamelessly to the emotions, while help wanted ads are usually an unemotional description of an opening; some date seekers try to make their case on the specifics of their personal credentials, while employment ads are required by law to be non-specific in a number of key ways. Thus, while the truth telling is similar for love seekers and job seekers, the appeals to emotion and use of logic provide a clear contrast.

These claims warrant some further exploration. Ordinarily, job ads tell the truth about the nature of the work and the qualifications needed for the position advertised. Sometimes the ads provide detailed information about the organisation doing the hiring. Universities, for instance, describe location, student body, type of institution (two-year, four-year, graduate, private, public), and so on. For example:

> The campuses of the University of California provide exciting environments that foster world-class education and research opportunities. The University of California continuously seeks applicants for faculty positions at each of its ten campuses. Links to campus Web sites announcing faculty and other academic appointments can be found at: http://www.ucop.edu/acadadv/aca-jobs.html The University of California is an Equal Opportunity Employer committed to excellence through diversity. (Chronicle.com, 2003)

To create an ethical base for any kind of ad or other argument, Aristotle suggests the need to establish the writer's moral character or authority. A contemporary rhetorical text describes ethos or character this way:

> Ethos is the persuasive aspect of a writer's or a speaker's persona.... People will, by nature, be more willing to believe the testimony of experts and authorities, even when these authorities are speaking outside their areas of expertise.... More important than

belonging to a credible category, however, is the kind of ethos that a writer or speaker creates. If an audience does not know who you are and what you believe in, it has no particular reason to believe what you have to say – or even to listen carefully. To make them pay attention, you have to somehow convey to them that you speak authoritatively. An advertiser, for example, who wants to sell a cold remedy will put an actor in a white coat and give him a microscope, thereby implying that physicians recommend the remedy. (Sudol, 1987, p. 193)

Job ads must not only establish ethos overtly as in Sudol's (1987) example, but also must be generally truthful about the nature of the work and the kind of employee being sought. Usually, ethos of both kinds is assumed. Sometimes, depending on the job, a salary range may be cited, or a specific job title will be used, such as, mechanical engineer or intensive care nurse. Areas of expertise, years of experience, and other key characteristics are often given, so that job seekers can tell whether the position is one for which they are qualified. These strategies help both job seekers, who can decide whether or not to apply, and employers, who will get applications from those reasonably qualified for the job. Accurate information is essential to draw appropriate candidates.

There is, ordinarily, or should be, a direct connection between what is in the job ad and the basic qualifications being sought. Inevitably, some people who are not qualified will apply, and then the employer must sort out, based on the specified qualifications, those who should or should not be in the candidate pool. Job ads do not reveal corporate culture or the boss's personality. On the whole, it is an orderly, honest process in which people's good character is presented fairly on both sides. As many people who have changed jobs know, employment ads may leave out key information that new employees must learn on the job. This problem is one of the frustrations online job seekers report (Feldman & Klaas, 2002).

However, this characteristic is quite different from outright lies, a common feature of personal ads, online, or otherwise. For instance, Cornwell and Lundgren (2001) note that in many forms of computer-mediated communication, people can easily 'mask various aspects of appearance, age, gender, personal attributes, or background characteristics' (p. 200). These researchers found that people making romantic connections by computer were significantly more likely to misrepresent themselves in terms of age and physical characteristics than those meeting face-to-face. However, Cornwell and Lundgren (2001) also found no significant difference in misrepresentation of other character-istics, such as, interests, background, occupation, and so on. Although Cornwell and Lundgren (2001) were looking at chat rooms, email, and other forms of computer communication, the point about the possib-ility of misrepresentation still holds. Whitty's (2002) survey of chat room behaviour supports this finding. In a survey of 320 chat users, she found lying to be common, especially among men, on gender, occupa-tion, education, and income, while women lie chiefly for safety reasons. While this study examined chat room behaviour and not online dating sites specifically, it seems reasonable to suggest similar behaviour would occur on dating sites.

The help-wanted ads make an effort to be truthful about the kind of job and kind of situation being offered. By contrast, online personals are not necessarily fully accurate in their content. In terms of ethos or 'truth value', then, while job ads are generally honest and the hiring process attempts to be fair, online dating is much more of an ethical free-for-all.

According to Aristotle, a second way to make an effective argument is through an appeal to the feelings of the audience (Aristotle as cited in Kennedy, 1991). Aristotle could reasonably be described as the first psychologist (Kennedy, 1991), since he describes the full range of human emotions in great detail to show how writers or speakers might sway an audience through emotion. He writes clearly about how an appeal to the emotions can work:

> For the speaker to seem to have certain qualities is more useful in deliberation; for the audience to be disposed in a certain way [is more useful] in lawsuits; for things do not seem the same to those who are friendly and those who are hostile, nor [the same] to the angry and the calm but either altogether different or different in importance: to one who is friendly the person about whom he passes judgment seems not to do wrong or only in a small way; to one who is hostile, the opposite; and to a person feeling strong desire and being hopeful, if something in the future is a source of pleasure, it appears that it will come to pass and will be good, but to an unemotional person and one in a disagreeable state of mind, the opposite. (Aristotle as cited in Kennedy, 1991, p. 120)

In one way, this discussion is nothing more than Aristotle saying, 'know your audience'. However, in another way, he is saying that a successful argument appeals to the emotions, that is, the speaker or writer must affect the feelings of the audience in a particular way to produce the desired response.

The rhetorical technique of appealing to readers' emotions is another area in which employment ads and personal ads are quite different. Employment ads seldom make any use of emotional appeal whatsoever. While job seekers, especially those who are unemployed, may have a substantial emotional investment in reading and responding to ads online, the intention of neither the advertiser nor the job seeker is to arouse the emotions positively or negatively.

Personal ads work in quite different ways. The goal is to catch the readers' eye and appeal to the emotions. The appeal is both that the ad is cleverly written, and that it uses some key words (for example, 'rare treasure' and 'highest standards and morals') to pull on the reader's feelings. Other scholars have explored the nature of online dating via the ads as a form of flirting or play, appealing to writers' sense of attractiveness or their sexuality (Whitty, 2003; Whitty & Carr, 2003). As Aristotle pointed out, an artistic argument that makes effective use of pathos can be highly persuasive.

Aristotle's last category of effective argument, the appeal to reason, provides a third approach to go along with ethos and pathos. He notes that 'persuasion occurs through arguments [logoi] when we show the truth or the apparent truth from whatever is persuasive in each case' (Aristotle as cited in Kennedy, 1991). Arguments are based on the 'common topics', which we know as the various rhetorical modes, such as, examples, definitions, cause and effect, comparison, contrast and so on (Aristotle as cited in Kennedy, 1991).

In logos, the advertiser uses reasoning to persuade, bringing in facts, data, and other kinds of specific information to make a point (Crowley & Hawhee, 2004). The kinds of specifics that can be included in the two categories of advertising are quite different. Personal ads are under no legal or other restrictions and do not hesitate to specify both the advertiser's personal characteristics and those of the person being sought. Online personals specify a remarkable amount of information, a key difference from their newspaper analogues. Dating profiles online, as described previously, ask for age, astrological sign, location, physical description, languages spoken, ethnicity, religion, education, occupation, income, smoking and drinking preferences, marital status, and whether or not the advertiser has or wants children. Then there is often space for two narratives, one in which the advertiser can describe him or herself, and another in which the advertiser can describe his or her match. Finally, there can be a section for personality preferences, which allows the advertiser to indicate feelings about TV, leisure activities, politics, musical tastes, pets, and so on. It is possible for the advertiser to set the search parameters to narrow the search for matches by location, religion, ethnicity or other of these characteristics. Clearly, personal ads often try to make their case on specific logical arguments using detailed information.

Neither job advertisers nor job seekers can present many personal specifics of this kind. Indeed, in advertising positions, employers are constrained by law from specifying the kinds of candidates they want by age, gender, race, ethnicity, sexual preference, and so on. The most they can say is 'equal opportunity, affirmative action employer' or 'minorities and women are encouraged to apply' or words to that effect. They can be specific in describing the job or position and usually are, to whatever extent it is possible to do so. However, unlike personal ads, job ads cannot define candidates by height, weight, religion, or personality traits, no matter how desirable these might be to the advertiser unless these relate directly to the ability to perform the work required.

To argue by specifics, according to Aristotle, is to try to convince readers of the writer's point through the use of facts, data, and other kinds of detailed information. In the details of online personals, writers use their individual characteristics hoping that readers will think 'This person is right for me', or perhaps 'We are right for each other'. In job ads, the goal in using specifics is similar, that is, advertisers hope that candidates will see a position and think 'I am qualified for this job'. However, the specifics in each case are markedly different, partly because the legal restrictions in employment advertising simply do not apply to personals. Additionally, because the goals of the ads, that is, to get dates or workers, are different, their content naturally includes distinct information.

Connecting and disconnecting

Online personal ads and online job ads seek connection by drawing on classical rhetorical techniques, including the well-known rhetorical modes of narration, description, exposition, and so forth. They also share other features, such as, their common goal of generating many responses in order to find the right person and their respective use of a set of credentials (online profile and online or paper résumé) to help people identify one another for love or work. Nonetheless, these two types of ads also differ in salient and classically rhetorical ways. Online personals and job ads make very different uses of ethos, pathos and logos to achieve their purposes. Rhetorical strategies described by Aristotle, including the rhetorical modes or topoi and the ethos, pathos and logos of argument, are the key mechanisms that help account for success or failure to connect by online advertising for love or work.

References

Bargh, J. A., McKenna, K. Y. A. & Fitzsimons, G. M. (2002). Can you see the real me? Activation and expression of the 'true self' on the internet. *Journal of Social Issues, 58* (1), 33–48.

Chronicle.com. Retrieved 28 February, 2003 from the World Wide Web: http://www.chronicle.com.

Cornwell, B., & Lundgren, D. C. (2001). Love on the internet: Involvement and misrepresentation in romantic relationships in cyberspace vs. realspace. *Computers in Human Behavior, 17*, 197–211.

Crowley, S., & Hawhee, D. (2004). *Ancient rhetorics for contemporary students* (3rd edn). New York: Pearson Education, Inc.

Ellin, A. (2003, 16 February). Mix and match, for many reasons. *New York Times*, p. 3:10.

Feldman, D. C., & Klaas, B. S. (2002). Internet job hunting: A field study of applicant experiences with on-line recruiting [Electronic version]. *Human Resource Management, 41* (2), 175–92.

Hardey, M. (2002). Life beyond the screen: Embodiment and identity through the internet. *Sociological Review, 50* (4), 570–85.

Harmon, A. (2003, 29 June). Online dating sheds its stigma as losers.com. *New York Times*, p. 1:1, 21.

Kennedy, G. A. (ed.) (1991). *On rhetoric: A theory of civic discourse*. New York: Oxford University Press.

Knox, D., Daniels, V., Sturdivant, L., & Zusman, M. E. (2001). College student use of the internet for mate selection. *College Student Journal, 35* (1), 158–60.

Lee, L. (2002, 24 November). Men on the internet are on another planet. *New York Times*, p. 9: 6.

Lehmann-Haupt, R. (2006, 12 February). Is the right chemistry a click nearer? *New York Times*, p. 9: 2.

Nussbaum, E. (2002, 15 December). Online personals are cool. *New York Times Magazine*, p. 106.

Ryze.com. Retrieved 11 December, 2005 from: http://ryze.com.

Sudol, R. A. (1987). *Textfiles: A rhetoric for word processing*. San Diego, CA: Harcourt Brace Jovanovich.

Whitty, M. T. (2002). Liar, liar! An examination of how open, supportive and honest people are in chat rooms. *Computers in Human Behavior, 18*, 343–52.

Whitty, M. T. (2003). Cyber-flirting: Playing at love on the internet. *Theory & Psychology, 13* (3), 339–57.

Whitty, M. T. & Carr, A. N. (2003). Cyberspace as potential space: Considering the web as a playground to cyber-flirt. *Human Relations, 56* (7), 869–91.

Williams, A. (2004, 12 December). E-dating bubble springs a leak. *New York Times,* p. 9: 1, 6.

Acknowledgments

The author gratefully acknowledges the help of several readers who provided feedback and/or information used in this article: Kate Epstein, Barbara and Gary Reetz, and David Snider. Monica Whitty's editorial advice improved the paper substantively and significantly. Errors and omissions are mine alone.

7

How do I Love Thee and Thee and Thee: Self-presentation, Deception, and Multiple Relationships Online

Julie M. Albright

Fifty women gathered in June 2003 at a television news conference to announce they had all been duped by a man they had met online: US Army Col. Kassem Saleh, a military officer whom each had met via an online dating site, had been wooing all 50 women simultaneously, even going so far as to propose to many of them, despite the fact that he was already married to another woman. At least two of the unwitting women had already bought wedding gowns before discovering the ruse. One woman called Colonel Saleh's email love letters 'intoxicating' and another said they were 'more romantic than the works of poets William Butler Yeats or Robert Browning' (Kleinfeld, 2003). 'You are my world, my life, my love and my universe', Saleh allegedly wrote in an email love note to one of his many mistresses (Kleinfield, 2003).

An estimated 16.3 million users accessed Internet dating sites in 2002 (Muriel, 2003). The most popular matchmaking website, Yahoo.com, claims almost 380 million visitors per month (Pasha, 2005). For those sincerely seeking it, many seem to be finding love online, with 8 per cent of men and 5 per cent of women in one study reporting that they had married someone they met online (Albright, 2001; Knapp, 2004). Though studies have examined meeting online (Albright, 2001; Wysocki, 1996), flirting online (Whitty, 2004), attraction via Internet personal ads (Strassberg & Holty, 2003), anonymity and trust online (Hardey, 2004), only a few studies have examined deception and infidelity online (Cornwell & Lundren, 2001; Whitty, 2002, 2003, 2005), and its impact on sincere communicators. Inspired by the story of Colonel Saleh, this chapter will attempt to explore how computer communication may foster the creation and maintenance of similar multiple, simultaneous intimate relationships.

Steps to attraction

People have been meeting and courting for centuries – usually face-to-face, but sometimes mediated by communication channels, such as, letter writing when separated by distance (Decker, 1998), by prison walls (Maybin, 2000), or by immigration as was the case of the 'picture brides' for Asian men in the United States, who viewed photos of potential brides in the hopes of meeting an overseas wife (Chow, 1987). Yet unlike previous mate selection methods, computer communication holds the possibility to change the 'dance' of courtship and intimacy, by providing an instantly accessible, large pool of availables in an environment which enhances romantic projections (Albright & Conran, 2003) and speeds up intimacy and self-disclosure relative to face-to-face interactions, in a process Walther (1996) calls 'hyperpersonal' communication.

Lying to get a lover

Strategies of self-presentation to create favourable first impressions in a potential romantic partner are important in forming a relationship. A person forms an impression of a potential mate through what Goffman has called 'sign activity' of two kinds: the *'expression given'* and the *'expression given off'* (Goffman, 1959). The 'expression given' involves symbols expressed during verbal and related communication, while the 'expression given off' includes such sign vehicles as clothing, appearance, sex, age, racial characteristics, size and looks, posture, speech pattern, bodily gestures, and so forth. Goffman calls that which serves to influence the other people present a 'performance', and states that any performance has a moral imperative that the character in front of them has a certain degree of verisimilitude, possessing the attributes he or she appears to possess (Goffman, 1959), otherwise the performance is deceptive. Typically, the audience is aware that the individual may be trying to present a favourable image of themselves, and therefore will pay more attention to the signs given off, since they are viewed as less intentional and less controllable by the actor. Despite the fact that most people seem to feel that deception in a romantic relationship is morally reprehensible (Peterson, 1996), a large majority (92 per cent) of people reportedly *have* lied to romantic partners, at least in face-to-face interactions (Boon & McCloud, 2001; Knox, Schacht, Holt, & Turner, 1993), sometimes in an attempt to fit what the other person seeks (Rowatt, Cunningham, & Druen, 1998). Computer communication enhances the ability to selectively self-present through an increased ability to control the signs given off, allowing the presentation of a care-fully crafted, edited impression, which can be more easily tailored to fulfil the romantic ideals of a desired partner (Whitty & Gavin, 2001). Lacking the visual cues available in offline interactions, an online lover may lie about many things, including age, marital status, income, looks, or other important factors in attraction (Cornwell & Lundgren, 2001).

I love thee and thee and thee

The story of Colonel Saleh and the broken hearted fiancées shows in a worst case scenario how computer communication can be used to deceive unwitting lovers. Infidelity in relationships is not new (Aviram & Amichai-Hamburger, 2005), and the distress caused by infidelity is well-known (Cann, Mangum, & Wells, 2003; Brown, 2001). Online, there are indications that at least infidelity may be quite common: One recent Canadian study estimated that 18 per cent of people on dating sites are married, while another dating site, Friendfinder.com, estimates that 48 per cent of its service subscribers are married (Reagan, 2002). Research has found that people may view sexual acts online, such as, chatting sexually with an online partner, as cheating, without even the need to involve bodies offline (Whitty, 2003, 2005). Computer communication enables new ways of carrying on illicit affairs, to an extent perhaps previously improbable, if not impossible: While one could imagine someone carrying on simultaneous affairs with multiple partners in 'real life', as in the sailor with a 'girl in every port', it would be hard to imagine someone being able to carry out 50 simultaneous, intense, and intimate affairs in the physical realm where the women were involved enough to see themselves as 'fiancées', as in the story of Colonel Saleh, without the hyper-intimate aspects of computer communication playing a role.

In order to study multiple relationships and infidelity online, this chapter will rely on data collected in two phases: Phase 1 consisted of an online survey of impression management and relationship forma-tion on the Internet consisting of 55 multiple choice questions and one open-ended question, which allowed respondents to tell the story of their online dating experience, worded as follows: Would you like to briefly tell the story of your online relationship, or make any addi-tional comments about your experience? If so, please feel free to do so here. Participants were recruited for the Phase 1 survey via online banner notices when they logged onto an Internet MUD site called DragonMud, and via a notice posted in chat areas. Respondents were also recruited from a second site, America Online, via notices posted on message boards and in chat rooms. Qualitative data for this chapter will be drawn from Phase 1, which yielded a sample of 513 participants, composed of 52 per cent men and 48 per cent women, ranging in ages from 18 to 71 years. Quantitative data will be drawn from Phase 2 of this study, which consisted of a second online survey of 31 multiple choice questions given to subscribers of a large Internet Matchmaking Service. Participants were solicited via an email letter containing a link to the survey. In all, 4726 people elected to answer the survey. Participants in Phase 2 were 33 per cent men and 67 per cent women, ranging in ages from 21 to 76 years. All respondents self-identify as single in order to subscribe to this particular matchmaking site.

Intentions online

Respondents in Phase 2 indicated a variety of reasons for using online matchmaking services: 53 per cent indicated they were seeking a committed relationship (monogamous dating), while 37 per cent indicated they were looking to get married. Only 8 per cent indicated they were only seeking 'casual dating' via these services. The majority of respondents indicated they had used more than one online matchmaking site in order to seek a partner, and about a third (30 per cent) reported they had actually met someone face-to-face that they had first contacted online.

Respondents were asked to rate the importance of character/honesty in a potential romantic partner on a 5-point Likert scale, ranging from 1 ('not at all important') to 5 ('very important'). Eighty-eight per cent of respondents rated character/honesty a '5,' or very important. Respondents were then asked to compare the character/honesty of the potential romantic partners they had met online, compared to those they had met face-to-face, on a 7-point Likert scale, ranging from 1 ('much worse) to 7 ('much better'). Only 7 per cent rated the potential romantic partners they had met online as worse than those they had meet face-to-face, while 40 per cent rated those they had met online as *better* in terms of character and honesty compared to those they had met first offline. Forty-three per cent rated them about the same.

Increased pool of availables and ease of communication

Many popular accounts say the online environment encourages deception and infidelity due to fostering a 'kid in the candy store' mentality by the wide availability of multiple potential romantic partners online, and the ease with which one can contact them (Albright, 2001; Whitty & Carr, 2005, 2006). In order to determine the frequency with which respondents were deceived about monogamy by those they met on an online dating site, they were asked to respond to the following: 'People who I have met online have said they were dating only me when they were also involved with someone else.' Respondents answered using a 5-point Likert scale, ranging from 1 ('never') to 5 ('constantly'). Forty-two per cent reported a 1 ('never happened') or 2 ('rarely happened'), 19 per cent reported a '3' or '4' (that it occasionally or frequently happened), while 39 per cent reported a '5', that it happened to them 'constantly.' Respondents were not asked how they found out about this deception.

To elaborate on the statistical findings of Phase 2, qualitative data from Phase 1 were analysed for recurrent themes in order to further explain how people use the Internet to foster multiple simultaneous relationships and infidelity. One recurrent theme which emerged was the ease with which one can meet a large pool of potential mates online, which may ease the process of committing infidelity, as evidenced by the surprised response of Sheryl, a 24 year old female:

This has been such a wild experience. I placed a personal ad with 'Digital City,' and received 200–300 replies. It was fascinating. The men I have expected to like I didn't and vice-versa. I did this so I could get over my ex, and it's working.

Abby, a 26 year old woman, was shocked to discover that the man whom she had been dating was involved in multiple other online relationships, some of which had traversed offline. She was pregnant, and discovered she was the '7th baby momma' – or seventh to have a child out of wedlock with this man. Abby tried to warn others away from the man, a 33 year old screen writer:

I am using email to contact the 1300+ women that Tony has been in contact for the past two and a half months.

It would probably take much longer, going to traditional singles locations, such as, bars and nightclubs to come away with 1300 plus phone numbers for potential dates. Online, one can meet many potential romantic partners, which makes it easy for those already in a relationship to initiate additional romantic relationships. As an example, Jill describes her experience of being lied to online by married men:

I have actually met a lot of people online. Most of the men seem much better online than they are in person. Most are married, and most lie.

Selective self-presentation and hyperintimacy

As the previous narrative shows, some people may be tempted to selectively self present or lie in order attract a romantic partner. Respondents in Phase 2 were asked if they had ever lied to a date in order to make them like them by responding to a 5-point Likert scale ranging from 1 'never' to 5 'constantly'. The majority (99 per cent) reported a 1 ('never') or 2 ('seldom'). They were then asked if they ever lied to someone online in order to appear more attractive, and on the same 5-point Likert scale, the majority (98 per cent) reported a 1 ('never') or 2 ('seldom'). Respondents were then asked if people they had met online had 'lied about important aspects of themselves in important ways'. On the same 5-point Likert scale, 39 per cent reported they had 'seldom' or 'never' been lied to; 25 per cent reported they had been occasionally lied to, while 11 per cent reported they had been frequently or constantly lied to by someone the had met online.

Lying about marital status or other relationships is one area of deception which is used to foster multi-personal relationships. Susan's story sheds light on the experience of such deception:

> It's a long and difficult story. Basically the guy was selling himself as this guy looking to settle down and get married. He made himself out to be the perfect husband. We did click intellectually and got along great so I thought it was great. He made it out that I was what he was looking for. Being a pilot he could fly to me and fly me to him so I let it happen. In the end I found out he had a lot of women like me thinking they were all his girlfriend too! He didn't lie about who he was or what he did. He only lied about his intentions and other relationships so it was hard to catch him in his lies.

Because of audience segregation, such lies are often difficult if not impossible to discover online. The next narrative by Audrey illustrates the major life changes a lover will go to in order to pursue such a relationship, only later to learn of the deception:

> He was very honest about his looks, personality, and occupation. Unfortunately, he was not completely honest about dating two

women at once. After I moved out there to be with him (although in separate apartments), and had been there for a year, I ran into him with another woman. After talking to him about it, it turns out that she moved out to be with him about a month before I did. So I was the other woman the whole time. I think he would disagree with my honesty ratings, and say that he was honest with me the whole way. It's true that he never lied directly, but I never asked the right questions which would force him to reveal the true situation.

In addition to lying about monogamy, it is easy to encourage interest in an online lover by presenting an idealised 'fantasy self', as illustrated by this next narrative from Anna:

> I was in the beginning stage of ending a marriage, and met a guy online, who said all the right things... after feeling like my wings had been clipped in a dead end marriage... this online guy gave me all the attention I was lacking... he swept me off my feet... before I knew it, I was in a fantasy world... he was good-looking, funny... and successful... treated me like a princess... Trusting him was easy... he was so easy to talk to... and would listen for hours... then... the bottom fell out... to make a long story short... I found out he was married... and the name I had been calling him for 10 months was not his... the job he spoke so highly of did not exist... I was crushed... But he is not an exception – in the 5 years of being single... there are a ton of people who lie... they do not see real people on the other side of their monitor.

Because people may present a fantasy image online which closely matches the other person's schema of what they are seeking in a mate, online relationships can become quite intoxicating and, some have argued, even addicting (see Whitty & Carr, 2005, 2006). As an example of this, the next narrative from 'Susan' describes her affair with an online Casanova as an 'emotional high':

> Experiencing the emotional highs of being open and honest about sexual wants, needs and desires, and having this other person respond back claiming similar wants, needs and desires, made me even more dissatisfied with my spouse then I already was. This caused me to be short tempered with him, and to become very easily annoyed by small things he did or did not do, or did or did not say. My partner online spoke of romance and romantic things, and seemed to have

the same sexual desires as I did and he shared in our role playing and made me feel wanted, sexy and needed like a man should need a woman and how a woman wants to feel. He lusted after me, and that was what I lacked at home. This did not work out when he ended up in the hospital, unknown to me, and I did not hear from him for a few weeks, and I wrote a letter to some of his online friends, whose addresses were included when he sent me jokes. This was when I found out he was very much with his wife, and had not moved from North Carolina to Georgia, as he claimed, and that everything he said to me, had been said to numerous other women, as I spoke to one of them online. She told me things he had said to her that were identical to what he had told me. This was a very painful experience for me and led to our no longer speaking to one another. But I sure do miss our talking, and if he had just told me the truth I think we could have remained talking online and continued in our role playing and fantasising.

Because they are hyperintimate (exceeding the speed and depth of intimacy compared to face-to-face relationships) (Walther, 1996), coupled with heightened levels of fantasy and projection fostered by anonymity (Whitty & Carr, 2005) online as discussed previously, online relationships may cause pre-existing relationships to pale in comparison, thereby encouraging cheating, as illustrated by Beatrice's narrative:

When I began to chat online, I never envisioned myself becoming involved with anyone. My marriage (we had been married over 25 years) was a little 'stale' and the thought of 'chatting' was exciting yet harmless. When I began to chat with this gentleman, I really felt a closeness that I feel was lacking in my marriage at the time. When we met face to face in July, I really felt a true connection to this man and he has made my life complete. I truly believe as human beings, that we are capable of loving more than one person in our lifetimes. This has proved true with me. My marriage is good . . . I love my husband and also love my lover. We have been together four times since we met online and each time it is wonderful. We share so many things. Our values are so much the same and we just enjoy being together.

Strategies for selective-self presentation online vary, from lies about being single when one is married, to the strategic use of photos. A photograph stands in as a sign for physical attractiveness, and those who are less confident of their physical appearance may omit the photo as a way to selectively self-present, as demonstrated by Terry's narrative:

> At that point in my life, I was very concerned about my 'image' since I was overweight. I thought the best way to meet people was to talk to them online, where I could hide behind the anonymity of a computer screen.

People who have lied about their appearance online may agree to a face-to-face meeting, probably hoping their personality will carry the day. The ruse is obviously quickly discovered upon a face-to-face meeting, which may cause a rupture in the relationship, as the other person realises they have been deceived. Joanne discussed such an experience as told to her by her current lover, Mark:

> Seems he had met a few people from online, and it had been a huge let down. One woman said she was 5'10", and a size 12. When they met she was 5'6", and could barely squeeze into the movie theatre seat. Then mid-way through the film said 'I can't contain myself anymore', and attacked him. He said he had to climb over the seats in front of him to get away from her.

Some respondents describe having experienced selective self-presentation techniques using a photo, typically through the potential partner providing a photo depicting them at a younger age, or when they were more physically attractive, thinner, had more hair, and so forth, or by providing a photo which is highly stylised and perhaps digitally enhanced, as in a 'glamour photo' type shot. Thirty-four per cent of the respondents in Phase 2 reported that someone had posted a photo that was more attractive than the person actually was in person.

Because a person can present an idealised self online (Walther, Slovacek, & Tidwell, 2001; Whitty & Carr, 2005, 2006), potentially negative personality characteristics can also be carefully edited and managed. Lina discusses her ultimate disappointment with her online lover, Doug:

> I met this person, we'll call him Doug, online. He was very interested in me and seemed very supportive. I talked to people who had met him in person previously, so I knew that he was an 'okay' person. When we finally met in person a few months later, he seemed far more moody and high-strung than I was expecting. Turns out he also

drank a fair amount and had a HORRIBLE tempter. Those traits were carefully masked from me during our long online sessions.

In sum, how does computer communication facilitate infidelity with multiple partners? First, through increasing the pool of potential partners one can easily meet and communicate with online. With email communication, it is possible to maintain multiple connections much more easily than via telephone or in person: Like Colonel Saleh, some of the men mentioned in the narratives cut and paste their romantic emails, copying the same messages to multiple women, thereby using email to persuade multiple women of their serious romantic interest.

Computer communication also allows deception about multiple relationships via enhanced 'audience segregation' (Goffman, 1959), or keeping partners physically separated from one another. The narratives presented in this chapter have shown that many who are deceptive about monogamy are often not found out until the lovers actually run into one another with alternate partners on the street, as was the case where the woman had moved to be near her online lover. Yet even the large percentage (47 per cent) that said they had been lied to about monogamy online may under-estimate the real percentage of having been deceived about this, since those reporting are presumably only the ones who discovered the ruse: Those who are dating more 'successful' liars may not have found out.

Lastly, the enhanced 'hyperpersonal' quality online and the ability to selectively self-present also fosters multiple relationships: Online Casanovas can construct an idealised image, which may bear little or no resemblance to offline reality, thereby fuelling the romantic fantasies and projections of their online lovers, leaving them to believe they've met a 'soul mate' (Albright & Conran, 2003; Seiden, 2001; Whitty & Carr, 2005, 2006). Love may indeed be blind in this case, because people may want to believe the romantic fantasy, rather than face the harsh reality that their lover may be seeing someone else. Although most relationships *do* start with some degree of projection and idealisation about the other, the Internet engenders it to a much higher degree due to the paucity of visual and other cues (Walther et al., 2001). It is noteworthy that one woman in this study, Anna, makes sense of online deception by saying that people who lie do not see 'real' people on the other side of the screen. Perhaps the lowered accountability levels of online interactions and the inability to pinpoint an online persona to a solid offline identity might foster such façades and lower people's inhibitions about lying. These people might rationalise that since the person on the other side of the screen 'isn't really real', no one is actually being hurt (Albright, 2001; Whitty, 2005; Whitty & Carr, 2005, 2006).

Although lying takes place online, data from this study suggests that people lie to romantic partners on and offline at almost equal levels. Perhaps only what is lied *about* differs: A large percentage (47 per cent) in this study reported that the person they were dating said they were dating only them, when they were in fact seeing others, a lie which may be more difficult to 'pull off' for an extended amount of time face-to-face, given that people offline often have social networks through which they can verify such information as marital status. New online services which attempt to create social networks online (e.g., Friendster and Myspace) have become instant successes – perhaps by encouraging trust through increased accountability, via the notion people are meeting a 'friend of a friend'.

This study supports prior research which suggests that people do lie to romantic partners (Boon & McCloud, 2001; Knox, Schacht, Holt, & Turner, 1993), but this study finds that people lie online and off at almost equal levels, and not more online despite the enhanced ability to selectively self-present. However, the types of lies told online and off may vary, and more research into the types of lies told in face-to-face versus online relationships should be undertaken. Further research is also suggested on infidelity online, to discern what differences there may be between carrying on extra-relational affairs online versus off, and if differences exist in 'uncovering' cheating partners online versus off. In addition, more research is warranted on the presentation strategies of deceptive versus sincere communicators seeking relationships online when flirting in the early relationship initiation stage.

References

Albright, J. (2001). *Impression formation and attraction in computer-mediated communication*. Unpublished doctoral dissertation, University of Southern California.

Albright, J., & Conran, T. (2003). Desire, love, and betrayal: Constructing and deconstructing intimacy online. *Journal of Systemic Therapies, 22*(3), 42–53.

Aviram, I., & Amichai-Hamburger, Y. (2005, April) Online infidelity: Aspects of dyadic satisfaction, self-disclosure and narcissism. *Journal of Computer Mediated Communication, 10*(3), Retrieved 11 April 2005 from: http://jcmc.indiana.edu/vol10/issue3/aviram.html

Boon, S., & McCloud, B. (2001). Deception in romantic relationships: Subjective estimates at success at deceiving and attitudes toward deception. *Journal of Social and Personal Relationships, 18*(4), 463–76.

Brown, E. M. (2001). *Patterns of infidelity and their treatment* (2nd edn). Ann Arbor, MI: Edwards Brothers.

Cann, A., Mangum, M., & Wells, M. (2003). Distress in response to relationship infidelity: the roles of gender and attitudes about relationships. *Journal of Sex Research, 38*(3), 185–90.

Chow, E. (1987). The development of feminist consciousness among Asian American women. *Gender and Society, 1*(3), 284–99.

Cornwell, B., & Lundgren, D. (2001). Love on the Internet: involvement and misrepresentation in romantic relationships in cyberspace vs. realspace. *Computers in Human Behavior, 17*, 197–211.

Decker, W. (1998). Epistolary practices: letter writing in America before telecommunications. Retrieved 15 October 2003 from: http://site.ebrary.com/lib/uscisd/Doc?id=2001276

Goffman, E. (1959). *The presentation of self in everyday life*. New York: Anchor Books.

Hardey, M. (2004). Mediated relationships: Authenticity and the possibility of romance. *Information, Communication & Society, 7*, 207–22.

Kleinfeld, N. (2003, 11 June). An officer and a gentleman? 50 women would disagree. *New York Times*, p. A1.

Knapp, D. (2004). 'Women gone wired.' Retrieved 30 December 2005 from: http://www.elle.com/article.asp?section_id=36&article_id=4574&page_number=1&preview=&magind=3804

Knox, D., Schacht, C., Holt, J., & Turner, J. (1993). Sexual lies among university students. *College Student Journal, 27*, 269–72.

Maybin, J. (2000). Death row penfriends: Some effects of letter writing on identity and relationships. In D. Barton & N. Hall (eds), *Letter writing as social practice*. (pp. 151–78). Amsterdam: John Benjamins.

Muriel, D. (2003, January). Netting a lover: Web sites cash in. *CNN.com/world*, 14 January 2003, Retrieved 31 December 2005 from: http://www.cnn.com/2003/WORLD/europe/01/14/internet.dating.

Pasha, S. (2005, August). Online dating feeling less attractive. *CNN/Money*, 18 August 2005, Retrieved 16 March 2006 from: http://money.cnn.com/2005/08/18/technology/online_dating/index.htm

Peterson, C. (1996). Deception in intimate relationships. *International Journal of Psychology, 31*(6), 279–88.

Reagan, B. (2002, 15 April). Bored of the rings. *The Wall Street Journal*, R4.

Rowatt, W., Cunningham, M., & Druen, P. (1998). Deception to get a date. *Personality and Social Psychology Bulletin, 24*, 1228–42.

Seiden, H. M. (2001). Creating passion: An Internet love story. *Journal of Applied Psychoanalytic Studies, 3*(2), 187–95.

Strassberg, D. S., & Holty, S. (2003). An experimental study of women's internet personal ads. *Archives of Sexual Behavior, 32*, 253–60.

Walther, J. (1996). Computer-mediated communication: Impersonal, interpersonal, and hyperpersonal interaction. *Communication Research, 23*, 3–43.

Walther, J. B., Slovacek, C., & Tidwell, L. (2001). Is a picture worth a thousand words? Photographic images in long-term and short-term computer-mediated communication. *Communication Research, 28*, 105–34.

Whitty, M. T. (2002). Liar, Liar! An examination of how open, supportive and honest people are in Chat Rooms. *Computers in Human Behavior, 18*(4), 343–52.

Whitty, M. T. (2003). Pushing the wrong buttons: Men's and women's attitudes towards online and offline infidelity. *CyberPsychology & Behavior, 6*(6), 569–79.

Whitty, M. T. (2004). Cyber-flirting: An examination of men's and women's flirting behaviour both offline and on the Internet. *Behaviour Change, 21*(2), 115–26.

Whitty, M. T. (2005). The 'Realness' of Cyber-cheating: Men and women's representations of unfaithful Internet relationships. *Social Science Computer Review, 23*(1), 57–67.

Whitty, M. T. & Carr, A. N. (2005). Taking the good with the bad: Applying Klein's work to further our understandings of cyber-cheating. *Journal of Couple and Relationship Therapy, 4*(2/3), 103–15.

Whitty, M. T. & Carr, A. N. (2006). *Cyberspace romance: The psychology of online relationships.* Basingstoke: Palgrave Macmillan.

Whitty, M. & Gavin, J. (2001). Age/sex/location: Uncovering the social cues in the development of online relationships. *CyberPsychology and Behaviour, 4*(5), 623–30.

Wysocki, D. (1996). *Love over the modem,* Unpublished doctoral dissertation, University of California, Santa Barbara.

Part 3

Online Dating Progression to Face-to-face: Success or Failure?

8

Expressing Emotion in Text: Email Communication of Online Couples

Andrea J. Baker

This chapter tells how people who have become attracted to each other online express emotion through text. Using quotes from their actual email, I will describe how people communicated their feelings of affection towards each other and about other emotions they expressed during their online writings before and after meeting offline. Effective communication online can contribute to the success or longevity of online relationships (see Baker, 2005).

People who meet online must communicate their thoughts and feelings in text, for a shorter or longer time. Those who form relationships online, especially long distance relationships, use email and chat or posts in blogs or discussion groups, public and private, to tell what they are doing, and to express their feelings. Modes of expression include text in words and pictorial signs such as emoticons and other created signals such as spelled-out sounds. Most of the shared communication online consists of shared words. The words are often expressed more informally than in traditional textual expression, leading some researchers to view online communication somewhere between 'speech-like' and 'writing like' (Danet, 2001) or what I and others have called 'talk/write' to indicate the mix of speaking and writing. While asynchronous media such as email may be closer to formal writing than chat, both usually contain features of 'digital writing' (Danet, 2001) a mode employing tactics to emulate informal speech and to save time by typing fewer characters.

Online pairs of friends, and in this case, lovers or intimate couples, 'talk/write' about everyday events, goals, values, and emotions toward their partners. Here exchanged email documents both feelings about the other and yearnings or longings for the partner's company offline. After an introduction to factors of online attraction, this chapter traces mainly the verbal and also the pictorial forms of expression of major strands of emotion, beginning with affection and extending to other forms of textual relating of feelings in relationships, such as longings, reassurances, apologies, and meta-talk about the progression of the relationship. The processes of 'mirroring' and gender presentation of feelings are then discussed, as well as the expression of feelings as the couples progress from online to offline.

Methodology

Detailed verbalisations of feelings in self-composed text appear in emails of the couples, contributed by a sub-group that voluntarily provided a selection of their written correspondence for the research. These people chose letters or sequences of notes from their email correspondence to share with the researcher, depicting style of communication and changes in their relationships. This paper is based primarily on the subset of couples (n=14) from the larger study of 90 online couples with both partners completing questionnaires, and sometimes follow-up telephone interviews about their online relationships. The subset provided data primarily from email records, with one chat log and one blog selection. The number of emails provided ranges from a few to several hundred with a median average of around ten. This paper also occasionally draws from data from the questionnaires and interviews that asked about use of emoticons and communication patterns. The data were collected between 1997 and 2005.

In providing email, usually only one partner sent email, with the permission of the other, sharing either both sides or only one side of the written conversation. One couple chose to send chat records to document their feelings. One wrote out some of their feelings in their online diaries or blogs, read by each other and many others. The email and chat transmitted during the relationship allow examination of people actually communicating with each other. Since both parties were queried for the main study, the research included many successful couples, such as those who married before or after they completed open-ended questionnaires. A few single people joined after the original research to contribute some email, but these are not used for this chapter.

People are identified by pseudonyms, not their real names. Because the self-selected samples of email and chat are not randomly drawn either from the general population or from the larger group studied, or from all the email exchanged by the participants, the author claims only exploratory results and does not attempt to quantify proportions of types of feelings in the messages. The selections used to illustrate types of emotions and processes in this chapter are neither inclusive nor exhaustive of emotions expressed by the couples. The examples of transmitted feelings combined with a discussion of the literature on emotions online are meant to start to build a typology of online feelings and to suggest directions for future research.

What others have said about emotions online

Researchers have found that people disclose more under certain conditions online than they do offline or face-to-face in physical space. Bargh, McKenna, and Fitzsimons (2002) conceptualise 'the true self' to distinguish those who can reveal more of themselves online, their 'real self' from those who cannot. The ability to express oneself authentically leads to close bonds among online participants (McKenna, Green, & Gleason, 2002). In a qualitative study of real-life online friendship, Henderson and Gilding (2004) document how people often feel closer to their online companions than their offline friends, because of faster self-disclosure and compensation in text for the lack of physical cues present online. These authors expand Walther's (1996) concept of 'hyperpersonal' online presentation of self in their interviews with people who made friendships that sometimes migrated offline. The couples studied here provide evidence supporting the 'hyperhonest' form of communication found in research on romantically involved partners (Baker, 2005).

A recent article by Rabby and Walther (2002) analysing transcripts of online and offline communication suggests that online, people send more supportive statements than other kinds. Using a modified form of Canary's typology of relationship maintenance strategies (Canary, Stafford, Hause, & Wallace, 1993), Rabby (1997) found that the 'narratives' and 'openness' accounted for most of email content among real-life couples, 22 per cent and 38 per cent, respectively or a total of 60 per cent. The objective reality of the couples or the events of their everyday lives, and the more subjective perceptions including self-disclosure and meta-talk occurred in these two categories. The research reported in this chapter concentrates on the subjective perceptions of the couples under the categories employed rather than on the narratives of daily activities contained in the couples' communications.

Also employing Canary's categories, Wright (2004) finds that in both exclusively Internet-based relationships and predominantly Internet-based relationships, 'positivity' and 'openness' characterise the bulk of online communications. People express affection, assurances, and support much more than other types of emotion online. He studied perceptions of people rather than their actual textual communications. The work of other researchers examining gender differences and similarities in expression of emotions online is reviewed later in this paper.

Factors of attraction, textual communications

First, some factors of attraction online are briefly presented in this chapter, with a look at how writing style can draw in or repel others. Then, examples from email and chat show the types of feelings people communicate including affection, encouragement, yearnings, meta-talk, and apologies. Next, the 'hows' or elements of the process of sharing feelings within intimate partnerships are examined, with sections about emoticons and gender differences and similarities. Finally, the chapter notes how people express emotions before meeting face-to-face and after, and how communication affects success.

The question of how people come to know each other in virtual environments (Rabby & Walther, 2002) is addressed. The data in this paper may add to ideas about how relating first online may affect the course of the relationship, and to the body of work on how people maintain relationships online (Wright, 2004). Unlike scholars who have studied the realm of face-to-face communication where nonverbal cues predominate, online researchers recognise that words constitute the bulk of the interaction in computer-mediated communication (Walther, 2004).

Online attraction and writing style

Whether in a dating site, an online game, chat room, or other online venue, a person's way of expressing oneself affects the quantity and kind of person who will engage him or her. Content and mode of expression both count.

Meeting online: what attracts people?

With little or nothing but text to go on, people meeting online must impress through words. How they impart their particular sense of humour (Baker, 1998) can make the difference between a positive impact, and someone ignoring them or thinking they are boorish. Common interests (Cooper & Sportolari, 1997; McKenna et al., 2002; Levine, 2000) articulated in detail can draw someone in, as can a similar ethnic identity or religion (Baker, 2005). The manner the person uses to express content, the 'writing style' (Baker, 1998, 2005), has an impact too, from the technical to the emotional level. Bad grammar and spelling act to cut potential dates or partners out.

How well a person writes relates to personal ability and effect on others, in that someone comfortable with composing in text has a head start towards communicating effectively online, and can attract people who share that comfort, and who admire skill in that area. The writing style is the vehicle to communicate the amount and type of humour preferred. It also reveals common interests, values and lifestyle, and the priorities placed on different life aspects.

Intelligence is desired online and offline and expressed through humour, in common interests and in writing style. The conversation that occurs online is primarily cognitive or intellectual (Ben Ze'ev, 2004), with emotions generated from the content of the conversation as well as the style.

If people's styles are 'in synch', they typically progress to later stages of relating. They go on to talk on the phone and meet online, while still maintaining text contact, though they do not depend upon it.

Writing style: repulsion and attraction

People who are not good writers have a more difficult time attracting others online. While they may have speaking skills or may nonverbally present themselves well in dress, gesture and physical appearance, they rank behind those who adeptly use text, the online medium. Those who routinely spell words wrongly or use them incorrectly, or write with bad grammar do not appeal to others judging the writing style. Another problematic area is risqué content. People who write sexually explicit messages risk driving away those who consider such content inappropriate, especially in initial or early online encounters.

Here are some quotes from people stating what they like or not in general about people's approaches in online writing. Bert describes a definite dislike:

> *I always avoid people who use bad language, or if they are English-speaking people who have poor writing abilities . . . Anybody who starts talking about sex I normally avoid as well.*

In speaking of her original attraction to her partner, Whitney refers to his writing ease:

I always say, since I'm a PR person, it was Grady's grammar and punctu-
ation that made my heart flutter.

Carla continued the theme when asked what she liked about Amanda:

Her writing style – she was fun to RP [role-play] with, lovely grammar,
good spelling, I can't stand chat room exchanges.

The ability to write well would imply at least a beginning facility in
communicating emotions in text.

Content of communication: types of emotions online

These categories emerged from the data of email of the couples written
online correspondence: positive, neutral and negative. Positive emotions
included indirect and direct signs of *affection* expressed through nicknames and verbal statements of liking or loving, *support* through
encouragement and appreciation, and *longing* for each other's physical presence. Neutral *meta-statements* about the relationship occurred
as people re-thought themselves and their involvements, and finally,
more negative or ambivalent emotions such as *apologies* and doubts
were expressed. Following Rabby (1997), most emotions, by far, were
positive.

Nicknames and salutations: indirect affection online

Often when people begin to like each other, they search for special
names and forms of address to individualise their relationships. Asking
what a person prefers is first in the process, and then people commence
to embellish on that name, usually with permission, in friend and
love relationships. If a person already has a nickname online, more
common in chat contexts, people may assume that's what they like to be
called.

For example, Justin began to call Frederick by a shortened form
of his name, adding the word 'my' to the salutation on the emails,
'My Freddie'. Terms of endearment peppered people's emails, such as
'Sweetie', 'Sweetums', 'honey', and 'dearest' in the greeting and body.
Signatures contain self-appellations and sentiments to the other. After
the couple meets offline, the nicknames, pet names, and affectionate
terms often escalate in their writings. In her salutations, Melinda referred
to Ferris as 'Dashing' shortly after their in-person encounter.

As with Melinda's case, one class of affection refers to appearance, stating how good-looking the other is, in the eyes of the partner. For example, in their email, Bert addresses Arabella as 'gorgeous' and she calls him 'handsome'.

Expressions of love and signatures: direct affection online

After establishing the mutual attraction, and usually after meeting in person, although sometimes before, some people speak of their fond feelings directly. Amanda greets her significant other in chat: 'Hey, love.' She elaborates upon the emotion, showing unconditional acceptance in the same chat: 'I love you anyway. Look at your card on the desktop. No matter how you are, you are love to me.' Jeff states with classic simplicity, 'I love you, Jenna,' before he meets her offline.

Affection often appears in closings, so that after a time, both Bert and Arabella use the term Dutch term 'Kusje' (little kiss), although Bert is British. Kisses and hugs in English are commonly pictured with 'x' and 'o', and the term 'hugs' occurs frequently in some text exchanges.

Declarations of tentative love can occur whenever people have committed to the relationship. Ferris hesitantly states 'I fear that I am falling faster and further than I intended.' In her blog, Kendra announces to all her readers,' . . . more importantly, I met the irrepressible OfficeGirl, made her my own, long live JournalWorld!' She and Kitty have decided to live together, closing the geographical distance between them.

Supportive remarks: encouragement and appreciation

Another kind of positivity is when people wish others luck, or hope things turn out for the best. Whitney sincerely and yet with tongue in cheek wishes Grady well: 'Hope you have a splendid mornin' with the dentist.' People reinforce their partner's goals or everyday activities that might contain difficulties with supportive words. They may express enthusiasm for an activity or a reassurance to the other that, indeed, the deed can be done or at least lived through. In closing, Justin often ends with the upbeat sentiment, 'Take care and have a good day.'

They also give thanks yous and your welcomes in response to gestures or gifts to show appreciation. These are sometimes abbreviated in chat or email: 'ty' and 'yw' or 't'anks', 'thanx' or 'thx' and 'yer welcome'. They react to compliments, which are supportive as well as affectionate, with thanks and gratitude. Kitty shows blog readers her gratitude for her Kendra's work: 'The Girl is downstairs building more things for the kitchen. She kills me.'

Yearnings and longings of partners

Before meeting and after visits the couple first imagines and then recalls sensations, feelings, or thoughts of each other's physiology, feel, and sound. The people often look back on their pleasures and express that they desire to join the other face-to-face again.

Arabella misses Bert and writes to him:

> *Hmmmmm another night without you, what to do??! I'll just dream of waking up with your face buried in the back of my neck :-)*

After his first meeting with Whitney, Grady looks back on what happened: 'Words cannot adequately express how wonderful you made me feel this past weekend.'

After meeting and becoming physically close offline, the partners have a sensory connection along with the cognitive or verbal. The emotion of longing may occur more frequently with long-distance couples than with those living in close proximity. The personal computer allows for ease and regularity of expression for people who miss each other's presence.

Meta-statements on the relationship status and technology

Sometimes couples find themselves discussing larger issues of their pairings such as how the relationship is progressing, or the technical mode of expression itself. Couples can run into glitches in technology and comment on them emotionally. How they handle technical problems with their computers or various modes of interaction such as chat and email can signal how successfully they can pursue their relationships (see Baker, 2005).

> *And hopefully, we can start off where we left. I sometimes need time to warm up in conversation; doesn't matter how long y'know me. But we can try just crashing on into this piece of conversation we've approached several times but have never quite gotten around to exploring in depth.*

Writing to Ferris, above, Melinda expresses optimism that they can revisit a difficult issue.

On technical problems in communication, on two occasions, Arabella talks of instant messaging, video and audio:

ICQ doesn't seem to work . . . I'll keep trying. . . . Well I sorted the web cam, but now I have screwed up my sound card. Don't know what is wrong with it. I will take a look at it next Monday. That will be the first day I have time to sort it out. Hopefully it won't be too big a problem to solve.

Couples often planned online meetings or took them for granted and then bemoaned misfires due to technological problems or poor timing. They often suggested ways to get their communications flowing again. On their relationships, they mused about how unusual they felt reacting so strongly to someone not yet met face-to-face or just after the first meeting, making projections about their future progression together.

Negative emotions: apologies and doubts

Members of the couples sometimes express negative views of themselves in the form of doubts or 'put-downs', and misgivings or fears about continuing the relationship. They will also apologise or try to redress their own wrongdoings, asking forgiveness from their partners.

Often communications occur that elicit apologies by the writer.

I am sorry if I sounded like some stupid 16 year old . . . Because I refused to tell you what it was about, you must have gotten the wrong idea! It was nothing sexual or anything (well at least not explicitly anyway). . . . I didn't tell you the dream, because it was really bizarre and surreal. You'll probably think I am as mad as a hatter.

Referring to a dream she had, Arabella corrects Bert on his negative impression. She had started to tell him on a video chat and then decided not to reveal the dream's contents, until later, in an email.

Even the so-called negative emotions are often attempts to right things with the partner. They include doubts or fears about the relationship or their own qualities, or concerns about what they have written or said on the phone. They can express ambivalence about going forward.

Process of communication: emoticons, mirroring, and gender

People have used emoticons and other graphic devices to fill in for the non-verbal expressions lost online. In couple communications and even for friends, a kind of 'mirroring' takes place, which allows people to type more in synch, to match each other, perhaps the way body language occurs offline (see for example, Rothschild, 2004). Also, gender differences in interpersonal communication have received much attention offline. (Tannen, 1990). Internet researchers have increasingly explored gender differences and similarities online (see, for example, Herring, 1996). Online communications may have different dynamics than those offline, with some overall similarities, depending on type of relationship and situation.

Emoticons, 'emphasisers' and sensory symbols

For some years now, starting before the WWW in BBSs where locals communicated online, people created acronyms or smileys for two reasons: (1) shorthand or abbreviation helped typing go faster, and (2) emotional content supplemented text words, adding the spin of inflection and mood. People become very creative when seeking to overcome the limitations of text (Preece & Ghozati, 2001).

Using several exclamation points in a row, writing in capital letters, extending vowels or consonants, and changing font size and colour are tactics of highlighting or calling attention to the text itself. These emphatics or 'emphasisers' are inserted for heightened emotion. Della describes how her emotions were expressed graphically:

> If I was embarrassed, I would use red coloured fonts! We usually communicated in purple further into our relationship because it is my favourite color. Also we used different sized fonts and bold for emphasis!

Sam writes 'I BET!!' to Joanie when she wrote of an exciting workday, affirming his agreement from his own experience.

Along with the basic smiley faces, from the ordinary smile ☺, the winky face ;-) and the laugh :-D, some correspondents abbreviate 'evil grin' (eg) or 'wide evil grin' (weg). Miranda's boyfriend Ferris represents himself as a devilish, bearded person who is grinning evilly: }-D >. The plain smiley is so common that chat, email and word processing programmes build in the graphic form with a round face, instead of the sideways characters.

To further indicate mirth, the acronym 'lol' is common, along with variations, among people who find something humorous. These acronyms, along with the sounds 'ha' or 'hehe' signal a good feeling, and often liking for the other person. Sounds can be drawn out with letters added, such as 'haaaaaaaaaaaaaaaahaaaaaaaa', or combined with capital letters, such as 'HEEHEE', signalling great mirth.

Pictures completely designed from ASCII exist to add texture and graphics to text. People sometimes use them in their signatures. The rose in various forms from simple to very complex is perhaps the best known, with others symbolising cats >^.^< and mythical creatures such as dragons.

Mirroring of openings, closings, and nicknames

A pattern of behaviour occurs online between people who like each other which imitates nonverbal 'mirroring' or synchronisation of gestures. After a period of communicating, many people quite quickly begin to reflect each other's openings and closings in email. They pick up forms of address and nicknames and style of expression.

One couple started with Jeff signing 'Love, J', and then the letters evolved to his 'l, j' and 'l, a' representing the mirrored emotion from Jenna, his partner. Jack copied Helen's 'Take care' closing.

The mimicking or mirroring of openings and closings ritualises the affection so that the hugs and kisses become an ongoing and easy to perform confirmation of the couple's closeness. The written expression also symbolises the equality or parity of the feelings.

Gender differences or similarities of partners

The data here and from the larger study supports conclusions about the similarities of gender expression online, rather than the differences. It does not find gender differences in use of emoticons, for example. One person can teach another and often men urge their use. For example, Leon taught Margo that emoticons could more easily signal mood than text, and Jay convinced Della to experiment with font size and colour. A finding from the couples early in the online couples research (Baker, 1998) through the present is that men may find expressing emotions online easier than expressing them offline. Perhaps the self-conscious attempt to compensate for physical cues leads to more demonstrativeness than men typically exhibit face-to-face.

In the creation of blogs, Huffaker and Calvert (2005) find more similarities than differences between men and women, wondering if the technology levels gender differences, or if this generation has become more androgynous. Their research shows that men use even more emoticons than women. Lee (2003) found that men chatting with women gravitated toward female styles in instant messaging, using almost as many greetings and closings as females taking to other females. Another study of chat communities looking at same-sex and other-sex pairs found little difference in emoticon use when men communicated with women online (Wolf, 2000) in comparison to differences in same-sex groups.

Context or situation may be crucial for determining when the gender differences emerge. For example in the discussion lists and newsgroups examined by Herring (1996, 2000), women tend toward supportiveness and men engaged in more aggressive disagreement with others. Here, in this study of online communication among couples that engage in ongoing dyadic relationships, the positive messages and negative seem equally dispersed between the genders, at least in their private communications. Same-sex couples of both genders appear geared toward the positive message as well.

The type of audience or group online and the type of relationship may influence whether gender differences occur or not. Perhaps equality within dyadic coupling is encouraged in online communication where the individual male or female can write as much or little as they like in a back-and-forth manner whether using asynchronous email, or in the synchronous mode of chat.

Progressing from online to face-to-face

When people 'click' at their first time face-to-face meeting, their communication typically intensifies. If they have presented themselves honestly and accurately online (Baker, 2002, 2005; Ben Ze'ev, 2004) they encounter few or minor surprises at the first meeting offline or later on in further encounters.

Process of liking or loving and the face-to-face

Attitudes towards each other before the first face-to-face encounter ranged from a strong liking to actually being in love. A few couples had not exchanged photos before meeting and felt attachment through text alone. Expressions of affection occurred before, during, and after meeting, along with plans to meet again. Further study of the trajectory of forms and content of statements and demonstrations of love can help us see what is unique about online romantic relationships, as well as what is similar to attraction and bonding among couples offline.

The meeting in real life (irl) determines where couples exceeded, met, or did not meet expectations, with reflections after the meeting. Building from initial impressions to forming a lasting relationship depends upon how well people irl match with what they have said, and the depth of their communication in text with or without photos.

In attraction, the process of 'cyberflirting' (Whitty & Carr, 2003) may be paramount, whereas in later stages, the self-disclosure of getting to know the person may take on the form of mutual appreciations and reassurances. Scholars in the future could productively analyse turning points to provide finer distinctions within the stages of online meeting and writing, progressing first to phone, and then to in-person contact. Perhaps an additional phase exists between initial attraction and further pursuit, as well as between text communication and voice, and then finally face-to-face meeting and then further text and phone interaction.

Factors of success and online communication

In the larger research project, the quality of online communication is related to the success or failure of the relationship. In looking at the 'POST' factors (Baker, 2005) of place, obstacles, self-presentation, and timing, effective online communication helped people negotiate optimal resolutions of any barriers to their progression. If couples could not agree on their primary mode of online communication, for example, they would possibly disagree on other issues. If they could work out solutions to their involvements with other partners, and geographical separation, they would have a higher chance of staying together.

Conclusions

Future research could benefit from offline and online comparisons of couples, when available, or from comparative reference to research on similar groups. Methodologically, we need to find new ways of obtaining actual communications between people without violating ethical responsibilities. For this paper, the researcher frequently developed some degree of rapport with the respondents before asking for their email.

To progress towards understanding of the varieties of types and processes in expressing emotion online, the demarcation of kinds of relationships would help. In friendships and love bonds, the closeness can develop literally by people expressing feelings. Words, emoticons and nonverbal sounds and emphasisers replace the physical cues of offline pairing. Frequency of communication alone may indicate that the bonds are growing stronger.

More research can help learn if online mirroring mimics offline body language to indicate attraction and bonding.

Rather than grouping all dyads or even all romantic couples together in drawing inferences, the issue of 'place' online where they first met can make a difference in how they communicate and the course of their relationships (Baker, 2005; McKenna, this volume; Baker & Whitty, 2006). The setting or place of initial encounter can determine how much information about a person is presented to a potential partner.

The study of how people talk/write online is only beginning now. This work contributes to a grounded approach in learning more about what is said and how. As one writer pointed out (Anderson, 2000), today we know the Internet is not so much merely about providing 'information' as about allowing us to express emotion. In observing individuals with cancer in chat rooms or online support groups, while noting that people do state facts, Anderson concludes: 'much of their discourse is emotive' (p. 1), which provides great solace to the participants. The couples of this research depend upon the Internet to build upon the foundation of their online attraction. They use text not only to share the activities of their day but to express caring and appreciation. The more successful among them may teach us more about the crucial aspects of relating well, and about optimal and various uses of email and chat.

References

Anderson, D. M. (2000). The false assumption about the Internet. *Computers and Society, 30* (1), 8–9.

Baker, A. J. (1998). Cyberspace couples finding romance online then meeting for the first time in real life. *Computer-Mediated Communication, 5* (7), 11–14. Retrieved 2 January 2006 from: http://www.december.com/cmc/mag/1998/jul/baker.html.

Baker, A. J. (2002). What makes an online relationship successful? *CyberPsychology and Behaviour, 5* (4), 363–75.

Baker, A. J. (2005). *Double click: Romance and commitment among online couples.* Cresskill, NJ: Hampton Press.

Baker A. J., & Whitty, M. T. (2006). *The role of 'place' in the initiation, development, and outcome of online relationships.* Manuscript in preparation.

Bargh, J. A., McKenna, K. Y. A., & Fitzsimons, G. J. (2002). Can you see the real me? The activation and expression of the 'true self' on the Internet. *Journal of Social Issues, 58,* 33–48.

Ben Ze'ev, A. (2004). *Love online.*Oxford: Oxford University Press.

Canary, D., Stafford, L., Hause, K., & Wallace, I. (1993). An inductive analysis of relational maintenance strategies: A comparison among young lovers, relatives, friends, and others. *Communication Research Reports, 10,* 5–11.

Cooper, A. & Sportolari, L. (1997). Romance in cyberspace. *Journal of Sex Education and Therapy, 22,* 7–14.

Danet, B. (2001). *Cyberpl@y: Communicating online.* Oxford: Oxford University Press.

Henderson, S., & Gilding, M. (2004). 'I've never clicked this much with anyone in my life': trust and hyperpersonal communication in online friendships. *New Media & Society, 6* (4), 487–506.

Herring, S. C. (1996). Posting in a different voice: Gender and ethics in computer-mediated communication. In C. Ess (ed.), *Philosophical Perspectives on Computer Mediated Communication* (pp. 115–45). Albany: SUNY Press.

Herring, S. C. (2000). Gender differences in CMC: Findings and implications. *Computer Professionals for Social Responsibility Journal* (formerly *Computer Professionals for Social Responsibility Newsletter*), *18* (1). Retrieved 22 October 2005 from: http://www.cpsr.org/publications/newsletters/issues/2000/Winter2000/herring.html.

Huffaker, D. A., & Calvert, S. L. (2005). Gender, identity, and language use in teenage blogs. *Journal of Computer-Mediated Communication, 10* (2). Retrieved 6 July 2005 from: http://jcmc.indiana.edu/vol10/issue2/huffaker.html.

Lee, C. (2003). How does instant messaging affect interaction between the genders? *The mercury project of instant message studies at Stanford.* Retrieved 10 February 2006 from: http://www.stanford.edu/class/pwr325/group2/projects/lee.html#.

Levine, D. (2000). Virtual attraction: What rocks your boat? *CyberPsychology & Behaviour, 3* (4), 565–73.

McKenna, K. Y. A., Green, A. S., & Gleason, M. J. (2002). Relationship formation on the Internet: What's the big attraction? *Journal of Social Issues, 58*, 9–32.

Preece, J., & Ghozati, K. (2001). Observations and explorations of empathy online. In R. R. Rice and J. E. Katz (eds), *The Internet and health communication: Experience and expectations* (pp. 237–60). Thousand Oaks: Sage Publications, Inc.

Rabby, M. K. (1997). Maintaining relationships via electronic mail. Paper presented at the annual meeting of the *National Communication Association*, Chicago, IL.

Rabby, M. K., & Walther, J. B. (2002). Computer-mediated communication impacts on relationship formation and maintenance. In D. Canary & M. Dainton (eds), *Maintaining relationships through communication: Relational, contextual, and cultural variations* (pp. 141–62). Mahwah, NJ: Lawrence Erlbaum Associates.

Rothschild, B. (2004). Mirror, mirror. *Psychotherapy Networker, 28*(5). Retrieved 6 January 2006 from: http://home.webuniverse.net/babette/mirror.htm.

Tannen, D. (1990). *You just don't understand.* New York: Harper Collins.

Walther, J. B. (1996). Computer-mediated communication: Impersonal, interpersonal, and hyperpersonal interaction. *Communication Research, 23*, 3–43.

Walther. J. B. (2004). Language and communication technology: Introduction to the special issue. *Journal of Language and Social Psychology, 23*, 384–96.

Whitty, M. T. & Carr, A. N. (2003). Cyberspace as potential space: Considering the web as a playground to cyber-flirt. *Human Relations, 56* (7), 869–91.

Wolf, A. (2000). Emotional expression online: Gender differences in emoticon use, *CyberPsychology and Behaviour, 3* (5), 827–33.

Wright, K. B. (2004). On-line relational maintenance strategies and perceptions of partners within exclusively Internet-based and primarily Internet-based relationships. *Communication Studies, 55* (2), 239–53.

9
A Progressive Affair: Online Dating to Real World Mating

Katelyn Y. A. McKenna

The dynamics of new relationship initiation and development can unfold somewhat differently on the Internet than occurs when individuals meet in more traditional, face-to-face settings.

Physical appearance, which has been found to be perhaps the most influential factor in what attracts us to others, is quite often absent in initial interactions on the Internet. Social mores dictate that conversational topics generally begin at the superficial level when we meet others in person and then gradually become more intimate, should we choose to pursue the relationship further. In contrast, introductory conversations online often leap-frog over the 'getting to know you' ice-breakers and into the meaty discussions that only rarely take place so early among fresh acquaintances in person. Indeed, individuals often discuss intimate issues with their relatively new online acquaintances that they have never discussed with their nearest and dearest. By following online group discussions or by reading through someone's personal blog prior to interacting, a reader can initiate a discussion with a new online acquaintance already armed with a great deal of knowledge about that person's opinions, values, background, and behaviour. It is rare, indeed, to be privy to this depth of information prior to making the acquaintance of another through traditional means and venues. And, while such conversation starters as 'hi, I've been following your life for quite some time now and just want to say...' are not uncommon nor unwelcome in the weblog sphere, imagine the reaction that would receive if it came from a stranger on the street or in a café.

That said, not all interaction venues on the Internet are alike nor are the motivations and personality characteristics of the users. The dynamics of attraction, relationship initiation, and development between users of online matchmaking services (see Baker and Whitty, this volume) can play out quite differently from that which takes place in an online discussion forum devoted to a specific interest, and differently again from that which takes place between bloggers and their readers. In this chapter, the principle differences between online and traditional interactions are discussed along with the factors influencing how, when, and why relationships that are initiated online will blossom into relationships that continue and thrive in person.

Relationship-facilitative aspects of the Internet

Identifiability

The ability to engage in anonymous communication is a difference between online and offline interaction that has been made much of in the past. For instance, people can be completely anonymous on the Internet. Internet service providers such as AOL or Yahoo allow individuals to choose screen names for themselves to use in chat rooms or instant messaging that have little or no relationship to their real name or true identity. In our face-to-face lives we frequently, and often repeatedly, interact with others (e.g., the clerk at our local drugstore, the woman who goes to our laundromat the same day of the week as we do) to whom we do not reveal personal information, such as our names, occupations, hometown, and so forth. However, despite the relative anonymity we have with these people, they may still be able to easily recognise us in a different setting. Occasionally, we do engage in what Zick Rubin (1976) called the 'strangers on a train' phenomenon. That is, we may share the most intimate details of our lives, details our closest friends may not even know, with the perfect stranger in the seat next to us. We feel safe making such disclosures to complete strangers whom we expect to never see again. In other words, when meeting someone in a face-to-face situation, it is very rare to develop lasting intimacy with that person while still retaining anonymity. However, on the Internet, such feelings can emerge between individuals who are completely anonymous to one another and can ultimately lead to the development of close relationships (e.g., Parks & Floyd, 1995; McKenna, Green, & Gleason, 2002; Walther, 1996).

Increasingly, however, people are choosing to interact online, to maintain personal weblogs, and to sign up with matchmaking sites with a great deal of identifying information about themselves freely available. They may post pictures of themselves, list their real names, and publicly provide information about their general location and career.

When talking to users of matchmaking sites, it is rare to hear of one who does not rush home from a first date with someone they met through the site and, now armed with the person's full name, run a 'Google' on their date to see what else they can turn up about the person and, if possible, to verify information given to them during the date.

And yet, even when people interact openly (i.e., using their true names, providing pictures and information about their profession) on the Internet, they often still feel relatively anonymous or, rather, non-identifiable – just one of the crowd (McKenna & Bargh, 2000; McKenna, Buffardi, & Seidman, 2005). As one blogger succinctly summed it up, 'There are millions of blogs online and my blog is just one of those millions. I use a nickname on my blog so if someone is searching for me by name online my personal blog won't show up. But I do post my picture and a lot of personal information. If someone *really* wanted to find out who I am I guess they could but I'm really not likely to run into someone who reads my blog on the street or anything. So I feel pretty anonymous.'

Due to this feeling of anonymity, online users often engage in a 'strangers on the Internet' phenomenon, disclosing personal, intimate information to others whom they may well encounter online again. These disclosures can thus become the groundwork for a continuing and close relationship. Additionally, the ability to interact anonymously or with a sense of non-identifiability allows people to join groups and explore aspects of self on the Internet that they might otherwise keep hidden in their existing relationships (e.g., McKenna & Bargh, 1998; McKenna et al., 2002).

Removal of gating features

Physical appearance and mannerisms play an essential role, not only in impression formation, but also in determining whom we will approach and, and even with whom we will develop friendships and romantic relationships (e.g., Hatfield & Sprecher, 1986). We tend to use physically available features to immediately categorise others (e.g., their ethnicity, attractiveness, age; Bargh, 1989; Brewer, 1988). For example, research on impressions at the zero-acquaintance level has shown that there is extremely high consensus among participants in their initial impressions of others, across a wide variety of personality measurements, based only on physical appearance (e.g., Allbright, Kenny, & Malloy, 1988; Kenny, 1994). Research has shown that it is rather difficult to get past our first impressions (e.g., Fiske & Taylor, 1991) because people tend to selectively focus on information that confirms rather than disconfirms their initial judgement, when they interact with these same people again (e.g., Higgins & Bargh, 1987).

Thus, those features that are most readily perceived, such as physical appearance (attractiveness), an apparent stigma (e.g., stuttering), or apparent shyness or social anxiety often serve as gates in our face-to-face interactions. These gates often open to admit those who are physically attractive and outgoing, but also often close when we encounter the less socially skilled or physically attractive, keeping these individuals out of our social and romantic circles.

When interactions with new online acquaintances take place in newsgroups, instant messengers, chat rooms, and so forth online, such gating features are not usually immediately apparent and thus do not become a barrier to potential relationships. Whitty (2004) found that even when individuals are engaging in romantic cyberflirting in chat rooms, the emphasis on physical aspects of self and other is much less than when individuals engage in flirting behaviour in person. Instead, impressions are formed on very different criteria. Rather than basing impressions on superficial features, such as attractiveness, the opinions expressed and the information about the self that is revealed become the basis of first impressions.

However, to the extent that such gating features *are* in evidence initially (for example, online dating services such as Match.com provide member profiles with an accompanying picture) then the same biases that operate in our face-to-face lives will come into play and we are likely to similarly bypass or reject out of hand from the outset potentially satisfactory and mutually profitable relationships.

Control

In online interactions, individuals are able to control interactions in a way that is not possible in face-to-face or telephone communication. In face-to-face and telephone interactions one is expected to respond immediately and 'off the cuff'. However, an immediate response is not expected in online communication. People realise that typing a reply can take time and that people tend to multi-task while chatting online and thus their attention may be momentarily devoted to something else on the computer screen. Pauses that may seem unnaturally long in speech can go unnoticed in an online instant message. Immediate replies to emails are not expected because we know that it often takes time for people to check their email and find the time to write a response.

The opportunity to delay response provides individuals with the chance to edit their message before sending it and it gives them more time to think about what they are going to say. This removes the pressure to respond immediately and allows for a more thoughtful response if the sender so chooses.

In addition, in person and telephone conversation norms require people to communicate in short bursts, rather than long speeches. This can inhibit the degree to which people can express themselves. However, online, long emails or instant messages are perfectly acceptable. Interaction partners therefore have more time to plan what they will say, they can type as much or as little as they want in a single reply, and they can edit responses before sending them. Bloggers can be as long and rambling as they wish in their posts, sometimes breaking down what amounts to short novellas about an experience they've had into separate posts with notes at the end indicating – 'Stay Tuned: Part 2 coming tomorrow.' All of these factors give individuals greater control over how they present themselves and their ideas and opinions to others than generally occurs in face-to-face or telephone exchanges.

Connecting to similar others

Another aspect of the Internet is the ease with which people can find and connect with similar others there. Even if we are aware of groups in the community that share our interests, we may not have the time or means to attend those get-togethers. Online, people can participate in interest groups at times that are most convenient for them, thus allowing interpersonal and group connections to be made. The Internet can be particularly useful for locating others who share very specialised interests (such as candle-making), who are experiencing similar health or emotional difficulties, or who share aspects of identity that are socially sanctioned and thus are often not readily identifiable in one's physical community.

Getting the goods before getting introduced

A final unique aspect that pertains to some forms of online communication is the ability to obtain a great deal of information about another person prior to initiating an interaction with him or her. This is particularly true when it comes to those who maintain personal blogs, but can also extend to those who take part in online dating sites and online discussion forums.

When we are introduced to a potential friend or love interest through family or friends, we may be told some information about him or her beforehand. Thus, before meeting we may know basic details such as the age, career path, and religious affiliation of the other, and as well, perhaps, a few anecdotal stories our friends share to assure us that he is a 'great and interesting guy' or that she is 'exceptionally smart and funny'. The information we know beforehand is generally somewhat limited, however, and it comes second-hand. By following a person's personal blog, however, we may know more about the person than their own mother does before we ever initiate contact and, rather than second-hand, our information comes right from the horse's mouth. As an active participant or as a lurker (someone who follows the threads of the discussion but does not participate him or herself) in online discussion groups we can observe how another individual formulates arguments and opinions, how he or she behaves during debates within the group, and glean other personality and behavioural characteristics through what they say and how they seem to conduct themselves within the group.

Summary

The qualities of computer-mediated communication discussed above can produce different outcomes than those that occur in traditional interaction settings. However, it is not the case that these qualities produce 'main effects' on the user. The particular aspects of the Internet interaction situation will, instead, interact with the goals, motivations, and personal characteristics of the individuals involved to produce effects on psychological and interpersonal outcomes (McKenna & Bargh, 2000; Spears, Postmes, Lea, & Wolbert, 2002). Anonymity provides a case in point. Anonymous interaction has been shown to produce anti-normative behaviour online (e.g., Kiesler, Siegel, & McGuire, 1984) but it has also been shown to produce even stronger normative effects online than in face-to-face situations (e.g., Spears et al., 2002). Yet other studies have shown that being identifiable rather than anonymous increases online participants' group-normative behaviour (e.g., Douglas & McGarty, 2001). While on the face of it these findings appear at odds, these differential outcomes are readily explained when one takes into account the way in which anonymity is interacting with other situational factors (see McKenna & Seidman, 2005).

Relationship formation

It is old hat now to note that relationships can and do form over the Internet and these relationships can become quite close (e.g., McKenna et al., 2002; Parks & Floyd, 1995). It is not for nothing that people have flocked to online dating sites to try their hand at meeting the perfect match. However, there are important differences in the way in which relationships are initiated and unfold in, for instance, common interest groups and those that take place between participants in online dating sites, although the outcomes are sometimes the same: the perfect mate is met or a good friend is made. Some of the important differences include the motivation for participation by the users (in dating sites the motivation is straightforwardly to find a mate; in common interests groups the motivation is generally to discuss and share with others an interest and any relationships that form are by-products), the manner in which 'the other' is selected and contacted, the length of time participants generally interact online prior to moving to the telephone or meeting in person, and the things discussed, to name only a few. Thus in this section, relationship formation will be discussed first in terms of findings that relate to 'naturally-forming' relationships – relationships that develop out of the interaction as opposed to those in which the interaction is specifically for the purpose of potential relationship formation – and then in terms of interactions through dating sites.

Naturally-forming relationships

Research has shown that an important factor in whether or not close relationships will form online between participants in electronic groups is the extent to which an individual feels better able to express his or her true or inner self online than in traditional interaction settings. McKenna et al. (2002) tested this prediction through structural equation modelling analyses of survey responses provided by hundreds of randomly selected Internet newsgroup members who were taking part in group discussions related to computer science, history, health, fashion, and so forth. 'Personals' groups were not included in the study.

While the participants in these groups were not actively seeking to find a romantic partner or close friendships from among the other members of their particular group, a significant percent of the survey respondents had done just that. The majority of respondents reported having formed friendships with other group members, and approximately 20 per cent of the participants had found a romantic partner through their online interactions. However, the critical mediator of whether an individual would form close Internet relationships was his or her responses to a 'Real Me' scale (for a copy of the scale, see Bargh, Fitzsimons, & McKenna, 2002). This scale measured whether or not the participant felt better able to express aspects of self and personality in Internet interactions than in his or her offline social life. Those who felt they expressed more of the 'real me' on the Internet were significantly more likely to have formed close, intimate relationships there and to have taken steps to integrate those online friends and romantic partners into their face-to-face interaction world, as compared to those who reported feeling more their true, inner self in traditional social settings. These close Internet relationships also turned out to be remarkably stable and durable over time, as a two-year follow-up study demonstrated (see McKenna et al., 2002).

Another important ingredient for the formation of close relationships over the Internet is the tendency to engage in greater self-disclosure there. Anonymity, connecting with similar others, and interacting in the physical absence of one's communication partner can produce this heightened disclosure tendency. The fact that people tend to more readily engage in acts of self-disclosure on the Internet has been well-documented (e.g., Joinson, 2001; Levine, 2000; Walther, 1996). As is argued by a number of theorists (e.g., Derlega, Metts, Petronio, & Margulis, 1993; Laurenceau, Barrett, & Pietromonaco, 1998), self-disclosure is important to the development of closeness and intimacy, as it entails being able to express and have accepted one's inner or true feelings and personality. Situation-appropriate self-disclosure fosters feelings of liking between communicants: We tend to like those to whom we self-disclose, to like those who disclose to us, and to disclose more to those we like (e.g., Collins & Miller, 1994). Early self-disclosure thus should lead to faster relationship development.

McKenna et al. (2002, Study 3) tested this premise in a laboratory experiment. Undergraduates were randomly assigned (in cross-sex pairs) to meet one another for the first time in an Internet chat room or to meet face-to-face. In line with predictions, those who met online both liked each other more and felt that they had gotten to know one another better than did those who interacted face-to-face. This effect held when participants met one another twice, once in person and once over the Internet. Importantly, these participants were unaware of the fact that they were talking to the same interaction partner in both situations. There was a significant correlation between the degree of liking for the partner and how well the participant felt he or she had gotten to know the other person for those who met over the Internet. However, there was no such correlation in the face-to-face condition. Along similar lines, Walther (1996, 1997) found that new acquaintances can achieve greater intimacy through online communication than they do in parallel face-to-face interactions.

Once intimacy has been firmly established and the online relationship becomes an integral part of a person's life, he or she is generally loath to leave the relationship solely in the virtual realm. Rather, people tend to be motivated to make their important online relationships into a social reality (see Gollwitzer, 1986) by incorporating them into their everyday, face-to-face lives if possible. As McKenna and colleagues found in their survey of newsgroup users, people tend to do this in a series of stages, moving first from online communication to telephone conversations and then to meeting in person.

Targeted relationships

The findings above, however, do not necessarily apply when it comes to interactions between participants in online dating sites. There are several critical differences between interactions that take place in forums where participants get together to discuss common interests and those that take place in the 'mating market' (see Baker, 2005, for additional ways in which these interactions differ).

The old adage 'a picture is worth a thousand words' may not be so apt when it comes to online dating. Users of dating sites routinely select potential interaction partners to contact based on the pictures in their profiles: if the picture passes muster they then look at the other attributes listed in the profile. In other words, they use physical attractiveness as the first and most important factor in their selection of potential partners in the same way that we tend to select potential partners and friends in our traditional interactions. Further, they form a priori assumptions about the person based on his or her evident physical characteristics and thus will tend to filter any further information they receive through these, often inaccurate, judgements.

Once a potential partner has passed the physical appearance test and been placed into the larger pool of 'possibles' the user then begins to narrow the contact options based on self-provided information about income and occupation, hobbies, previous marital status, and so forth. If all of these factors seem to be 'good', the participant will send off an introductory email and wait to see if he or she, in turn, passes the other person's 'shopping list' of acceptable criteria and is contacted in return.

Once reciprocal contact is established between two members on the dating sites, the next step – establishing a face-to-face meeting – generally happens quite quickly. A recent study of dating site users found that participants generally move to telephone contact after exchanging an average of three emails and the first (and more often than not only) face-to-face meeting is frequently arranged during that initial phone conversation (McKenna, Seidman, & Buffardi, 2005). This is in marked contrast to those who meet through common interest forums online: Participants in these groups communicated regularly online for an average of four months prior to picking up the telephone.

Conclusions

Because of the unique aspects of online communications, online relationships can unfold quite differently than can those formed in traditional spheres. Relationship formation and development within different types of online meeting places also do not conform to a single model. As discussed above, impression and relationship formation in common interest forums and in dating sites, two different kinds of online venues, often unfold quite differently. The initial motivations for contact are often different. In the one venue contact is made for the express purpose of possibility hitting it off romantically; in the other the motive is to engage in a discussion of an interest that is important or enjoyable to both. Interacting based on common interests may give these potential relationships a better chance of coming to fruition as we know, from research on traditional relationships, that sharing similar interests and values are important factors for successful relationship formation and the longevity of the relationship (e.g., Byrne, Clore, & Smeaton, 1986; Hatfield & Sprecher, 1986).

Interacting with the presence or absence of one's own and the other's physical appearance initially in evidence also has a strong influence on the initial impressions made and the subsequent course of the relationship. Critically, it is a major determinant of whether a potential relationship will ever be initiated in the first place. In many kinds of common interest forums online, interactions take place without having a picture available prior to contact initiation. Instead, initial impressions are formed on the basis of the opinions, values and behaviour the 'person of interest' expresses and contacts are made without knowing the physical details. In dating sites, the physical attractiveness of the other is what fuels the contact, with his or her opinions and interests coming in much lower on the scale. The opinions, values, and interests of those who fail to measure up on an individual's 'attractiveness meter' are never explored at all. Thus, in this respect, dating sites closely resemble traditional face-to-face 'meeting places' such as bars, parties, and cafes.

Increased self-disclosure over that which occurs in typical face-to-face interactions can occur in both common interest and dating venues online. Yet here too there are differences. Interactions that take place in common interest groups often are initiated and early disclosures made with no intent on the part of the participants to ever meet. It is on the very basis of the closeness that develops through mutual self-disclosure that many of these participants do eventually decide to meet. In contrast, contacts are made through dating sites with the very intent of meeting the other (should he or she seem remotely suitable) in person. Under these conditions participants may be more reticent about making intimate disclosures.

The transference of a potential dating-site relationship from online to offline is generally a fast-forwarded version of what occurs between participants in other kinds of online venues. Thus these relationships are unlikely to have the same depth and importance for the participants, which may be important for getting beyond a first in-person meeting. When considerable time and effort have been invested in a relationship people may be more motivated to maintain a positive opinion of the other and to wish to continue that relationship even if, upon meeting, the other's physical and personality attributes are less than expected or optimally desired.

On the other hand, dating sites allow people to connect with many more 'potentials' living in their immediate geographic region than he or she will generally encounter in everyday life or more than will be encountered through a typical common interest group on the Internet. Simply having a wider pool of potential partners can increase the chance that one will meet Mr or Ms Right.

Thus, it is clear that many factors influence relationship formation online. In some cases, these factors will mirror those that influence relationships in the face-to-face world and in others they will differ. The Internet is no panacea when it comes to relationships and it offers no instant solutions for the currently mateless. It does, however, widen the opportunities and existing options for connecting with possible partners. Like in the face-to-face world, some meeting venues are more likely to bring together two compatible partners than others. For instance, traditionally relationships have been more successfully initiated and developed through common interest or goal settings in the face-to-face world (e.g., through church, hobby groups, places of work) than through the 'meat market' venues (e.g., bars). When it comes down to it, the online world seems to parallel this, with a few interesting twists.

References

Allbright, L., Kenny, D. A., & Malloy, T. E., (1988). Consensus in personality judgments at zero acquaintance. *Journal of Personality & Social Psychology, 55*, 387–95.

Baker, A. (2005). *Double click: Romance and commitment among online couples.* Cresskill, NJ: Hampton Press.

Bargh, J. A. (1989). Conditional automaticity: Varieties of automatic influence in social perception and cognition. In J. S. Uleman & J. A. Bargh (eds), *Unintended thought* (pp. 3–51). New York: Guilford Press.

Bargh, J. A., Fitzsimons, G. J., & McKenna, K. Y. A. (2002). The self, online. In S. Spencer & S. Fein (eds). *Motivated social perception: The 9th Ontario Symposium on Social Cognition.* Mahwah, NJ: Erlbaum.

Brewer, M. B. (1988). A dual process model of impression formation. In T. K. Srull & R. S., Wyer, Jr. (eds), *A dual process model of impression formation. Advances in social cognition, Vol. 1* (pp. 1–36). Hillsdale, NJ, England: Lawrence Erlbaum Associates, Inc.

Byrne, D., Clore, G. L., & Smeaton, G. (1986). The attraction hypothesis: Do similar attitudes affect anything? *Journal of Personality & Social Psychology, 51*, 1167–70.

Collins, N. L., & Miller, L. C. (1994). Self-disclosure and liking: A meta-analytic review. *Psychological Bulletin, 116*, 457–75.

Derlega, V. L., Metts, S., Petronio, S., & Margulis, S. T. (1993). *Self-disclosure.* London: Sage.

Douglas, K. M., & McGarty, C. (2001). Identifiability and self-presentation: Computer-mediated communication and intergroup interaction. *British Journal of Social Psychology, 40*, 399–416.

Fiske, S. T., & Taylor, S. E. (1991). *Social cognition* (2nd edn). New York: Scott Foresman.

Gollwitzer, P. M. (1986). Striving for specific identities: The social reality of self-symbolizing. In R. Baumeister (ed.), *Public self and private self* (pp. 143–59). New York: Springer-Verlag.

Hatfield, E., & Sprecher, S. (1986). *Mirror, mirror: The importance of looks in everyday life.* Albany: State University of New York Press.

Higgins, E. T., & Bargh, J. A. (1987). Social cognition and social perception. *Annual Review of Psychology, 38*, 369–425.

Joinson, A. N. (2001). Knowing me, knowing you: Reciprocal self-disclosure in internet-based surveys. *Cyberpsychology and Behaviour, 4*, 587–91.

Kenny, D. A. (1994). *Interpersonal perception: A social relations analysis.* New York: Guilford Press.

Kiesler, S., Siegel, J., & McGuire, T. (1984). Social psychological aspects of computer-mediated communication. *American Psychologist, 39*, 1129–34.

Laurenceau, J., Feldman Barrett, L., & Pietromonaco, P. R. (1998). Intimacy as a process: The importance of self-disclosure and responsiveness in interpersonal exchanges. *Journal of Personality and Social Psychology, 74*, 1238–51.

Levine, D. (2000). Virtual attraction: What rocks your boat. *Cyberpsychology & Behavior, 3*, 565–73.

McKenna, K. Y. A., & Bargh, J. A. (1998). Coming out in the age of internet: Identity 'de-marginalization' through virtual group participation. *Journal of Personality and Social Psychology, 75*, 681–94.

McKenna, K. Y. A., & Bargh, J. A. (2000). Plan 9 from cyberspace: The implications of the internet for personality and social psychology. *Journal of Personality and Social Psychology, 4*, 57–75.

McKenna, K. Y. A., Buffardi, L. & Seidman, G. (2005). Self-presentation to friends and strangers online. In Karl-Heinz Renner, Astrid Schutz & Franz Machilek (eds). *Internet and Personality*. Göttengen: Hogrefe & Huber Publishers.

McKenna, K. Y. A., Green, A. S., & Gleason, M. E. J. (2002). Relationship formation on the Internet: What's the big attraction? *Journal of Social Issues, 58*, 9–31.

McKenna, K., & Seidman, G. (2005). You, me, and we: Interpersonal processes in electronic groups. In Y. Amichai-Hamburger (ed.), *The social net: Human behavior in cyberspace* (pp. 191–217). New York: Oxford University Press.

McKenna, K. Y. A., Seidman, G., & Buffardi, L. (2005). The changing faces of online dating. *Manuscript in preparation*.

Parks, M. R., & Floyd, K. (1995). Making friends in cyberspace. *Journal of Communication, 46*, 80–97.

Rubin, Z. (1975). Disclosing oneself to a stranger: Reciprocity and its limits. *Journal of Experimental Social Psychology, 11*, 233–60.

Spears, R., Postmes, T., Lea, M., & Wolbert, A. (2002). When are net effects gross products? The power of influence and the influence of power in computer-mediated communication. *Journal of Social Issues, 58*, 91–107.

Walther, J. B. (1996). Computer-mediated communication: impersonal, interpersonal, and hyperpersonal interaction. *Communication Research, 23*, 3–43.

Walther, J. B. (1997). Group and interpersonal effects in international computer-mediated collaboration. *Human Communication Research, 23*(3), 342–69.

Whitty, M. T. (2004). Cyber-flirting: An examination of men's and women's flirting behaviour both offline and on the Internet. *Behaviour Change, 21*, 115–26.

Part 4
Darker Sides of Online Dating

10

Cyberstalking as (Mis)matchmaking

Brian H. Spitzberg and William R. Cupach

Online technologies, such as online matchmaking services, are increasingly becoming a normal and normative medium through which relationships are initiated, developed, maintained, and ended. This chapter examines the phenomenon of *stalking* and obsessive relational intrusion, with special emphasis on *cyberstalking* as one variant that is particularly likely in the online matchmaking environment. To elaborate these processes, the interrelationship of impression management theory, socioevolutionary theory, and relational goal pursuit theory are examined as they inform an understanding of relationship matchmaking, and *mis*matchmaking, in the online environment.

In mediated matchmaking contexts there are impression management motives for participants to adapt their image so as to optimally match the goals their target audience is seeking. The ability to manage impressions strategically is facilitated in a computer-mediated communication (CMC) environment, which tends to be more intentional, more asynchronous, more verbal, and less nonverbal than oral or face-to-face (FtF) interaction. From a socioevolutionary perspective, for example, males will tend to emphasise their status characteristics (e.g., income, education, career), whereas females will tend to emphasise their youth and physical attractiveness so as to appeal optimally to the presumed goals of the intended target audience. Such manipulation of impressions is designed to optimise both short-term and long-term mating strategies, but also serves to link one's persona specifically to the seeker's goals.

By emphasising certain characteristics relative to others, and targeting the attributed goals of the intended partners, online matchmaking may facilitate the formation of *apparent*, relative to *actual*, compatibility of potential mates. To the extent that goal linking occurs in the context of biased impression management, it increases the risks of forming non-mutual and obsessive relationship attachments. In the CMC context, obsessive attachments can easily transform online court-ship into a process of cyberstalking.

A synopsis of stalking, cyberstalking, and Obsessive Relational Intrusion

Courtship is an intrinsically tricky affair. Humans must develop attach-ments but there are many motives for being selective in the process. Courtship is a process that permits participants to test the relational waters with their prospective partners to see if further pursuit is warranted. It follows that many courtships go only so far, and then are ended by one or both participants, due to a simple lack of mutual compatibility, or due to disorders and dysfunctions of the partners or relationship.

There are many ways and reasons that courtship becomes a dysfunc-tional process. One particular disorder that has become recognised by modern society is stalking. *Stalking* is an intentional process of persistent and threatening pursuit, intrusion, and harassment. A common stereo-type of stalking is that it involves crazed or psychotic killers hunting celebrities. This is not an accurate portrait of the spectrum of stalking behaviour. Approximately three-quarters of all stalking emerges from the context of a previous acquaintance, with almost half of all stalking emerging from a previously romantic relationship (Cupach & Spitzberg, 2004). In other words, most stalkers creep in under people's 'relational radar screen' long enough to establish some form of acquaintance.

Given that the majority of stalkers are seeking romantic interests (or are seeking revenge for having these interests rejected), the process of obsessive relational intrusion is of distinct interest. *Obsessive relational intrusion* (ORI) 'is the repeated pursuit of intimacy with someone who does not want such attentions' (Cupach & Spitzberg, 2004, p. 3). It is distinct from stalking in two respects. First, ORI involves the pursuit of a relationship, whereas some stalking is solely intended to harm or harass the target of pursuit. Second, ORI may only be annoying or troublesome rather than threatening or fearful. Nevertheless, research to date indicates that most ORI could qualify as stalking (Cupach & Spitzberg, 2004; Spitzberg & Cupach, 2001, 2002, 2003). Taking ORI and stalking together, across over 140 studies, as many as 26 per cent of women and 10 per cent of men can expect to be persistently pursued in unwanted ways. Approximately 75 per cent of victims of unwanted pursuit are women (Cupach & Spitzberg, 2004; Spitzberg, 2002).

The creativity, resourcefulness, and variegation of stalking activities are impressive. The topography of stalking and ORI activity can be described in terms of eight forms of behaviour (Cupach & Spitzberg, 2004). *Hyperintimacy* consists of inappropriate expressions of desire, affection, attraction, and desire for relationship escalation. It includes verbal and nonverbal messages of desire, ingratiation (e.g., compliments), bids for relationship enhancement, and an excessive emphasis on sexual aspects of relating. The difference between a single rose on the doorstep after the first date and three-dozen roses laid inside one's car in an otherwise deserted parking lot signals the distortion of the boundaries of propriety and normative expectations.

The second form of unwanted pursuit, particularly relevant to the online matchmaking context, involves *mediated contacts*. The use of the telephone, pagers, text messaging, mail, email, photos, and CMC all become tools in the stalking toolbox. The experience of becoming saturated with calls, faxes, and e-mails from an 'ex' or would-be paramour has become almost an iconic image of the person who cannot 'let go'.

Third, unwanted pursuit also seeks affiliation through *interactional contacts*, which consist of both direct and indirect forms. Direct interaction contacts involve conversational engagement, physical approaches in public, appearances (e.g., showing up at a person's work or gym), interactional intrusions (i.e., interrupting and inserting oneself into an ongoing conversation), personal space invasions (i.e., getting too physically close to someone), and involvement in activities (e.g., joining one's volunteer group). Indirect interaction involves pursuit through others, such as friends and family of the target or through the pursuer's own friends, family, or hired professionals (e.g., private investigators).

Perhaps the most prototypical stereotype of stalking involves the use of *surveillance*. Surveillance includes synchronising activities (e.g., matching one's movements and schedules to keep tabs on someone), loitering in places the person may frequent, watching (i.e., setting up station to observe covertly), following physically, and the use of drive-by observations of a person's location. Surveillance involves relatively public monitoring. In contrast, *invasion* involves more covert intrusion to obtain information. Information theft (i.e., the acquisition of private information, such as diaries, identity information, etc.), property theft (e.g., underwear, personal tokens, etc.), property invasions (e.g., breaking and entering), and exotic surveillance (e.g., bugging, inserting Trojan horses into a computer, hidden video monitors, etc.) illustrate types of invasion.

The sixth type of unwanted pursuit is *harassment and intimidation*. These forms of pursuit attempt to introduce problems into someone's life. Nonverbal intimidation (e.g., leaving implicitly threatening objects on a doorstep) and verbal or written harassment are common. A pursuer can also harass a person's reputation (e.g., spreading negative rumours), network (e.g., intimidating one's social or business relationship partners), or by trying to isolate the person by disenfranchising the social network. A pursuer can also harass a person through regulatory (e.g., signing someone up for unwanted subscriptions, entangling in legal proceedings) or economic means. Sometimes intimidation is achieved through sheer unrelenting persistence of pursuit and intrusion. Finally, harassment and intimidation are sometimes accomplished through bizarre behaviour or artefacts, such as leaving a bloodied stuffed animal on the person's doorstep.

Harassment and intimidation tend to operate at a level just under the threshold of true threats. When pursuit escalates, often due to rejection or a perceived lack of cooperation with the pursuer's intentions for the relationship, tactics often turn to *coercion and threat*. Threats can be directed at one's reputation, property, economic livelihood, social and task network, and even the pursuer (e.g., threaten suicide if the person does not accept the relationship). In addition, more serious harms, such as, sexual coercion and the prospect of physical violence can be threatened.

When threats turn to threats fulfilled, it represents the final and most severe forms of stalking, *aggression and violence*. Aggression can be directed against the same targets of the threats, but sometimes take other forms such as kidnapping and rape. Approximately one-third of stalking victims experience violence at the hands of their pursuer, and this appears to rise to half or more when there has been a previous romantic or sexual relationship between the victim and the pursuer (Cupach & Spitzberg, 2004; Spitzberg, 2002).

The experience of violence is suggestive of the seriousness of stalking. Research reveals that victims of stalking and unwanted pursuit tend to experience a wide range of unpleasant symptoms (Cupach & Spitzberg, 2004; Spitzberg, 2002). These symptoms include behavioural (e.g., changing one's routine activities), affective health (e.g., anxiety, depression), cognitive health (e.g., distrust, alienation), physical health (e.g., sleep and eating disorders), social health (e.g., isolation from one's social relationships), resource health (e.g., depleting one's economic resources), and spiritual health (e.g., loss of faith in God) effects. In addition, there are costs to society in fighting stalking, as well as the general level of fear that people in society experience as a result of the occurrence of stalking. It is important to point out, however, that at least some stalking victims find silver linings to their experience. Some victims become more resolved, more resilient, more cautious, or more determined (Spitzberg & Rhea, 1999). Some even find they experience ambivalent effects (Haugaard & Seri, 2003), feeling both flattered and more attractive, while simultaneously experiencing a sense of fear and threat (Dunn, 2002). Such ambivalence may open spaces for continued pursuit, especially in the context of developing relationships in which explicit discussions of relationship definition may be avoided in order to save face.

In order to understand how such forms of unwanted pursuit may intrude into the realm of online matchmaking, it is important to set the theoretical stage that will help navigate the potentially treacherous waters of courtship. We find three theories particularly relevant to charting our course: relational goal pursuit theory, impression management theory, and socio-evolutionary theory.

Relational goal pursuit theory

Relationship goal pursuit theory (Cupach & Spitzberg, 2004; Cupach, Spitzberg, & Carson, 2000; Spitzberg & Cupach, 2001, 2002) explains how ordinary efforts to form, develop, and maintain interpersonal relationships can become inappropriate and obsessive. The theory begins with the premise that activity designed to pursue a relationship is motivated by a *relational goal*. When one desires some level of interdependence and/or intimacy with another, then one possesses a relational goal (e.g., to develop a romantic relationship). The more important the goal is, the more motivated one is to pursue it and the greater the effort one will exert (e.g., Beck, 1983). Relational goal pursuit manifests itself in activities designed to establish or maintain an interpersonal relationship, including creating opportunities for interacting with the target, cultivating the target's affinity, and gathering information about the target.

Progress in attaining an important goal is regularly monitored. It is possible to believe that progress is being made in cultivating a relationship, even when objectively that is not the case. Because relationship definitions and implications inferred from interactions are tacitly exchanged, there is often opportunity for misperception and mismatching of relational goals (Cupach & Spitzberg, 2004; Metts & Spitzberg, 1996; Spitzberg, 1998). Moreover, social rejection is normally conveyed in tactful and polite ways, the ambiguity of which fuels misperception.

When one's efforts at relational goal achievement appear to be thwarted or blocked, two options are considered. First, if the relational goal seems unrealistic (i.e., unattainable or unworthy of further effort), pursuit is abandoned and efforts are directed at other more important goals. Alternatively, if the goal retains its importance, then pursuit efforts are intensified accordingly.

An individual's goals are organised in a hierarchical fashion. Goals lower in the hierarchy are often instrumental in accomplishing higher order goals. Goal *linking* occurs when one perceives that the achievement of a higher order goal, such as life happiness (McIntosh & Martin, 1992; McIntosh, Harlow, & Martin, 1995) or self-worth (Pomerantz, Saxon, & Oishi, 2000; Pyszczynski & Greenberg, 1987), *requires* the accomplishment of a particular lower order goal (McIntosh & Martin, 1992). Individuals who obsessively pursue a relationship tend to link the lower order relational goal to higher order goals. 'Hence, the lower-order relational goal takes on the enduring quality of the higher order goal to which it is linked' (Cupach & Spitzberg, 2004, p. 101).

Thus, obsessive relationship pursuit is grounded in the pursuer's exaggeration of the importance of a relational goal. Persistence of pursuit is further fuelled by three reinforcing thought processes and emotions. First, the obsessive pursuer *ruminates* about the unmet relational goal. Ruminative thoughts are repeated, intrusive, and distressing (Martin & Tesser, 1989, 1996), and goal linking contributes to rumination (McIntosh et al., 1995; McIntosh & Martin, 1992). Rumination itself is persistent and escalates over time until the relational goal is achieved or abandoned (Miller & Tesser, 1986, 1989). Rumination drives persistence in striving for the relational goal.

Second, obsessive pursuers rationalise the consequences of their actions (Cupach & Spitzberg, 2004). Feeling the pressure to accomplish the relational goal, obsessive pursuers exaggerate both the expected benefits of relational goal success and the dire consequences of relational goal failure. They experience corresponding anticipatory emotions associated with relational goal success (i.e., imagined happiness) and relational goal failure (i.e., imagined sadness). Moreover, obsessive relationship pursuers tend to see their own persistence as noble, to misinterpret cues of resistance or rejection from the target as signs of encouragement, and to underestimate the negative effects of their persistence on the target. These various forms of rationalisation disinhibit the relationship pursuer's normal comprehension of appropriate goal-pursuit behaviour, thereby legitimating aggressive and excessive relational pursuit.

Third, the frustration of the relational goal, coupled with rumination over time, lead the obsessive pursuer to feel flooded with negative emotion. The frustration of an important goal produces distressing levels of negative affect (Martin & Tesser, 1989, 1996). The negative emotion reinforces the persistence of both rumination and relational goal pursuit.

Impression management theory

Individuals routinely control the impressions of themselves they create for others (see Leary, 1995; Metts & Grohskopf, 2003; Schlenker, 1980). By influencing the impressions of others, people can maximise their rewards and minimise their costs (Schlenker, 1980). *Self-presentation* refers to 'the process by which individuals, more or less intentionally, construct a public self that is likely to elicit certain types of attributions from others, attributions that would facilitate the achievement of some goal...' (Metts & Grohskopf, 2003, p. 360). The extent of success at getting others to form desired impressions enhances the chances of obtaining desired behavioural responses from others (Jones & Pittman, 1982).

Any enacted behaviour can leave others with impressions, whether or not the actor is intending strategic manipulation of others' attributions. Leary and Kowalski (1990) indicate that there are three general features that determine the extent of an individual's impression motivation in a given situation: (a) the goal relevance of the impressions; (b) the value of the desired outcomes; and (c) the discrepancy between one's desired image and the image currently portrayed.

'When a person is dependent on others for valued outcomes, the impressions he or she makes on them are more important, and the individual will be more motivated to engage in impression management' (Leary & Kowalski, 1990, p. 38). In the case of matchmaking and relationship formation, goal achievement is critically dependent on creating the right impressions in the target partner. Moreover, the relevance of making good impressions to accomplishment of the relationship goal is magnified by the expectation of continued future interactions with the target (Leary & Kowalski, 1990).

The more important a goal is the greater goal-striving motivation tends to be. To the extent that relationship formation hinges on creating favourable impressions in the target partner, impression motivation is high. When progress toward relational goal achievement is insufficient, then a likely inference is that appropriate impressions have not been promoted effectively. This perceived discrepancy between the image apparently conveyed and the image that is desired (in order to attain the relational goal) serves to sustain impression motivation. In order to rectify the discrepancy between current versus desired image, a person may either work harder (or smarter) at creating the desired image, or attempt to portray a different image that could more effectively attain the relational goal.

The nature and content of impressions that individuals promote depend on their desired outcomes and the expectations attendant on the social context (Leary & Kowalski, 1990). In the case of matchmaking where a relational goal is being pursued, a suitor attempts to present a desirable image that enables continued interaction and promotes affinity. In order to facilitate the development of a relationship, people normally portray an identity that is attractive, interesting, and likeable – features conveying that worthiness as a desirable partner. Consequently, the corresponding self-presentation strategies of ingratiation (e.g., giving compliments, expressing similar opinions) and self-promotion (e.g., demonstrating one's own abilities, commenting on one's own accomplishments or assets) are commonly exhibited during matchmaking endeavours (e.g., Jones & Pittman, 1982).

Self-presentations vary somewhat between face-to-face and CMC interactions. First, nonverbal behaviour normally plays a prominent role in impression formation during face-to-face interaction (e.g., Schlenker, 1980). Physical appearance, proxemic behaviour, kinesic cues, and paralanguage substantially supplement and qualify the interpretations of verbal communication. People often rely on such cues that are often unconsciously 'given off' to verify the accuracy of verbal cues that are consciously 'given' (Goffman, 1959). When interaction occurs in a CMC environment, the availability of nonverbal cues is greatly diminished and actors must rely more heavily on verbal cues for drawing inferences. Such inferences may suffer in their reliability. Second, some individuals may intentionally select leaner communication channels when they wish to 'ambiguate, or obscure completely, unattractive or embarrassing' characteristics that would lead to unfavourable impressions (O'Sullivan, 2000, p. 408). For example, if one perceives that physical appearance could undermine relationship initiation in face-to-face interaction, then one might choose to initiate a relationship through CMC to better regulate the impressions initially created in the target. Surprisingly, some of these self-presentational tendencies may be influenced by factors deep in our evolutionary pasts.

Socio-evolutionary theory

Socio-evolutionary theory is a family of theories that claim natural selection influences social behaviour patterns. Darwin proposed that random changes in organisms' traits would be more or less adaptive to survival in local environments. Those traits that happened to be more adaptive would facilitate survival, and therefore mating and subsequent progeny, than would those traits that were less adaptive. Over many generations, those adaptive traits would be more selected, and therefore a species would be more and more characterised by those traits. Social behavioural tendencies are viewed in terms of whether they (1) are reflections of historical adaptive functions or (2) are optimising current reproductive fitness through the maximisation of potential progeny.

Humans are a sexually dimorphic species; males and females are fairly distinct anatomically, and both their genetic material is required for mating and the production of offspring. It so happens that one of the evolutionary products of primate history is the development of long gestation periods for females, and the birth of relatively helpless infants who require very long developmental periods of parental investment in care for infants to mature into relatively autonomous progeny. This means that females invest enormously in the carrying and care of the next generation. In contrast, males may elect to invest enormous energies into the care of their offspring, but are also relatively free to seek other pair bonds and mating opportunities. Furthermore, 'because fertilization and gestation occur internally within women and not men, men over evolutionary history have faced an adaptive problem simply not faced by women – less than 100% certainty of parenthood' (Buss, 1995, p. 14). Thus, men could end up investing decades in assisting the rearing of offspring that are not their own genetic progeny.

Given these sexual differences in the relative required investments in offspring, various sex differences in social behaviour might be anticipated. For example, females should become relatively selective of their mates, given the enormous consequences that mating implies. In contrast, motivated to mate extensively and produce offspring, males should be more sexually motivated (Baumeister, Catanese, & Vohs, 2001; Pedersen, Miller, Putcha-Bhagavatula, & Yang, 2002), seek multiple mating partners, and be less inclined to invest in long-term pair bonds (Buss, 1994; Hirsch & Paul, 1996, Paul & Hirsch, 1996; Trivers, 1972). Males will be more attracted to cues of physical attractiveness as signs of physical health and therefore reproductive fitness, whereas females will be more attracted to cues of status and stability as signs of willingness to commit to the long-term and to protect the family unit (Buss & Schmitt, 1993). These tendencies are qualified in at least two significant ways. First, even though males are likely to pursue sex (i.e., short-term mating strategies), and females are likely to pursue attachments (i.e., long-term mating strategies), both sexes may employ either or both sets of strategies if such strategies facilitate pair-bonding and mating (Buss, 1998; Buss & Schmitt, 1993; Koziel & Pawlowski, 2003). Second, males and females, recognising these tendencies, may well adapt their mating strategies to appeal to the preferences of the opposite sex. For example, once pair-bonded in a long-term relationship, males will likely be motivated by jealousy to engage in mate-guarding activities (e.g., surveillance possessiveness, competition with rivals, etc.) in order to protect and assure paternity. So, males may prefer short-term mating strategies, but advertise long-term mating characteristics. Females may prefer long-term mates, but advertise themselves as seeking short-term partners (Tooke & Camire, 1991).

Adapting mating strategies to the presumed preferences of the opposite sex, while potentially duplicitous, may actually facilitate successful mating for both sexes, as it promotes opportunities to encounter potential partners. Indeed, research indicates that males and females are becoming more similar over time in their most preferred characteristics (e.g., mutual attraction and love, physical attractiveness, financial resources, chastity) of a potential mate (Buss, Shackelford, Kirkpatrick, & Larsen, 2001). Culture interacts with adaptive tendencies to produce such variations in mating strategies, which makes the role of personal advertising for the purpose of mating a particularly intriguing nexus of theoretical and empirical questions (McGuirl & Wiederman, 2000). In order to ground such inquiry in existing understandings, the personal ads, video-dating, and person matchmaking literatures provide an analogue for examining the potential evolution of mating into the CMC environment.

Cyberstalking and the construction of online matchmaking

New media of communication inevitably and systemically influence the social structure within which those media are adopted. Many people view the Internet as an alternative route to relationship development (Goodson, McCormick, & Evans, 2000). There is evidence that many people are using online media for precisely such purposes (e.g., Goodson et al., 2001; Jones, 2002; Knox, Daniels, Sturdivant, & Zusman, 2001;

Lenhart, Rainie, & Lewis, 2001; McKenna, Green, & Gleasan, 2002; Nice & Katzev, 1998; Parks & Floyd, 1996; Parks & Roberts, 1998; Pew, 2000; Rumbough, 2001; Scharlott & Christ, 1995; Wolak, Mitchell, & Finkelhor, 2002). Despite predictions and some findings that CMC relationships tend to escalate in artificial and accelerated ways (e.g., Bargh, McKenna, & Fitzsimmons, 2002; McKenna et al., 2002; Merkel & Richardson, 2000; Tidwell & Walther, 2002; Whitty, 2002), most research to date suggests that those who develop intimate CMC relationships both find them highly comparable to real space (RS) and primarily face-to-face relationships, and they tend to extend those relationships across these domains of interaction (Cornwell & Lundgren, 2001; McKenna et al., 2002; Nice & Katzev, 1998; Wildermuth, 2001). However, the new media of communication permit varieties of access that are simply not possible in RS. That these forms of access would be sought by those who would use them to exploit, coerce, or stalk others is little surprise.

Computer technologies permit the design of relatively anonymous and strategically designed mating messages. Such media facilitate the efficient use of both broadcasting (i.e., sending out similar messages to multiple audiences) and narrowcasting (i.e., delimited searches and parameter) approaches to pursuer display as well as target acquisition. Finally, the relative sense of security permitted by communicating at a distance is likely to promote accelerated disclosures, and thus, an exaggerated sense of intimacy and accessibility. Such hyper-intimate interaction may stimulate the impression of intimacy despite a relative lack of intimacy across other relationship domains. Such a sense of instant intimacy can easily promote passionate obsessions and subsequent unwanted pursuit predicated on the impression that more of a relationship has been established than actually *has* been established. In this context, cyberstalking seems likely.

Cyberstalking is 'the use of the Internet, email, or other electronic communications devices to stalk another person' (US Attorney General, 1999, p. 2). It typically involves 'a group of behaviors in which an individual, group of individuals, or organization uses information and communication technology to harass another individual, group of individuals, or organization' (Bocij, 2004, p. 14). Anecdotally, about a fifth of stalking crimes involve some aspect of electronic communications (US Attorney General, 1999). Working to Halt Online Abuse (WHOA, 2003) reported on a subsample of 827 cases of online harassment reported to their organisation between 2000 and 2002. About 62 per cent of victims are female, and an average of 60 per cent of harassers are thought by the victim to be male. In terms of prior acquaintance, 27 per cent in 2002 were considered an 'ex', 28 per cent were known from online interaction, and another 16 per cent were considered a 'friend'. Harassment occurred in a variety of media, including email ($M = 33\%$), message boards ($M = 16\%$), instant messaging ($M = 10\%$), websites ($M = 6\%$), and chat spaces ($M = 12\%$). A majority of victims perceive that the online harassment escalated once begun, and a majority of approximately 65 per cent of victims claimed to have received a threat of off-line harassment.

A large-scale study of 1500 youth Internet users aged 10–17 years found one-fifth had received online sexual solicitations in the previous year, of which a quarter experienced fear or distress as a result (Finkelhor, Mitchell, & Wolak, 2000). In a multi-study investigation, Spitzberg and Hoobler (2002) found a three-factor structure to cyberstalking behaviours: hyper-intimacy (e.g., sending exaggerated messages of affection, sending tokens of affection, etc.), RL transfer (e.g., meeting first online and then threatening you, meeting first online and then following you, etc.), and threat (e.g., sending threatening written messages, sending threatening pictures or images, etc.). They also found that the percentage of college students who experienced any of 24 unwanted cyberstalking tactics at least once ranged from 1 per cent to 31 per cent. Importantly, the experience of cyberstalking tactics correlated significantly to the experience of terrestrial obsessive relational intrusion tactics. If the available studies of obsessive relational intrusion and stalking that report some type of cyberstalking incidence are averaged (see Table 10.1), to date only about 14 per cent of stalking takes place through electronic means. However, there is every reason to expect that this proportion will increase as such media increasingly saturate social adoption (Hitchcock, 2002; Spitzberg & Hoobler, 2002).

Beyond the pathological models of child molesters, little to nothing is known about the motives of cyberstalkers. One motive for cyberstalking may simply be that those people who are prone to stalking for love or intimidation will extend their toolbox to new media, which hold the promise of relative anonymity, access from a distance, and enormous efficiency in terms of time and resources. A second motive is that increasingly there is evidence that some people are prone to Internet addiction, or excessive use of the Internet (Anderson, 2001; Griffiths, 1999; Pratarelli, Browne, & Johnson, 1999; Schneider, 2000), and some people are also prone to sexual Internet pursuit (Cooper & Sportolari, 1997) and addictions (Cooper, Delmonico, & Burg, 2000; Cooper, Putnam, Planchon, & Boies, 1999; Edelson, 2000; Lamb, 1998; Schwartz & Southern, 2000) via the Internet.

Table 10.1 Estimates of cyberstalking tactics

- 0% web pages (LeBlanc, Levesque, & Berka, 2001)
- 1% first meeting online and then stalking you (Spitzberg & Hoobler, 2002)
- 1% meeting first online and then following (Spitzberg & Hoobler, 2002)
- 1% meeting first online and then harming you (Spitzberg & Hoobler, 2002)
- 1% Internet (Meloy et al., 2000)
- 2% fax (Oddie, 2000)
- 2% telephoned/sent mail (McLennan, 1996)
- 2% stalked by means of the Internet (Kamphuis & Emmelkamp, 2001)
- 3% cyber-attempting to disable your computer (Spitzberg & Hoobler, 2002)
- 3% meeting first online and then intruding in life (Spitzberg & Hoobler, 2002)
- 3% meeting first online and then threatening (Spitzberg & Hoobler, 2002)
- 5% cyber-sending threatening pictures/images (Spitzberg & Hoobler, 2002)
- 6% computer (Oddie, 2000)
- 9% cyber-sending threatening written messages (Spitzberg & Hoobler, 2002)
- 12% cyber-sabotaging reputation (Spitzberg & Hoobler, 2002)
- 17% cyber-exposing private information to others (Spitzberg & Hoobler, 2002)
- 18% cyber-sending sexually harassing messages (Spitzberg & Hoobler, 2002)
- 19% unwanted faxes, letters, or e-mails (Purcell, Pathé, & Mullen, 2002)
- 19% cyber-sending pornographic/obscene messages (Spitzberg & Hoobler, 2002)
- 20% cyber-pretending to be someone she or he wasn't (Spitzberg & Hoobler, 2002)
- 25% cyber-sending excessively 'needy' or demanding messages (Spitzberg & Hoobler, 2002)
- 25% stalking cases involved e-mail incidents (Fisher, Cullen & Turner, 1999)
- 26% cyber-sending excessively disclosive messages (Spitzberg & Hoobler, 2002)
- 31% cyber-sending exaggerated messages of affection (Spitzberg & Hoobler, 2002)
- 31% cyber-sending tokens of affection (Spitzberg & Hoobler, 2002)
- 39% counter-allegations of stalking (Sheridan, Davies, & Boon, 2001)
- 58% tried other communications (Lemmey, 1999)

Source: Adapted from Cupach & Spitzberg, 2004.

A third motive structure for cyberstalking may be the prospect of exploitation. There is already evidence that some people who use the Internet employ deception in the process of communicating with others. In a large sample study, Cooper et al. (2000, p. 16) found only '5% of the entire sample reported having ever changed their gender while online. However, the data suggested that it is common for people to misrepresent their age' (> 48%) and race (38%). A large-scale Pew Internet study of teen life online found '24% of teens who have used IMs [instant messages] and email or been to chat rooms have pretended to be a different person when they were communicating online' and '33% of these teens report having someone give them fake information about themselves in an email or instant message' (Lenhart et al., 2001, p. 4). In a study of chat room users, Whitty (2002) found that men reported lying more than women, and the more they used chat rooms, the more likely they were to lie. The typical topics of deception were age, gender, occupation, education and income, all of which are factors that would be sources of personal advertisements. In a study of seeking romance on the Internet, Cornwell and Lundgren (2001) found that 50 per cent of their sample of cyberspace, compared to 35 per cent of the RS, respondents misrepresented themselves in some way. The difference was significantly greater in cyberspace in regard to age and physical characteristics. Rumbough (2001, p. 225) found 18 per cent of students reported having 'pretended to be someone else while using e-mail', 28 per cent 'pretended to be someone else while in a chat room', 27 per cent 'lied about age', 15 per cent 'lied about weight', 11 per cent 'lied about gender', almost 10 per cent 'lied about geographic location' while using e-mail or participating in chat rooms. It could be that such deceptions represent people exploring the implications of such identities, but it is also possible that such behaviour normalises the process of deception and manipulation of others. It could be a small step from such deceptions to more intrusive manipulative actions. From an impression management perspective, deception is more likely when an interactant has a motive to ingratiate another and win his or her affection (Feldman, Forrest, & Happ, 2002).

Such deception can serve at least three functions. First, it can facilitate attracting a person under false pretences in the early stages of interaction. Second, it could facilitate manoeuvres to attract a person back to the relationship after an attempted detachment. Third, deception could be employed to inveigle oneself back into a person's electronic life through hacking or surreptitious insinuation into that person's network of correspondents.

Conclusion

People are increasingly drawn to online media for initiating, developing, maintaining, and ending their relationships with others. Online media are attractive for a variety of reasons, including efficiency, interactional control, and accessibility. Such technological advantages are a double-edged blade, providing expanded opportunities both for those seeking relationships with benign and exploitative intentions. Furthermore, even those benignly inspired can become intrusive harassers who invade and inveigle themselves through the various technological media through which we increasingly live our lives. More ominously, these cyberstalkers may view such electronic means of pursuit as only a prelude to stalking in real space. Online matchmaking is a natural nexus for the understanding of both the normal and abnormal processes of relationship pursuit. Those seeking relational union through online means are motivated to adapt their impression to suit those who are also using those online means to seek a partner. These adaptations will likely be guided by intuitive understandings of evolved sex differences in romantic preferences in seeking partnership. Such management of impressions is therefore likely to link directly into the goals people seeking relationship partners are most likely to possess. It is perhaps inevitable that as the use of online matchmaking increases, the likelihood of cyberstalking victimisation will also increase. Such ominous portents bear a close and vigorous watch by scholars and would-be paramours alike if a relationally embedded technological dystopia is to be avoided.

References

Anderson, K. J. (2001). Internet use among college students: An exploratory study. *Journal of American College Health, 50*, 21–6.

Baize, H. R., Jr., & Schroeder, J. E. (1995). Personality and mate selection in personal ads: Evolutionary preferences in a public mate selection process. *Journal of Social Behavior and Personality, 10*, 517–36.

Bargh, J. A., McKenna, K. Y. A., & Fitzsimmons, G. M. (2002). Can you see the real me? Activation and expression of the 'true self' on the Internet. *Journal of Social Issues, 58*, 33–48.

Baumeister, R. F., Catanese, K. R., & Vohs, K. D. (2001). Is there a gender difference in strength of sex drive? Theoretical views, conceptual distinctions, and a review of relevant evidence. *Personality and Social Psychology Review, 5*, 242–73.

Beck, R. C. (1983). *Motivation: Theories and principles* (2nd edn). Englewood Cliffs, NJ: Prentice-Hall.

Bocij, P. (2004). *Cyberstalking: Harassment in the internet age and how to protect your family*. Westport, CT: Praeger.

Buss, D. M. (1994). *The evolution of desire*. New York: Basic Books.

Buss, D. M. (1995). Evolutionary psychology: A new paradigm for psychological science. *Psychological Inquiry, 6*, 1–30.

Buss, D. M. (1998). The psychology of human mate selection: Exploring the complexity of the strategic repertoire. In C. Crawford & D. L. Krebs (eds), *Handbook of evolutionary psychology: Ideas, issues, and applications* (pp. 405–29). Mahwah, NJ: Lawrence Erlbaum Associates.

Buss, D. M., & Schmitt, D. P. (1993). Sexual strategies theory: An evolutionary perspective on human mating. *Psychological Review, 100*, 204–32.

Buss, D. M., Shackelford, T. K., Kirkpatrick, L. A., & Larsen, R. J. (2001). A half century of mate preferences: The cultural evolution of values. *Journal of Marriage and Family, 63*, 491–503.

Cooper, A., Delmonico, D. L., & Burg, R. (2000). Cybersex users, abusers, and compulsives: New findings and implications. *Sexual Addiction & Compulsivity, 7*, 5–29.

Cooper, A., Putnam, D. E., Planchon, L. A., & Boies, S. C. (1999). Online sexual compulsivity: Getting tangled in the net. *Sexual Addiction and Compulsivity, 6*, 79–104.

Cooper, A., & Sportolari, L. (1997). Romance in cyberspace: Understanding online attraction. *Journal of Sex Education and Therapy, 22*, 7–14.

Cornwell, B., & Lundgren, D. C. (2001). Love on the Internet: Involvement and misrepresentation in romantic relationships in cyberspace vs. realspace. *Computers in Human Behavior, 17*, 197–211.

Cupach, W. R., & Spitzberg, B. H. (2004). *The dark side of relationship pursuit: From attraction to obsession and stalking*. Mahwah, NJ: Lawrence Erlbaum Associates.

Cupach, W. R., Spitzberg, B. H., & Carson, C. L. (2000). Toward a theory of stalking and obsessive relational intrusion. In K. Dindia & S. Duck (eds), *Communication and personal relationships* (pp. 131–46). New York: John Wiley & Sons.

Dunn, J. L. (2002). *Courting disaster: Intimate stalking, culture, and criminal justice*. New York: Aldine de Gruyter.

Edelson, E. (2000, 8 Feb.). Fleeting thrills or cybersex addiction? Retrieved from: http://www.apbnews.com/safetycenter/famil . . . rsex0208_01.html?s=_ad_cybersex1_netscape.

Feldman, R. S., Forrest, J. A., & Happ, B. R. (2002). Self-presentation and verbal deception: Do self-presenters lie more? *Basic and Applied Social Psychology, 24*, 163–70.

Finkelhor, D., Mitchell, K. J., & Wolak, J. (2000). *Online victimization: A report on the nation's youth*. Alexandria, VA: National Center for Missing and Exploited Children.

Fisher, B. S., Cullen, F. T., & Turner, M. G. (1999). *The extent and nature of the sexual victimization of college women: A national-level analysis*. Final Report submitted to the National Institute of Justice (NCJ 179977). Washington, DC: US Department of Justice.

Goffman, E. (1959). *The presentation of self in everyday life*. Garden City, NY: Doubleday Anchor.

Goodson, P., McCormick, D., & Evans, A. (2001). Sex and the Internet: A survey instrument to assess college students' behavior and attitudes. *CyberPsychology & Behavior, 3*, 129–49.

Griffiths, M. (1999). Internet addiction: Fact or fiction? *Psychologist, 12*, 246–50.

Haugaard, J. J., & Seri, L. G. (2003). Stalking and other forms of intrusive contact after the dissolution of adolescent dating or romantic relationships. *Violence and Victims, 18*, 279–97.

Hirsch, L. R., & Paul, L. (1996). Human male mating strategies: I. Courtship tactics of the 'quality' and 'quantity' alternatives. *Ethology and Sociobiology, 17*, 55–70.

Hitchcock, J. A. (2002). *Net crimes & misdemeanors*. Medford, NJ: Information Today.

Jones, E. E., & Pittman, T. S. (1982). Toward a general theory of strategic self-presentation. In J. Suls (ed.), *Psychological perspectives on the self* (Vol. 1, pp. 231–62). Hillsdale, NJ: Lawrence Erlbaum Associates.

Jones, S. (2002, 15 September). *The Internet goes to college: How students are living in the future with today's technology*. Pew Internet & American Life Project. Washington, DC: Author.

Kamphuis, J. H., & Emmelkamp, P. M. G. (2001). Traumatic distress among support-seeking female victims of stalking. *American Journal of Psychiatry, 158*, 795–8.

Knox, D., Daniels, V., Sturdivant, L., & Zusman, M. E. (2001). College student use of the Internet for mate selection. *College Student Journal, 35*, 158–60.

Koziel, S., & Pawlowski, B. (2003). Comparison between primary and secondary mate markets: An analysis of data from lonely hearts columns. *Personality and Individual Differences, 35*, 1849–57.

Lamb, M. (1998). Cybersex: Research notes on the characteristics of the visitors to online chat rooms. *Deviant Behavior, 19*, 121–35.

Leary, M. R. (1995). *Self-presentation: Impression management and interpersonal behavior*. Madison, WI: Brown & Benchmark.

Leary, M. R., & Kowalski, R. M. (1990). Impresion management: A literature review and two-component model. *Psychological Bulletin, 107*, 34–47.

LeBlanc, J. J., Levesque, G. J., & Berka, L. H. (2001). Survey of stalking at WPI. *Journal of Forensic Sciences, 46*, 367–9.

Lemmey, D. (1999). *Stalking of battered women before and after seeking criminal justice help*. Unpublished doctoral dissertation, Nursing Program, Texas Women's University, Denton.

Lenhart, A., Rainie, L., & Lewis, O. (2001). *Teenage life online: The rise of the instant-message generation and the Internet's impact on friendships and family relationships*. Washington, DC: Pew Internet & American Life Project.

Martin, L. L., & Tesser, A. (1989). Toward a motivational and structural theory of ruminative thought. In J. S. Uleman & J. A. Bargh (eds), *Unintended thought* (pp. 306–26). New York: Guilford.

Martin, L. L., & Tesser, A. (1996). Some ruminative thoughts. In R. S. Wyer (ed.), *Ruminative thoughts* (pp. 1–47). Mahwah, NJ: Lawrence Erlbaum Associates.

McGuirl, K. E., & Wiederman, M. W. (2000). Characteristics of the ideal sex partner: Gender differences and perceptions of the preferences of the other gender. *Journal of Sex & Marital Therapy, 26*, 153–9.

McIntosh, W. D., & Martin, L. L. (1992). The cybernetics of happiness: The relation of goal attainment, rumination, and affect. In M. S. Clark (ed.), *Emotion and social behavior* (pp. 222–46). Newbury Park, CA: Sage.

McIntosh, W. D., Harlow, T. F., & Martin, L. L. (1995). Linkers and nonlinkers: Goal beliefs as a moderator of the effects of everyday hassles on rumination, depression, and physical complaints. *Journal of Applied Social Psychology, 25*, 1231–44.

McKenna, K. Y. A., Green, A. S., & Gleason, M. E. J. (2002). Relationship formation on the Internet: What's the big attraction? *Journal of Social Issues, 58*, 9–31.

McLennan, W. (1996). *Women's safety, Australia, 1996*. Canberra, Commonwealth of Australia: Australian Bureau of Statistics.

Meloy, J. R., Rivers, L., Siegel, L., Gothard, S., Naimark, D., & Nicolini, J. R. (2000). A replication study of obsessional followers and offenders with mental disorders. *Journal of Forensic Sciences, 45*, 147–52.

Merkel, E. R., & Richardson, R. A. (2000). Digital dating and virtual relating: Conceptualizing computer mediated romantic relationships. *Family Relations, 49*, 187–92.

Metts, S., & Grohskopf, E. (2003). Impression management: Goals, strategies, and skills. In J. O. Greene & B. R. Burleson (eds), *Handbook of communication and social interaction skills* (pp. 357–99). Mahwah, NJ: Lawrence Erlbaum Associates.

Metts, S., & Spitzberg, B. H. (1996). Sexual communication in interpersonal contexts: A script-based approach. In B. R. Burleson (ed.), *Communication yearbook 19* (pp. 49–91). Thousand Oaks, CA: Sage.

Millar, M. G. & Tesser, A. (1986). Effects of affective and cognitive focus on the attitude–behavior relation. *Journal of Personality and Social Psychology, 51,* 270–6.

Millar, M. G. & Tesser, A. (1989). The effects of affective–cognitive consistency and thought on the attitude–behavior relation. *Journal of Experimental Social Psychology, 25,* 189–202.

Nice, M. L., & Katzev, R. (1998). Internet romances: The frequency and nature of romantic on-line relationships. *CyberPsychology & Behavior, 1,* 217–23.

O'Sullivan, P. B. (2000). What you don't know won't hurt *me*: Impression management functions of communication channels in relationships. *Human Communication Research, 26,* 403–31.

Oddie, J. (2000). *The prediction of violence in stalkers.* Unpublished doctoral dissertation, California School of Professional Psychology, Fresno, CA.

Parks, M. R., & Floyd, K. (1996). Making friends in cyberspace. *Journal of Communication, 46,* 80–97.

Parks, M. R., & Roberts, L. D. (1998). 'Making MOOsic': The development of personal relationships online and a comparison to their off-line counterparts. *Journal of Social and Personal Relationships, 15,* 517–37.

Paul, L., & Hirsch, L. R. (1996). Human male mating strategies: II. Moral codes of 'quality' and 'quantity' strategists. *Ethology and Sociobiology, 17,* 71–86.

Pedersen, W. C., Miller, L. C., Putcha-Bhagavatula, A. D., & Yang, Y. (2002). Evolved sex differences in the number of partners desired? The long and the short of it. *Psychological Science, 13,* 157–61.

Pew Internet & American Life Project. (2000, 10 May). *Tracking online life: How women use the Internet to cultivate relationships with family and friends.* Washington, DC: Author.

Pomerantz, E. M., Saxon, J. L., & Oishi, S. (2000). The psychological trade-offs of goal investment. *Journal of Personality and Social Psychology, 79,* 617–30.

Pratarelli, M. E., Browne, B. L., & Johnson, K. (1999). The bits and bytes of computer/Internet addiction: A factor analytic approach. *Behavior Research Methods, Instruments, & Computers, 31,* 305–14.

Purcell, R., Pathé, M., & Mullen, P. E. (2002). The prevalence and nature of stalking in the Australian community. *Australian and New Zealand Journal of Psychiatry, 36,* 114–20.

Pyszczynski, T., & Greenberg, J. (1987). Self-regulatory perseveration and the depressive self-focusing style: A self-awareness theory of reactive depression. *Psychological Bulletin, 102,* 122–38.

Rumbough, T. (2001). The development and maintenance of interpersonal relationships through computer-mediated communication. *Communication Research Reports, 18,* 223–9.

Scharlott, B. W., & Christ, W. G. (1995). Overcoming relationship-initiation barriers: The impact of a computer-dating system on sex role, shyness, and appearance inhibitions. *Computers in Human Behavior, 11,* 191–204.

Schlenker, B. R. (1980). *Impression management: The self-concept, social identity, and interpersonal relations*. Monterey, CA: Brooks/Cole.

Schneider, J. P. (2000). Effects of cybersex addiction on the family: Results of a survey. In A. Cooper (ed.), *Cybersex: The dark side of the force* (pp. 31–58). Philadelphia: Brunner-Routledge.

Schwartz, M. F., & Southern, S. (2000). Compulsive cybersex: The new tea room. In A. Cooper (ed.), *Cybersex: The dark side of the force* (pp. 127–44). Philadelphia: Brunner-Routledge.

Sheridan, L., Davies, G. M., & Boon, J. C. (2001). The course and nature of stalking: A victim perspective. *Howard Journal of Criminal Justice, 40*, 215–34.

Spitzberg, B. H. (1998). Sexual coercion. In B. H. Spitzberg & W. R. Cupach (eds), *The dark side of close relationships* (pp. 179–232). Mahwah, NJ: Lawrence Erlbaum Associates.

Spitzberg, B. H. (2002). The tactical topography of stalking victimization and management. *Trauma, Violence, & Abuse, 3*, 261–88.

Spitzberg, B. H. (2004, February). Preliminary development of a model and measure of computer mediated communication (CMC) competence. Paper presented at the Western States Communication Association Conference, Albuquerque, NM.

Spitzberg, B. H., & Cupach, W. R. (2001). Paradoxes of pursuit: Toward a relational model of stalking-related phenomena. In J. A. Davis (ed.), *Stalking crimes and victim protection: Prevention, intervention, threat assessment, and case management* (pp. 97–136). Boca Raton, FL: CRC Press.

Spitzberg, B. H., & Cupach, W. R. (2002). The inappropriateness of relational intrusion. In R. Goodwin & D. Cramer (eds), *Inappropriate relationships: The unconventional, the disapproved, and the forbidden* (pp. 191–219). Mahwah, NJ: Lawrence Erlbaum Associates.

Spitzberg, B. H., & Cupach, W. R. (2003). What mad pursuit? Obsessive relational intrusion and stalking related phenomena. *Aggression and Violent Behavior, 8*, 345–75.

Spitzberg, B. H., & Hoobler, G. (2002). Cyberstalking and the technologies of interpersonal terrorism. *New Media & Society, 4*, 71–92.

Spitzberg, B. H., & Rhea, J. (1999). Obsessive relational intrusion and sexual coercion victimization. *Journal of Interpersonal Violence, 14*, 3–20.

Tidwell, L. C., & Walther, J. B. (2002). Computer-mediated communication effects on disclosure, impressions, and interpersonal evaluations: Getting to know one another a bit at a time. *Human Communication Research, 28*, 317–48.

Tooke, W., & Camire, L. (1991). Patterns of deception in intersexual and intrasexual mating strategies. *Ethology and Sociobiology, 12*, 345–64.

Trivers, R. L. (1972). Parental investment and sexual selection. In B. Campbell (ed.), *Sexual selection and the descent of man, 1871–1971* (pp. 136–79). Chicago, IL: Aldine.

U. S. Attorney General. (1999, August). *Cyberstalking: A new challenge for law enforcement and industry*. Report from the Attorney General to the Vice President. Retrieved 9 September 1999, from: http://www.usdoj.gov/ag/cyberstalkingreport.htm.

Whitty, M. T. (2002). Liar, liar! An examination of how open, supportive and honest people are in chat rooms. *Computers in Human Behavior, 18*, 343–52.

Wildermuth, S. M. (2001). Love on the line: Participants' descriptions of computer-mediated close relationships. *Communication Quarterly, 49*, 89–95.

Wolak, J., Mitchell, K. J., & Finkelhor, D. (2002). Close online relationships in a national sample of adolescents. *Adolescence, 37*, 441–55.

Working to Halt Online Abuse. (2003). Online harassment statistics. Retrieved 11 November 2003, from: http://www.haltabuse.org/resources/stats/index.shtml.

11
Cyber-Victimisation and Online Dating

Robert A. Jerin and Beverly Dolinsky

Online dating Internet sites are one of the newest devices being used to help people find love and companionship. However, it is possible that these individuals who use online dating services might also experience cyber-victimisation as a result of using this dating strategy. The purpose of this chapter is to describe the use of online dating services, their advantages and disadvantages especially as it relates to cyber-victimisation, and online dating safety precautions. Specifically, the chapter will define cyber-victimisation. It will describe actual and perceived risk of cyber-victimisation as a result of online dating. The safety precautions recommended by online dating sites will be described and compared to the precautions actually used by online dating service members.

An analysis of interpersonal Internet relationships indicates that using an online dating service can result in more intimate, informal, and immediate communication (Gerlander & Takala, 1997). The use of online dating services is described as booming and there are many Internet sites whose sole purpose is the business of helping individuals find romantic partners. Skriloff and Gould (1997) listed 42 such sites in their 1997 book devoted to assisting women to be successful in 'flirting, dating and finding love on-line' (p. 1). By 2005, this number had increased to over 1000 with the sites ranging from the broad audience (e.g., eharmony.com and Yahoo! Personals) to sites targeting specifics interests (e.g., Black Singles Connection, Christian Soulmates, and Senior Friend Finder). One of the more popular sites is Match-maker.com that boasts over 7 million registrations and purportedly more than 50,000 new members joining weekly. A second major player is Match.com claiming more than 724,000 paying subscribers and more than 8 million members with profiles posted or who are active users (Sage-Hearts.com, n.d.). One of the newest online dating services is poddater.com which launched a video dating site that allows members to download videos of people they are interested in to their iPod.

The debate over online dating

As online dating has become more mainstream people have started to debate its effect on social relationships (Gerlander & Takala, 1997; Katz & Aspden, 1997; Merkle & Richardson, 2000; Parks & Floyd, 1996). The popular literature is filled with mixed messages describing either the value of online dating in helping people meet Mr/Mrs Right or warning of its danger to the individual's safety. Interestingly enough, there is a noticeable lack of systematic research specifically examining online relationships (Spitzberg & Hoobler, 2002; Whitty, 2003). Katz and Aspden (1997) have noted that with the development of each new form of communication technology there have been critics espousing its evils. They argue that such innovations as the telegraph, telephone, and automobile have all radically altered society. While each of these innovations has improved the quality of life, critics believe it has also resulted in detrimental changes in relationships and society as a whole (Stoll, 1995). For example, critics have charged that both the telephone and automobile have caused individuals to have fewer face-to-face interactions and to become more isolated from society (Berger, 1979; Katz, 1990).

As with these earlier technologies, Internet communication has its advocates and critics (Gerlander & Takala, 1997; Katz & Aspden, 1997; Merkle & Richardson, 2000; Parks & Floyd, 1996). Advocates argue that genuine and meaningful communication can occur, and in fact can be enhanced, using online methods (Merkle & Richardson, 2000; Parks & Roberts, 1998; Scharlott & Christ, 1995; Walther, Loh, & Granka, 2005). Some claim that this method actually harkens back to the old days of courtship (Benson, Harrison, & Koss-Feder, 2000; Canon, 1997). Merkle and Richardson (2000) have described computer-mediated relationships as occurring through an inverted developmental sequence. That is, individuals get to know each other first and then later discover whether there is 'true' attraction following a face-to-face meeting. Similarly, Van Acker (2001) states that online dating allows individuals to talk and truly get to know each other's backgrounds, opinions and life goals, and those who use the method describe a level of intimacy often not found in face-to-face dating. How often computer-mediated relationships lead to

Robert A. Jerin and Beverly Dolinsky 149

face-to-face relationships remains to be determined (Baker, 2002; Cooper & Sportolari, 1997; Houran & Lange, 2004; Schnarch, 1997).

A second major argument for the value of online dating is its ability to allow individuals to 'meet' each other from around the world. Online communication is said to be creating an Internet 'global village', and with this individuals have more choice and hence more of a possibility of meeting someone who reflects the attributes of their 'ideal' lover (Feng, 2005; Katz & Aspden, 1997; Krakowka, 1998; Skriloff & Gould, 1997).

The critics charge that computer mediated communication and relationships are shallow, impersonal, and potentially dangerous. In reviewing the literature, both Katz and Aspden (1997), and Parks and Floyd (1996) found that the majority of dangers discussed in the popular and professional literature dealt more with the deterioration of meaningful social relationships as compared to criminal victimisation issues. Furthermore, most of the charges were anecdotal and based on personal impressions and case studies. For example, Ann Landers warned her readers to be wary of online romance because she received approximately 250 letters from individuals who had described their emotional, and in one instance, physical trauma, as a result of using computer mediated communication methods (Stein, 1996). As a second example, one man was both surprised and disappointed that some of the women who were responding to his online personal advertisement were in fact prostitutes making solicitations (Daniel, 2002). Recently, the State of Florida has considered creating legislation that would regulate online dating sites to require informing their clients whether they perform criminal background checks on their members. The law has been lobbied for by True.com and offers the screenings that would be required by the new law it is lobbying for. Government officials in California, Ohio, Virginia, Michigan, and Texas are also considering similar laws. Interestingly, neither Match.com nor the Florida police Computer Crimes Centre have noted any significant victimisation cases that would warrant statewide legislation regarding the use of online dating services (Farrell, 2005).

Cyber-victimisation and online dating

Cyber-victimsation can include receiving threatening email, unsolicited obscene email, spamming (junk email), flaming (online verbal abuse), leaving improper messages on message boards, and receiving electronic viruses (Whitty & Carr, 2005). Additionally, cyber-victimisation can take the form of cyberstalking. Cyberstalking can include a number of illegal behaviours including being followed or spied on, receiving unsolicited letters, receiving unsolicited phone calls, being left unwanted items, property being vandalised, description or harm of something loved, physical harm, and electronic identity theft (Whitty & Carr, 2005). One of the first initial studies to examine cyberstalking using social scientific research was completed by Spitzberg and Hoobler (2002). In three pilot studies, their research indicated that approximately one-third of their respondents had reported 'some form of cyber-based unwanted pursuit, albeit most of which was relatively harassing but benign' (Spitzberg & Hoobler, 2002, p. 86).

Actual and perceived risk of victimisation as a result of engaging in online relationships was systematically investigated for the first time, to our knowledge, in 2000 (Jerin & Dolinsky, 2001). The purpose of the study was to explore the actual and perceived risk of victimisation of women who use Internet dating services as a means of pursuing interpersonal relationships. A computer survey of a randomly selected international sample of female customers of three popular Internet dating services was conducted over a month long period. To select a representative sample of participants using Internet dating sites the authors used a clustered sampling method. Establishing the online dating services age group limitations (18–27 years, 28–37 years, 38–47 years, 48 years and above) as the only profile requirement, the dating services selection services provided a randomly selected list of members. Of the 1400 surveys that were sent out, 154 were returned as undeliverable. Of the remaining 1246 surveys, 134 were completed resulting in a 10.75 per cent participation rate.

The survey instrument was developed after reviewing available literature on stalking, cyberstalking, and dating violence prevention (Cyberangels, n.d, Jerin, 1998). The survey asked women to describe their perceived risk of specific forms of cyber-victimisation, knowledge and use of safety measures recommended by online dating services, and any victimisation experience as a direct result of the use of an online dating service. A list of possible detrimental cyber-victimisation experiences were developed by using the safety precaution information provided by the Internet dating services and Internet sites dedicated to online safety (Cyberangels, n.d). Forms of cyber-victimisation included threatening email, unsolicited obscene email, receiving a multitude of junk email (spamming), verbal online verbal abuse (flaming), leaving improper messages on message boards, receiving electronic viruses, and being the subject of electronic identity theft. The survey also asked online dating members their experiences with cyberstalking.

This included being followed or spied on, receiving unsolicited letters or written correspondence, receiving unsolicited phone calls, having someone stand outside their home, school or workplace, being left unwanted items, property being vandalised, the destruction or harm of something loved, and physical harm.

The basic thrust of the analysis examined perceived risk and victimisation experiences. The majority of respondents perceived the risk of experiencing cyber-victimisation as a result of using online dating services to be within minimal or acceptable levels. Length of time as measured by how many months they had used online dating services did not change perceptions of risk. Perceptions of risk also did not vary between different age groups. The age of the respondent and their education level did not influence cyber-victimisation experiences. The analysis did show a difference in cyber-victimisation experiences based upon the length of time one uses a dating service. Specifically, the results indicated that individuals who used the services for longer than one year were more likely to receive online verbal, threatening, and junk email. The increase in cyber-victimisation did not translate into a significant amount of traditional stalking behaviour among the groups. Among current users the incidents of stalking that had occurred was almost negligible (Jerin & Dolinsky, 2001).

Online dating safety precautions

The popular literature and online dating services all provide safety precaution advice. Stories abound in newspapers, radio, television, and web-based services that stress the importance of learning safe practices when using online services. There are hundreds of websites whose primary purpose is to promote safe use practices, with one of the most frequently referenced being 'cyberangels.org' (Cyberangels, n.d.). A second example is 'sage-hearts.com' (Sage-hearts.com, n.d.) an online site whose sole purpose is to review the best online dating sites available and also posts many safety tips including information on Internet dating safety precautions, background checks, and safety strategies when meeting someone in person. Such precautions include remaining anonymous by never giving out real email addresses, last names, home addresses, phone numbers or workplace information, using email redirection services, using gender neutral nicknames, and remembering to adjust automatic signature replies to avoid giving out personal information. Prior to meeting the individual background checks are recommended. In the simplest form this entails asking for references of the individual's friends, family, or workplace. These online websites also provide web based services that provide background checks for a fee (e.g., WhoisHe.com/WhoisShe.com, CheckMate.com, and True.com).

When meeting someone in person the online dating sites advise to first talk on the phone. If this is successful they then advise to meet in a public place and to meet the individual with a friend or to tell a friend of when and where the meeting is. The sites advise individuals to make their own car and hotel reservations if travel is necessary to meet the individual, to never go home with the individual, and to report individuals who violate the rules to the dating service (Cyberangels, n.d; Match.com, n.d.; Sage-hearts.com, n.d.; Skriloff & Gould, 1997). The online dating services have this information available for members. In fact, Match.com places the information on its homepage and makes it available to all web users, not just members.

As there has been very limited research on actual and perceived risk of victimisation as a result of engaging in online relationships, there has been equally limited research on the safety precautions used by individuals who are members of online dating services. In our 2001 study, we asked women about their knowledge and use of safety strategies they use when using online dating services. Women were asked whether they were aware of various safety precautions and whether they actually used them. Women were also asked to evaluate the perceived risk of using an online dating service. With respect to respondents' knowledge of online dating safety precautions, 84 per cent stated they were aware of such precautions. However, it was noteworthy that many of the respondents never read the safety messages provided by the online services (34.7 per cent), and of those who did, only 57.4 per cent found the messages helpful.

The percentage of respondents who used the various safety precaution measures recommended by online dating services ranged from 44 per cent to 90 per cent. With the exception of giving out one's phone number, over 80 per cent of the respondents consistently reported using the various safety precaution methods. However, the use of safety precaution measures did vary across different age groups. Respondents aged 18 to 27 years were less likely to tell a friend of the meeting, and to meet in a public location than women older than 27 years. Women older than 27 years were also less likely to give out a home address.

Women who used online dating services for more than one year also employed more safety measures. They were much more likely to meet in a public location, and were more likely to have told a friend about the meeting. The research also found that there was no difference in giving out phone numbers, going home with a person, or giving out their home address based upon length of experience in using online dating services.

Conclusion

Dating modalities are continuing to evolve. As has been observed, 'a major trend in the 20th century has been the expansion and differentiation of the courtship process' (Makepeace, 1997, p. 29). This continues to be true in the 21st century with the use of Internet dating services. A limited amount of research has shown that the Internet is also expanding the ways women can be victimised. Even with the Internet as the intermediary, victimisation of women still occurs within dating and developing interpersonal relationships. Moreover, there are expanding forms of victimisation, what is being called 'cyber victimisation'. Flaming, obscene emails, and spamming are all serious methods of victimisation that use the web and email. Additionally, sexual harassment, intimidation, and stalking opportunities may occur because of this new communication medium. Our research in 2001 also found that the greater the experience a woman has using an Internet dating service, the more likely she is to be cyberstalked.

Many online daters see no greater danger in online dating than in traditional blind dating. Some even found meeting people online to be safer than other ways of meeting possible dates. Why they believe this to be true needs to be examined in future research. Our research shows that women do recognise some safety issues and are somewhat careful with their encounters over the Internet. However, the amount of effort seems to be no greater than with traditional dating methods. The greater the experience of women with the Internet, the more precautions they use. This suggests that Internet online dating services would be serving their customers better if they provided professional crime prevention guidelines that were required reading before someone joined the service.

Using email solicitation is a relatively new way of studying social behaviour (Babbie, 2004). With this new methodology, limitations are expected (Cho & LaRose, 1999; Hamilton, 1999; Tse, 1998). These limitations include the method of sampling and the low response rate that can impact both internal and external validity. It is recognised that non-probability sampling is acceptable when probability sampling is not feasible (Babbie, 1990). Such is the case when sampling web users (Kaye & Johnson, 1999). Research also is limited in its sample response rate. Low response rates can impact external validity and this has been acknowledged by researchers using online surveying (Cho & LaRose, 1999). Additionally, sampling on the web and using email to contact subjects make it impossible to distinguish between those who actually received and declined to respond to a survey as compared to surveys that never reached their intended audience (Kaye & Johnson, 1999). It is also possible that women who have been victimised over the Internet may have stopped using it. Strategies should be developed to identify these women who have been victimised and no longer use the Internet and to examine their cyber-victimisation experiences. There is also a need for additional social scientific research on individuals' experiences with online dating and how it compares to traditional methods of meeting romantic partners although the research in this area is certainly growing (e.g., Baker, 2002; Houran & Lange, 2004; Whitty, 2003). Additional inquiry into cyber-victimisation is the only way to develop better prevention methods. Although the web and email both offer individuals tremendous potential for positive experiences, victimisation through this new medium can have the same impact as traditional victimisation. The research indicates that women can be victimised by this new medium in many ways. Gaining an understanding of the types of victimisation that can occur, its frequency and severity, and establishing effective crime prevention modalities for potential victims is increasingly important.

References

Babbie, E. (1990). *Survey research methods*. Belmont, CA: Wadsworth.

Babbie, E. (2004). *The practice of social research* (10th edn). Belmont, CA: Wadsworth.

Baker, A. (2002). What makes an online relationship successful? Clues from couples in cyberspace. *CyberPsychology and Behavior, 5* (4), 363–75.

Benson, J., Harrison, L., & Koss-Feder, A. (2000). The love machines: Valentines may now be wired, but online dating is also fostering some very 19th century courtship. *Time, 155* (6), 73–5.

Berger, M. L. (1979). *The devil wagon in god's country: The automobile and social change in rural America 1893–1929*. North Haven, CT: Archon Books.

Canon, J. (1997). Love connections. *Computer Life, 4* (2), 14.

Cho, H., & LaRose, R. (1999). Privacy issues in Internet surveys. *Social Science Computer Review, 17* (4), 421–34.

Cooper, A., & Sportolari, L. (1997). Romance in cyberspace: Understanding on-line attraction. *Journal of Sex Education and Therapy, 22*, 7–14.

Cyberangels (n.d.) Online dating. Retrieved 4 January 2006, from: http://www.cyberangels.org/dating.html.

Daniel, D. (2002, October). Online services don't always ad up. *Boston Globe*, 7 October 2002, Retrieved 7, October 2002 from http://www.boston.com.

Farrell, N. (2005, April). Florida wants to regulate online dating. *The Inquirer*, 7 April 2005, Retrieved 16 February 2006 from: http://www.theinquirer.net/?article=22383.

Feng, M. (2005). Choosing online partners in the virtual world: How online partners' characteristics affect online dating. *Dissertation Abstracts International*. (AAT 3171606).

Gerlander, M., & Takala, E. (1997). Relating electronically: Interpersonality in the net. *Nordicom Review, 18*, 77–81.

Hamilton, J. C. (1999, 3 December). The ethics of conducting social-science research on the Internet. *Chronicle of Higher Education*, p. B6

Houran, J., & Lange, R. (2004). Expectations of finding a 'soul mate' with online dating. *North American Journal of Psychology, 6* (2), 297–308.

Jerin, R. (1998). *Victims of Crime*. Chicago, IL: Nelson-Hall.

Jerin, R.., & Dolinsky, B. (2001). You've got mail! You don't want it. *Journal of Criminal Justice and Popular Culture, 8* (1). Retrieved 9 December 2005 from: http://www.albany.edu/scj/jcjpc/vol9is1/jerin.html.

Katz, J. (1990). Caller-ID, privacy, and social process. *Telecommunications Policy, 14* (5), 372–411.

Katz, J., & Aspden, P. (1997). A nation of strangers: Patterns of friendship and involvement in Internet users. *Communication of the ACM, 40* (12), 81–6.

Kaye, R., & Johnson, T. J. (1999). Research methodology: Taming the cyber frontier. *Social Science Computer Review, 17* (3), 323–37.

Krakowka, L. (1998). The rules go online: Online romance rules. *American Demographics, 20* (4), 33.

Makepeace, J. M. (1997). Courtship violence as process: A developmental theory. In A. P. Cardarelli (ed.), *Violence between intimate partners: Patterns, causes and effects* (pp. 29–47). Boston: Allyn and Bacon.

Match.Com. (n.d.). Eleven safety tips for your next date. Retrieved 4 January 2006, from: http://www.match.com/help/safetytips.aspx?lid=4.

Merkle, E., & Richardson, R. (2000). Digital dating and virtual relating: Conceptualizing computer mediated romantic relationships. *Family Relations, 49* (2), 187–92.

Parks, M. R., & Floyd, K. (1996). Making friends in cyberspace. *Journal of Communication, 46* (1), 80–97.

Parks, M. R., & Roberts, L. D. (1998). 'Making MOOsic': The development of personal relationships online and a comparison to their off-line counterparts. *Journal of Social and Personal Relationships, 15*, 517–37.

Sage-hearts.com (n.d.). Date smart online. Retrieved on 9 December 2005 from: http://sage-hearts.com/dating_services/match.html.

Scharlott, B., & Christ, W. (1995). Overcoming relationship-initiation barriers: The impact of a computer-dating system on sex role, shyness, and appearance inhibitions. *Computers in Human Behavior, 11* (2), 191–204.

Schnarch, D. (1997). Sex, intimacy, and the internet. *Journal of Sex Education and Therapy, 22*, 15–20.

Skriloff, L., & Gould, J. (1997). *The single woman's guide to flirting, dating, and finding love on-line*. New York: St. Martins Griffin.

Spitzberg, B., & Hoobler, G. (2002). Cyberstalking and the technologies of interpersonal terrorism. *New Media and Society, 4* (1), 71–92.

Stein, M. L. (1996). Landers takes on online romances. *Editor and Publisher, 129* (32), 33–4.

Stoll, C. (1995). *Silicon snake oil.* New York: Doubleday.

Tse, A. C. B. (1998). Comparing the response rate, response speed, and response quality of two methods of sending questionnaires: E-mail vs. mail. *Journal of the Market Research Society, 40,* 353–61.

Van Acker, E. (2001). Contradictory possibilities of cyberspace for generating romance. *Australian Journal of Communication, 21* (1), 102–16.

Walther, J., Loh, T., & Granka, L. (2005). Let me count the ways: The interchange of verbal and nonverbal cues in computer-mediated and face-to-face affinity. *Journal of Language and Social Psychology, 24* (1), 36–65.

Whitty, M. T. (2003). Cyber-flirting: Playing at love on the internet. *Theory and Psychology, 13* (3), 339–57.

Whitty, M. T. & Carr, A. N. (2005). Electronic bullying in the workplace. In B. Fisher, V. Bowie, & C. Cooper (eds), *Workplace violence.* (pp. 248–62). Cullompton, UK: Willan Publishing Ltd.

Part 5
Online Dating Sub-groups

12
Sexual Orientation Moderates Online Sexual Activities

Robin M. Mathy

This article is dedicated to the memory of Al Cooper.

This chapter discusses the relationships between online sexual activities, sexual orientation, and sexual activities in physical space. It aims to help readers explore the possibility that online sexual activities are moderated by sexual orientation, defined here as one's self-identification as heterosexual, bisexual, or gay or lesbian. Online sexual 'activities include, but are not limited to, seeking information or advice about sexual health, romance and relationships, online chatting with a sexual focus, viewing erotic acts, buying erotic materials, or arranging for erotic encounters offline' (Cooper, Scherer, & Mathy, 2001, p. 437). If this chapter were a documentary film, it might be necessary to admonish readers that anyone who requires a definition for 'sexual behaviors in physical space' may proceed only if accompanied by a parent or adult guardian (i.e., an 'R' rating by the Motion Picture Association of America). In reality, human sexual activities – whether engaged in online or in physical space – have in common a central theorem of Human Sexuality. Specifically, the brain is *Homo sapiens'* primary sex organ.

Let us review a few physiological facts that support the thesis that the brain is central to all human sexual experience. The pituitary gland is a tiny (pea-sized), bi-lobed gland that lies at the base of the brain. As the 'Master Gland,' the pituitary signals the production of hormones, including estrogen and testosterone, as well as cortisol and thyroid hormone. In addition to sexuality, these hormones have significant effects on blood pressure, metabolism, reproduction (ovulation, gestation, and lactation), and the human growth hormone that affects normal development of height. The pituitary is connected to the hypothalamus by a thread-like stalk containing nerves and blood vessels. Located immediately above it, the hypothalamus is a small (almond-sized) gland that interacts with the pituitary to control and regulate the endocrine system. Rich in ganglia, nerve fibers, and synaptic connections, the hypothalamus is associated with primitive emotions, such as, fear and rage, the regulation of emotions, and sexual behaviours. The hypothalamus regulates physiological homeostasis, the autonomic nervous system, and interacts with the thalamus to control circadian rhythm, including sleep–wake cycles.

Because the brain is central to human sexual experience, it may not be so surprising that both online and physical sexual activities are mediated by human thought. We need only recall from the epistemology of Descartes the dictum *cogito, ergo sum* to appreciate the importance of thought in human sexuality. Insofar as thoughts are shaped, in part, by experience, we can use phenomenology to examine similarities and differences in online and physical sexual activities. Phenomenology is both a field within philosophy as well as a movement in the history of philosophy. Here, we shall refer to phenomenology as the structures of experience (i.e., consciousness). In its most literal sense, phenomenology is the study of phenomena. However, as a field within philosophy, phenomenology argues that consciousness is shaped by the first-person meanings we ascribe to our experience. These meanings are influenced by other experiences, social and situational contexts, and interpersonal interactions in which our self-perception is shaped, in part, by our own perception of how others perceive us. Importantly, phenomenology holds that we simultaneously assume that those with whom we interact are also engaged in a similar inter-subjective process. Consequently, each person's social reality is the sum total of the products of all of their first-person inter-subjective negotiations.

For example, in earlier ethnographic research by Mathy, Schillace, Coleman, and Berquist (2002), the author once witnessed an interaction in a defunct Internet chat room (*'Girl Chat'*) in which two self-identified lesbians had been engaged in an ongoing romantic relationship that included a substantial amount of intimate interaction. The relationship had continued for approximately three months when, as noted in Mathy's ethnographic notes, one of the lesbians suddenly wrote, 'Honey, {kissing your hand and sitting down next to you on the sofa} you know I love you, but there's something I have to tell you {holding your hand and gazing into your beautiful eyes, stroking your hair}'. The other lesbian wrote back, 'It's okay, {kiss} you can tell me anything! WU? [What's Up?] {Kissing your cheek and handing you a drink from the end table.}' There was a long pause, and the first lesbian wrote, 'Honey,

I don't know how to tell you this. But I'm really a male (still – I'm preop TS) [preoperative transsexual]. But inside I feel like a lesbian and I really, truly, passionately love you as a lesbian {holding your hand, nervously}.' The second lesbian logged off. Chatroom users reacted in various ways, some providing the first 'lesbian' with emotional support and reinforcement for 'coming out'. Others were infuriated and felt betrayed, which led to a fair amount of 'flaming' (i.e., the equivalent of yelling profanities and name-calling). Suddenly, after about 15 minutes the second lesbian logged back in and wrote, 'Is [Name] still here? {looking around}'. The first 'lesbian' responded, 'Yes {looking sheepish}'. 'I'm sorry. But I really do love you!' The second lesbian replied, 'I know. It's okay. I understand. Really.' One of the chatroom participants who had been leading the support of the first 'lesbian' wrote, 'Wow! Way cool {Huge Hug}. I don't know if I would've been able to deal with it.' The second lesbian reiterated, 'No, really, it's okay. I understand. I'm a TG [transgender] male. I can't pass [appear convincingly female], so I like to hang out in here.' Their 'lesbian' relationship did not continue, and their participation in *'Girl Chat'* attenuated due, in part, to friction and hostilities with other community members.

Phenomenologically, one might argue that the differences between virtual and physical reality appear more distinct than they really are. In the preceding example, two self-identified 'lesbians' were in actuality males (a preoperative male-to-female transsexual and a transgender male, respectively). Because they could conceal their anatomy, they were able to 'virtually' be females and lesbians. In physical space, we find a corollary in the fact that our assumptions of others' physiological sex is based almost exclusively on physical and social characteristics we associate with being male vis-à-vis female. In essence, we assume that individuals who appear male vis-à-vis female based on our perception of their attire, grooming, and physical characteristics (stance, posture, gesture) have male as opposed to female genitalia, respectively. However, we seldom have the opportunity to verify our assumptions. There is insufficient space here to address the obvious complications imposed by the reality that anatomical sex is a continuum that includes individuals who are intesexed (e.g., congenital adrenal hyperplasia, or adrenogenital syndrome; Klinefelter's syndrome). The more removed we are from physical cues to guide our assumptions, the more dependent we become upon virtual cues. Consider, for example, the ease with which respondents may misrepresent themselves when participating in a survey being conducted by mail or random digit dialling. In essence, our consciousness is shaped by our assumptions about others, others' assumptions about us, and the processes by which we mutually and simultaneously negotiate a shared social reality that enables us to navigate physical reality and complex social situations without constantly stumbling into walls (due to distraction) or awkwardly asking each person we meet, 'What sex are you?' or, perhaps, 'Are you a potential sexual partner or a potential sexual competitor?'

From the perspective of evolutionary biology, nothing could be more important than success in competition for, and selection of, sexual partners with whom to have a greater number of surviving, reproducing offspring than other members of the species. For most sexually dimorphic species, mate selection and sexual competition are brutishly here-and-now affairs that are, at most, augmented by pheromones and marking one's territory. In contrast, human consciousness, mate selection, and sexual competition appear to be evolving beyond the confines of propinquity. As consciousness has evolved, technological innovations have provided humans the opportunity, if not luxury, to transcend time and place. Reading and writing made it possible for experience to transcend the presence of an oral storyteller. However, literacy and ownership of printed materials were relatively rare until the 19th century. In the 20th century, radio (developed ca. 1920s) and television (developed ca. 1930s) expanded the distance between events and one's experience of them. For the first time in human history, some visual and auditory aspects of wars and catastrophes could be experienced safely, from the comfort of one's living room or bedroom. With the development of the videocassette recorder in the mid 1970s, *Homo sapiens* transcended the temporal confines imposed by the need to synchronise one's schedule with that of the storyteller. Individuals no longer needed to rush home to watch the evening news or their favourite sitcom; they could merely record it and enjoy the experience at a later time.

The Internet represents nothing less than the evolution of consciousness beyond the limitations that had been imposed on human experience by propinquity. The development of the Internet can be traced to 1957 when the Advanced Research Projects Agency (ARPA) was formed as part of the US Department of Defense. Notably, it was developed in response to concerns that the launch of Sputnik could reflect Soviet superiority in the nation's ability to apply science and technology to military applications. In 1969, the Advanced Research Projects Agency Network (ARPANET) became the first active operational packet switching network (the progenitor of the Internet) when UCLA, Stanford Research Institute, the University of California Santa Barbara, and the University of Utah established a four-node network. The packet switching technology was revolutionary because it enabled a computer system to assemble discrete packets of data and route them independently of other packets, as well as making it possible to send one data packet to multiple locations simultaneously. Previous data communication depended upon circuit switching (e.g., early telephone systems) in which a dedicated circuit was monopolised for the entire duration of transmission and receipt of data. The World Wide Web was created in 1989 by scientist Tim Berners-Lee of CERN (the world's largest particle physics laboratory), and released in 1991. Just over a decade prior to writing this chapter (1995), a number of traditional Internet Service Providers (ISPs), such as, America Online, CompuServe, and Prodigy, began to provide Internet access to the World Wide Web.

Like its somewhat primitive, audio-based predecessor, the telephone, a person experiencing a winter day can communicate in real-time, in the present, with another person experiencing a summer night. Unlike its predecessors, the Internet enables one to send audiovisual messages as well as sounds, pictures, and words to a virtually unlimited number of recipients simultaneously. Moreover, the totality of those experiences can be experienced synchronously or asynchronously, stored and retrieved on a range of electronic media, and they can be repeated and shared with others at various times. More importantly, perhaps, those experiences can be shared without any semblance of a physical presence. Hence, the Internet has made it possible for *Homo sapiens* to transcend time, place, and space. Precisely because time, place, and space frame the assumptions that people make about each other, the Internet enables individuals to create a shared social reality without having to expend the effort needed to negotiate one's corporeal presentation of self.

If we are to substantiate the thesis that the technological development of the Internet is part of an evolutionary process associated with an expansion in human consciousness, we must examine the underlying hypothesis that human sexuality affects, and is affected by, the use of this medium. In fact, because the Internet facilitates online sexual activities, as well as physical sexual interaction, this venue has come to be recognised as a newly emerging risk environment for sexually transmitted diseases (Bull & McFarlane, 2000; Elford, Bolding, & Sherr, 2001; Jayaraman, Read, & Singh, 2003; McFarlane, Bull, & Reitmeijer, 2000). For example, in June to August of 1999, a syphilis epidemic among gay men in San Francisco was traced to users of an Internet chat room (Klausner, Wolf, Fischer-Ponce, Zolt, & Katz, 2000). Additionally, researchers have found gender differences in Internet usage for shopping (Dittmar, Long, & Meek, 2004), which has implications for evolutionary sex differences in resource acquisition and allocation. Ono and Zavodny (2003) examined trends in Internet usage by gender and found a narrowing in the gap even as differences in frequency and duration of use have persisted. Re-examining data regarding Americans' Internet usage from telephonic surveys conducted between March 2000 and September 2005, Fallows (2005) reported that women have closed the gap with men in most indices of online activities. However, 'Men like the internet for experiences it offers, while women like it for the human connections it promotes' (p. 1). Madden and Lenhart (2006) reported that nearly three-fourths (74 per cent) of single Americans searching for partners have used the Internet to facilitate their romantic pursuits. They noted that about 15 per cent of American adults acknowledged knowing someone who met their spouse or long-term significant other online.

This chapter examines the possibility that sexual orientation moderates online sexual activities, as well as sexual activities in physical space. Further, it tests the hypothesis that sexual activities antedating Internet usage are associated with online sexual activities, controlling for self-identified sex and sexual orientation. Gender-based differences in Internet usage have decreased but not disappeared (Fallows, 2005); therefore, we shall examine each group separately. Although it is common for social science research to collapse groups of self-identified gays or lesbians with their same-sex bisexual participants, this chapter delineates these as three distinct groups of individuals.

Method

Procedure

All data were gathered from 1–20 June 2000. Participants were able to access the questionnaire via an interactive website located on the home page of a major news organisation with a server connected to the World Wide Web. Access to the questionnaire required participants to check a box indicating that they had read, understood, and agreed to the informed consent. Minors were excluded because the questionnaire involved sexual behaviour. Global user identification numbers (GUIDs) and cookies were used to minimise duplicate submissions. Data from completed surveys were stored on a database linked to the news organisations' server. Every thousandth unique visitor to the website was invited to participate via a pop-up window. A systematic sampling design (Rubin & Babbie, 1997) with a 1 in 1000 sampling interval yielded 7037 valid responses, with unreliable data excluded based on a priori and post hoc reliability criteria. The overall response rate was 25 per cent, which approximates the response rate of random digit dialling protocols without replacement (Members of the Federal Committee on Statistical Methodology, 1984). However, because 'response rate is one guide to the representativeness of the sample respondents' (Rubin & Babbie, 1997, p. 352), the sampling design permits generalisation only to June 2000 users of an (anonymous) major news organisation who would have chosen to respond to a survey if every participant who visited that website had been invited to participate. The present study includes all US participants aged 18 to 80 years who were not otherwise excluded by a priori or post hoc reliability criteria. The study was approved by the Institutional Review Board at the Pacific Graduate School of Psychology. Associated probabilities of $p \leq .05$ are considered statistically significant for this study.

Analyses of Variance (ANOVA) were performed to test hypotheses that within each variable tested the means of each sexual orientation were equivalent. Levene's Test for Equality of Variance was performed to test the hypothesis that for each variable the variance about the means of sexual orientations were equivalent, and post hoc pairwise analyses with Dunnett's C were performed when the results of this test were statistically significant.

Instrument

The survey consisted of 76 items. It has been reproduced in its entirety in Cooper, Morahan-Martin, Mathy, and Maheu (2002). The survey is an expansion and refinement of an instrument used in previous studies of online sexual activity (Cooper, Delmonico, & Burg, 2000; Cooper, Scherer, Boies, & Gordon, 1999). It includes 15 items regarding participant demographics and 41 items concerning participants' sexual attitudes and behaviours. This chapter focuses on online sexual activities and sexual activities prior to using the Internet. Three demographic items from the survey are included here: 'My age is: ——,' 'I am' with response categories including male, female, and transgender (the latter group excluded in this study); and 'I identify my sexual orientation as' with response categories including 'Heterosexual/Straight,' 'Gay/Lesbian,' 'Bisexual,' and 'None of the above' (the latter group excluded in this study).

Variables regarding general Internet usage included: 'Prior to today I have been logging on to the Internet' measured in months, and 'The total amount of time I go online for all my Internet uses is' measured in hours per week. Participants also were asked to respond to, 'The total amount of time I go online for sexual pursuits is' with a response measured in hours per week.

Variables regarding online sexual activities were measured as binary (yes/no) responses. They included: 'The reason(s) I go online for sexual activities' with response categories including, 'To Educate myself', 'To distract myself/take a break', 'To deal with stress', 'To meet people to date', 'To meet people to have offline sexual activities with', 'To "socialize" with people who share my interests', 'To engage in sexual activities I would not do in real time', 'To get support around sexual concerns', and 'To buy sexual materials'.

Variables regarding sexual activities in physical space prior to engaging in Internet use (i.e., 'Prior to becoming involved with the Internet I engaged in:') were measured on a 5-point Likert scale ranging from 'Never' (0) to 'All of the time' (4): 'Prior to becoming involved with the Internet I engaged in'; 'Viewing sexually explicit magazines'; 'Viewing explicit videos'; 'Paying for phone sex'; 'Frequenting strip clubs'; 'Paying for sexual services at a massage parlor;' 'Paying for prostitutes'; 'Anonymous sex with strangers'; 'Casual sexual relations'; and 'Illegal sexual activities (i.e., voyeurism, exhibitionism, etc.)'; and 'I engage in online sexual activities that I would not engage in real time.'

Sample

The selected random sampling design yielded 7037 responses (5925 males and 1112 females). After excluding participants based on a priori and post hoc criteria (Cooper et al., 2001) and limiting the study to US participants, the sample included 5385 males (89.8 per cent heterosexual, 6.4 per cent gay, and 3.8 per cent bisexual) and 1038 females (84.4 per cent heterosexual, 4.4 per cent lesbian, and 11.2 per cent bisexual). For statistical purposes, the Central Limit Theorem permits us to assume that each sub-sample is sufficiently large (i.e., $n > 30$) to rely upon a normal sampling distribution and parametric statistics. However, readers are cautioned to remember that the sampling distributions about the means of the sexual minority populations (gay, lesbian, and bisexual) are considerably larger than those of the heterosexuals, given that their sample sizes are substantially smaller.

Findings

There were no statistical differences in mean ages of male participants ($M = 33.96, SD = 10.74$) by sexual orientation. However, self-identified bisexual females were on average 3.44 years younger than heterosexual peers ($M = 30.46$, $SD = 9.50$) and 5.91 years younger than lesbian peers ($M = 32.93$, $SD = 8.07$), $F(2, 1035) = 9.14$, $p < .001$.

Internet usage

Among males, neither prior months of Internet usage ($M = 52.44$, $SD = 24.15$) nor current hours per week spent online ($M = 39.83$, $SD = 23.90$) varied by sexual orientation. However, the total hours per week in which participants engaged in online sexual activities varied significantly by sexual orientation among males, $F(2, 5382) = 34.80$, $p < .001$. Gay ($M = 3.69$, $SD = 4.72$), as well as bisexual males ($M = 5.71$, $SD = 11.82$) spent significantly more time online in sexual activities than their heterosexual peers ($M = 2.65$, $SD = 5.15$).

Among females, all these variables varied significantly by sexual orientation. Lesbian females ($M = 46.87$, $SD = 24.43$) reported that they had been online longer than both bisexuals ($M = 43.89$, $SD = 23.42$) and heterosexuals of the same sex ($M = 38.92$, $SD = 23.84$), $F(2, 1035) = 4.33$, $p < .01$. Lesbian females ($M = 26.15$, $SD = 20.68$) also reported that they spent more hours per week online currently than their bisexual ($M = 23.45$, $SD = 24.67$) and heterosexual ($M = 19.22$, $SD = 18.29$) peers. However, when females were asked how many hours per week they had spent online in sexual activities, there were no statistically significant differences among the three sexual orientations

Multivariate regression analyses yielded equivocal results, although it is perhaps most important to note here that the variance explained by sexual orientation when controlling for age did not increase significantly at $p < .01$.

Motivations for online sexual activities

Among males, all but one reason for engaging in online sexual activities (education) varied by sexual orientation (see Table 12.1). Please note, in the table, only pairwise significance below .01 are delineated, as an F test may detect significance in one-way analyses of variance, even though there are no statistically significant pairwise difference at $p < .05$. Levene's test for homogeneity of variance led to rejection of the null hypothesis of equality of variance about the means of different sex and sexual orientation groups. Therefore, Dunnet's C was used to conduct post hoc pairwise analyses to determine whether variances in reasons for engaging in online sexual activities could be attributed to differences between gays or lesbians relative to bisexuals and heterosexuals. In general, these tests indicated that the percentages of heterosexuals who engaged in online sexual activities for particular reasons (distraction, meet dates, meet for sex, socialise, explore fantasies, obtain support for sexual concerns, and purchase sexual materials) were significantly lower than those of their gay and bisexual male peers. In a few cases (meeting dates, meeting for sex, and exploring sexual fantasies) there were also statistically significant differences between the percentages of gay and bisexual males who engaged in these activities. Relative to gay males, bisexuals of the same sex were significantly less likely to engage in online sexual activities to meet dates or arrange meetings for sex. Conversely, bisexual males were significantly more likely than gay males to use the Internet to explore sexual fantasies.

The data for females (see Table 12.1) indicate that several reasons for engaging in online sexual activities (education, distraction, and coping with stress) did not vary by sexual orientation. Post hoc tests with Dunnett's C were conducted to detect significant pairwise differences. These tests revealed that bisexual females were significantly more likely than their heterosexual and lesbian peers to use the Internet to meet for sex, as well as to socialise. Lesbians were significantly less likely than both bisexual and heterosexual females to engage in online sexual activities to explore sexual fantasies. Heterosexuals were significantly less likely than bisexual females to use the Internet to obtain support for sexual concerns.

Frequency of sexual activities prior to Internet usage

As shown in Table 12.2, the data indicated that prior to engaging in online sexual activities participants' sexual activities varied significantly by sex and sexual orientation. Only pairwise significance below .01 are delineated here, as an F test may detect significance in one-way analyses of variance, even though there are no statistically significant pairwise difference at $p < .05$. Among males, statistically significant variance by sexual orientation was found for most variables. These variables included: viewing sexually explicit videos, frequenting strip clubs, engaging in anonymous sex with strangers, engaging in casual sexual relations, engaging in illegal sexual relations, and engaging in fantasy sex. Among females, there were fewer variables that varied by sexual orientation. Statistically significant findings were evident for viewing sexually explicit magazines, viewing sexually

Table 12.1 Reasons for engaging in online sexual activities (per cent of participants who endorsed item) by gender and sexual orientation

	Heterosexual		Gay/Lesbian		Bisexual		F	p
	M	SD	M	SD	M	SD		
Education								
Male	.31	.46	.29	.45	.32	.46	0.42	.665
Female	.55	.50	.59	.50	.59	.50	0.43	.649
Distraction								
Male	.82	.38	.76	.43	.78	.41	5.07	.006**H<G
Female	.58	.49	.65	.48	.65	.48	1.15	.317
Cope with stress								
Male	.31	.46	.28	.45	.39	.49	3.45	.032* B<G
Female	.17	.38	.17	.38	.17	.38	0.00	.996
Meet dates								
Male	.08	.28	.27	.44	.18	.39	71.98	.000***H<B<G
Female	.08	.27	.15	.36	.16	.36	4.58	.010*
Meet for sex								
Male	.09	.28	.30	.46	.28	.45	108.07	.000***H<B<G
Female	.03	.18	.02	.15	.13	.34	11.937	.000***B>H, L
Socialise								
Male	.15	.35	.42	.50	.41	.49	132.76	.000***H<G, B
Female	.20	.40	.26	.44	.51	.50	27.28	.000***B>H, L
Explore fantasies								
Male	.21	.40	.23	.42	.37	.48	16.00	.000***H<G<B
Female	.20	.40	.07	.25	.26	.44	3.87	.021*L<H, B
Support sexual concerns								
Male	.05	.22	.11	.32	.14	.34	23.08	.000***H<G, B
Female	.13	.34	.11	.32	.24	.43	4.98	.007**H<B
Purchase sexual materials								
Male	.11	.32	.19	.39	.21	.41	17.60	.000***H<G, B
Female	.15	.36	.22	.42	.24	.43	0.83	.022*

Note: *$p < .05$, **$p < .01$, ***$p < .001$; H = Heterosexual, G = Gay, L = Lesbian, B = Bisexual.

explicit videos, frequenting strip clubs, engaging in anonymous sex with strangers, having casual sexual relations, and engaging in illegal sexual relations. Levene's tests for equality of variance were statistically significant, $p < .05$; therefore, Dunnet's C was performed to conduct post hoc tests for significant pairwise differences.

Among the significant findings ($p < .01$) in Table 12.2, heterosexual males reported that they viewed sexually explicit videos and engaged

Table 12.2 Frequency of engaging in sexual activities prior to Internet usage, by gender and sexual orientation

	Heterosexual		Gay/Lesbian		Bisexual		F	p
	M	SD	M	SD	M	SD		
View sexually explicit magazines								
Male	1.53	0.85	1.62	0.98	1.60	0.90	2.20	.111
Female	0.90	0.84	0.98	0.72	1.34	0.97	13.31	.000***H < L < B
View sexually explicit videos								
Male	1.49	0.86	1.75	1.00	1.72	.935	20.13	.000***H < G, B
Female	1.11	0.92	1.22	0.87	1.59	1.01	14.13	.000***H < B
Pay for phone sex								
Male	0.06	0.31	0.10	0.39	0.11	0.35	3.27	0.038*
Female	0.02	0.20	0.02	0.15	0.03	0.23	0.15	0.862
Frequent strip clubs								
Male	0.83	0.79	0.47	0.68	0.76	0.84	34.02	.000***G < H, B
Female	0.25	0.54	0.54	0.84	0.50	0.72	13.92	.000***H < B < L
Pay for sex at massage parlour								
Male	0.10	0.39	0.07	0.30	0.16	0.53	3.37	.034*
Female	0.01	0.12	0.04	0.30	0.02	0.19	1.46	.233
Pay for prostitutes								
Male	0.12	0.42	0.10	0.36	0.17	0.51	1.77	.171
Female	0.01	0.13	0.07	0.44	0.03	0.16	3.54	.029*
Anonymous sex with strangers								
Male	0.26	0.58	0.93	1.04	0.67	0.87	210.37	.000***H < B < G
Female	0.10	0.35	0.17	0.44	0.03	0.16	16.14	.000***H < B < L
Casual sexual relations								
Male	0.81	0.91	1.38	1.02	1.18	1.05	73.54	.000***H < B, G
Female	0.71	0.84	0.72	0.66	1.28	0.97	23.31	.000***H > L, H
Illegal sexual relations								
Male	0.20	0.52	0.37	0.70	0.44	0.86	32.57	.000***H < G < B
Female	0.13	0.43	0.13	0.40	0.39	0.72	15.59	.000***H > L, H
Engage in fantasy sex								
Male	0.60	.90	0.83	1.00	1.07	1.04	33.86	.000***H < G < B
Female	0.68	0.96	0.54	0.75	0.92	1.02	3.84	.022*

Note: $*p < .05$, $**p < .01$, $***p < .001$; H = Heterosexual, G = Gay, L = Lesbian, B = Bisexual.

in casual sexual relations significantly less often than gay as well as bisexual males, whereas gay males indicated that they frequented strip clubs significantly less frequently than their heterosexual and bisexual peers. With the exception of frequenting strip clubs, the frequency of physical sexual activities was lower for heterosexual males than it was for both gay and bisexual males. Bisexual males were significantly more likely than their gay male peers to engage in some physical sexual activities (engaging in illegal sexual relations and engaging in fantasy sex). However, gay males were significantly more likely than their bisexual peers to engage in anonymous sex with strangers. Relative to bisexual females, heterosexual females indicated that they had a significantly lower frequency of viewing sexually explicit materials, viewing sexually explicit videos, frequenting strip clubs, and engaging in anonymous sex with strangers. However, relative to both heterosexual and lesbian peers of the same sex, bisexual females reported a significantly greater frequency of engaging in casual sexual relations as well as illegal sexual relations. Relative to lesbians, bisexual females reported a greater frequency of viewing sexually explicit magazines and a lower frequency of frequenting strip clubs and engaging in anonymous sex with strangers.

Binary logistical regressions were performed separately by gender to determine whether sexual orientation was a statistically significant factor in predicting online sexual activities when controlling for physical sexual activities in which participants had engaged prior to using the Internet. Sexual orientation significantly increased the goodness of fit of a model predicting online sexual activities to meet dates. Controlling for all other variables, analyses revealed an Odds Ratio [OR] of 1.72 and a 95 per cent Confidence Interval [95% CI] of 1, 10, 2.68 for gay males and OR = 0.48, 95 per cent CI = 0.33, 0.71 for heterosexual males engaging in online sexual activities to meet dates. Heterosexual orientation among males (OR = .36, 95% CI = .25, .52), as well as females (OR = .30, 95% CI = .15, .60) was associated with a significantly decreased likelihood of engaging in online sexual activities to find someone to meet for sex. Among males, heterosexual sexual orientation was associated with a decreased likelihood of engaging in online sexual activities to socialise (OR = .32, 95% CI = .23, .43). Among females, heterosexual and lesbian sexual orientations were associated with a decreased likelihood of engaging in online sexual activities to socialise (OR = .26, 95% CI = .17, .39; OR = .40, 95% CI = .18, .85, respectively). For males, gay sexual orientation was associated with a decreased likelihood (OR = .56, 95% CI = .36, .88) of engaging in online sexual activities to explore sexual fantasies. For males, heterosexual sexual orientation was associated with a decreased likelihood (OR = .36, 95% CI = .24, .55) of engaging in online sexual activities to obtain support for sexual concerns. Among females, both heterosexual and lesbian sexual orientations were associated with a decreased likelihood (OR = .43, 95% CI = .27, .70; OR = .35,

95% CI = .12, .97) of engaging in online sexual activities to obtain support for sexual concerns. Among males, heterosexual sexual orientation was associated with a decreased likelihood (OR = 0.55, 95% CI = .38, .79) of engaging in online sexual activities to purchase sexual materials.

Discussion

This study found that self-identified sexual orientation moderates sexual activities in physical space, as well as online sexual activities. Variables moderated by sexual orientation appear to differ for males and females. However, the sample of males was much larger than that of females, so one cannot rule out the possibility that these sex differences may reflect the effects of statistical power when conducting data analyses.

Overall, the data indicate that relative to heterosexual males a significantly greater percentage of gay and bisexual males in this study had engaged in online sexual activities. Relative to gay and bisexual males, there were no domains in which a greater percentage of heterosexual males had engaged in online sexual activities. In general, this suggests that heterosexuals are significantly less likely than others of the same sex to use the Internet to explore their sexuality. It would also suggest that gay and bisexual males are significantly more likely than heterosexuals to use the Internet to engage in risky sexual behaviours (e.g., engaging in anonymous sex with strangers). A greater percentage of bisexual than gay males in this study reported that they had engaged in online sexual activities to engage in exploration of sexual fantasies. Conversely, a greater percentage of gay than bisexual males engaged in online sexual activities to cope with stress, meet dates, and meet for sex.

The data reported here suggest that greater care is warranted in delineating groups of 'men who have sex with men'. Although gay men and 'men who have sex with men' are frequently groups targeted for HIV and STD prevention and intervention efforts (Johnston et al., 2005), the findings presented here suggest that bisexual, as well as gay males are generally more likely than heterosexual males to engage in sexual risk-taking behaviours online. Further, the relationships between 'men who have sex with men' and self-identified bisexual, gay, and heterosexual identities requires further consideration. This is important precisely because some men who engage in same-sex sexual behaviour identify as heterosexual (Ross, Mansson, Daneback, & Tikkanen, 2005). Although the term 'men who have sex with men' may capture the scientific essence of same-sex sexual behaviour among males, it fails to address the phenomenology of being gay or of being a bisexual or heterosexual man who has sex with men – even if only online.

To the extent that self-reflective consciousness and inter-subjective realities affect sexual behaviour, one must be cautious about superimposing 'scientific' realities on those whose experiences of everyday life become the 'subject' of our study. In addition, further research is needed to understand how the process of 'becoming' gay or bisexual transcends the meaning of being (identity) in ways that differ from heterosexually identified men who have sex with men. For example, Ross et al. reported that 11 per cent of the self-identified heterosexual men in their study acknowledged that they had engaged in online sexual activities with other men. Fundamentally, the Internet has facilitated the expansion of consciousness beyond propinquity and even corporealness. It is, therefore, worth asking how participation in online sexual activities affects, and is affected by, the development of human sexuality, including gender identity (one's sense of oneself as masculine, feminine, or androgynous) and sexual orientation.

When comparing the three sexual orientation groups of females this study found that heterosexuals generally had the smallest percentage of participants who had engaged in online sexual activities. A smaller percentage of heterosexual females than lesbians and bisexual females acknowledged that they had viewed sexually explicit magazines, frequented strip clubs, or engaged in anonymous sex with strangers. A significantly greater percentage of bisexual females than lesbians or heterosexual females acknowledged that they had engaged in illegal sexual relations and had engaged in anonymous sex with strangers. Conversely, a smaller percentage of lesbians than bisexual females reported that they had viewed sexually explicit magazines.

The data analysed in this study suggest that bisexual and lesbian females sometimes, but not always, comprised two distinct groups. This warrants further research. When post hoc pairwise analyses were performed with Dunnett's C, bivariate differences between bisexuals and lesbians were found for several online sexual activity variables. These variables included meeting to engage in sex, socialise, and explore sexual fantasies. However, for variables with somewhat less emphasis on sexually intimate interaction (engaging in online sexual activity for education, distraction, coping with stress, or meeting dates, purchasing sexual materials), there were no statistically significant different pairwise differences among the three groups of females. Nonetheless, differences among the three groups of female sexual orientations emerged when examining variables that require more interpersonal or intimate interaction (meeting for sex, socialising, and exploring sexual fantasies). This suggests that online sexual activities vary by sexual orientation where more social interaction and/or sexually intimate behaviour are involved. This warrants further research.

The data concerning frequency of engaging in physical sexual behaviours prior to using the Internet also substantiate the hypothesis that sexual orientation moderates sexual activities beyond merely sex of one's partner. Where differences were found among males, in all but one case (frequenting strip clubs), heterosexuals had the lowest frequency of engaging in physical sexual behaviour. One might have predicted that a greater percentage of bisexual, as well as heterosexual males would frequent strip clubs, and this finding is not particularly remarkable. However, it is notable that pairwise post hoc analyses with Dunnet's C revealed that bisexual males were significantly more likely than gay males to engage in anonymous sex with strangers. One might hypothesise that engaging in sex with anonymous strangers is socially safer than having sex with someone known. Conversely, pairwise analyses indicated that gay males engaged in illegal sexual relations and fantasy sex at a significantly lower frequency than did bisexual males.

In general, heterosexual females engaged in physical sexual activities at a significantly lower frequency than bisexual or lesbian females. However, bisexual females engaged in casual sexual relations and illegal sexual relations at a significantly greater frequency than their heterosexual or lesbian peers. They also viewed sexually explicit magazines at a frequency greater than either lesbians or heterosexual females. Although significantly greater attention is given to sexual risk-taking behaviours among men who have sex with men, these findings are noteworthy for several reasons. First, sexual orientation moderates engaging in anonymous sex with strangers, and this puts females at high risk of sexual trafficking, sexual assault, and exploitation. Second, sexual orientation moderates engagement in casual sexual relations, which may have adverse psychosocial and physical consequences. Third, sexual orientation moderates engagement in illegal sexual relations, which carries substantial liability as well as risks for civil and criminal prosecution.

Finally, bivariate regression analyses yielded substantial evidence that sexual orientation is a significant factor predicting engagement in certain online sexual activities. Controlling for all other behaviours antedating participation in online sexual activities, gay sexual orientation significantly predicted use of the Internet to meet dates. Conversely, under the same controls heterosexual males were significantly less likely to use the Internet to meet dates. Controlling for all physical sexual characteristics antedating online sexual activities, heterosexual males, as well as females were significantly less likely to use the Internet to socialise. Gay sexual orientation was associated with a decreased likelihood of engaging in online sexual activities to explore sexual fantasies. Among males, heterosexual sexual orientation was associated with a decreased likelihood of engaging in online sexual activities to obtain support for sexual concerns or purchase sexual materials. Among females, both heterosexual and lesbian sexual orientations were associated with a decreased likelihood of engaging in online sexual activities to obtain support for sexual concerns. In sum, these analyses indicate that self-identified sexual orientation is a significant factor in predicting online sexual activities, even after controlling for all other physical sexual activities in which participants engaged.

This study has a number of limitations. First, it is cross-sectional. We do not know whether sexual orientation changed from the time before, during, and after engaging in online sexual activities. Second, the study has limited generalisability. It cannot be generalised to the general population, nor can inferences be made about the present. Third, questions contained in this study were framed after the study was conducted. Therefore, the possibility of subtle post hoc reasoning vis-à-vis genuine hypothesis testing may be involved. Fourth, the study was limited to a secondary analysis of a pre-existing data set from research conducted six years ago. Given the rapid advances in Internet technology, replication of this study with more recent data is indicated.

Nonetheless, this study has substantiated the hypotheses that sexual orientation moderates (a) physical sexual activity, (b) online sexual activities, and (c) that sexual orientation significantly contributes to the prediction of online sexual activities after controlling for all physical sexual activities antedating Internet usage. The brain is the primary organ involved in human sexual activity and sexual orientation moderates physical sexual activity, as well as online sexual activity. Therefore, greater efforts must be made to understand the ways in which experience with the Internet affects, and is affected by, our lived experiences online and in physical space when taking sex (male, female, intersex), gender (masculine, feminine, androgynous), and sexual orientation into consideration. As we evolve into consciousness beyond propinquity and corporealness, we will transcend previous concepts and limitations of what it means to be sexed, gendered, or classified based on the sex or gender of those we love.

References

Bull, S. S., & McFarlane, M. (2000). Soliciting sex on the Internet: What are the risks for sexually transmitted diseases and HIV? *Sexually Transmitted Diseases, 27*, 545–50.

Cooper, A., Delmonico, D., & Burg, R. (2000). Cybersex users, abusers, and compulsives: New findings and implications. In A. Cooper (ed.), *Cybersex: The dark side of the force* (pp. 5–29). Philadelphia: Brunner Routledge.

Cooper, A., Morahan-Martin, J., Mathy, R. M., & Maheu, M. (2002). Toward an increased understanding of user demographics in online sexual activities. *Journal of Sex & Marital Therapy, 28*, 105–29.

Cooper, A., Scherer, C. R., Boies, S. C., & Gordon, B. L. (1999). Sexuality on the Internet: From sexual exploration to pathological expression. *Professional Psychology: Research and Practice, 30* (2), 154–64.

Cooper, A., Scherer, C., & Mathy, R. M. (2001). Overcoming methodological concerns in the investigation of online sexual activities. *Cyberpsychology & Behavior, 4* (4), 437–47.

Dittmar, H., Long, K., & Meek, R. (2004). Buying on the Internet: Gender differences in on-line and conventional buying motivations. *Sex Roles, 50* (5–6), 423–44.

Elford, J., Bolding, G., & Sherr, L. (2001). Seeking sex on the Internet and sexual risk behaviour. *AIDS, 15*, 1409–15.

Fallows, D. (2005). *How women and men use the Internet.* Washington, DC: Pew Internet & American Life Project.

Jayaraman, G. C., Read, R. R., & Singh, A. (2003). Characteristics of individuals with male-to-male and heterosexually acquired infectious syphilis during an outbreak in Calgary, Alberta, Canada. *Sexually Transmitted Diseases, 30* (4), 315–19.

Johnston, W. D., Holtgrave, D. R., McClellan, W. M., Flanders, W. D., Hill, A. N., & Goodman, M. (2005). HIV intervention research for men who have sex with men: A 7-year update. *AIDS Education and Prevention, 17* (6), 568–89.

Klausner, J. D., Wolf, W., Fischer-Ponce, L., Zolt, I., & Katz, M. H. (2000). Tracing a syphilis outbreak through cyberspace. *JAMA: Journal of the American Medical Association, 284*, 447–9.

Madden, M., & Lenhart, A. (2006). *Online dating.* Washington, DC: Pew Internet & American Life Project.

Mathy, R. M., Schillace, M., Coleman, S. M., & Berquist, B. E. (2002). Methodological rigor with Internet samples: New ways to reach underrepresented populations. *CyberPsychology & Behavior, 5*, 253–66.

McFarlane, M., Bull, S. S., & Reitmeijer, C. A. (2000). The Internet as a newly emerging risk environment for sexually transmitted diseases. *JAMA: Journal of the American Medical Association, 284* (4), 443–6.

Members of the Federal Committee on Statistical Methodology (1984). Statistical policy working paper 12 – The role of telephone data collection in federal statistics. Washington, DC: Office of Management and Budget. Retrieved 13 April 2006, from: http://www.fcsm.gov/working-papers/wp12.html.

Ono, H., & Zavodny, M. (2003). Gender and the Internet. *Social Science Quarterly, 84* (1), 111–21.

Ross, M. W., Mansson, S., Daneback, K., & Tikkanen, R. (2005). Characteristics of men who have sex with men on the Internet but identify as heterosexual, compared with heterosexually identified men who have sex with women. *CyberPsychology & Behavior, 8* (2), 131–9.

Rubin, A., & Babbie, E. (1997). *Research methods for social work*, 3rd edn. Belmont, CA: Wadworth Press.

13
Whips and Chains? Fact or Fiction? Content Analysis of Sadomasochism in Internet Personal Advertisements

Diane Kholos Wysocki and Jennifer Thalken

> 'Bind my ankles with your white cotton rope so I cannot walk. Bind my wrists so I cannot push you away. Place me on the bed and wrap your rope tighter around my skin so it grips my flesh. Now I know that struggle is useless.'
>
> (Apostolides, 1999, p. 6)

In order to study the sexual attitudes, identities, and behaviours of individuals involved in sadomasochism (S & M) it is necessary to understand the role of culture which heavily influences sexual behaviour. Historically, psychologists have viewed sexual behaviour as a biological or psychological phenomenon that reflects the drives, motives, and needs of an individual (Freud, 1962; Krafft-Ebing, 1886/1965). Horney (1967) believed that masochism in women was a result of the cultural constraints they faced with regards to social status, the sexual, and roles in society that kept women in a place of submissiveness. Sexuality has traditionally been explained by three paradigms – instinct, drive, and energy and unfortunately has assumed that sexuality equals heterosexuality, making heterosexuality the norm (Fergunson, 1989). Popular sexologists, such as, Ellis (1903/1926), Kinsey (1953), and Masters, Johnson, and Kolodny (1986) have constructed models of sexuality that reflect and reproduce male supremacy, which then becomes viewed as natural and universal, giving the impression that 'normal' male sexuality has control over female sexuality and that female sexuality should be passive and dependent (Coveney, Jackson, Jeffreys, Kay, & Mahony, 1984).

In contrast, other researchers have stressed that culture is the shaping force of sexuality and sexuality is therefore socially constructed

(Foucault, 1978; Gagnon & Simon, 1973; Giddens, 1992; Green, 1987; Simon & Gagnon, 1984; Vance, 1993; Weeks, 1986). Jeffery Weeks (1986) in *The Invention of Sexuality* stated that:

We must learn to see that sexuality is something which society produces in complex ways. It is a result of diverse social practices that give meaning to human activities, of social definitions and self-definitions, of struggles between those who have power to define and regulate, and those who resist. Sexuality is not given; it is a product of negotiation, struggle and human agency. (p. 25)

Sexual identity includes the categories individuals use to locate themselves in relation to others (Michener, DeLamater, Schwartz, & Merton, 1990). This begins very early in life with the onset of puberty (Gagnon & Simon, 1973) and begins as a result of the sexual scripts that are available to teach us how to live our lives, which includes being sexual (Doctor, 1988; Laws & Schwartz, 1977; Simon & Gagnon, 1984, 1998). Sexual scripts refer to abstractions about sexuality that most individuals in a particular culture would recognise. For instance, in an American culture the term 'hooking up' has become known for meeting someone and having sex. Furthermore, the traditional heterosexual sexual script in our culture emphasises the different expectations for male and female behaviour and sets up a controversial relationship between the male who is expected to be aggressive, oversexed, and emotionally insensitive, verses the passive, unassertive female who must put up a façade that her sexuality is unattainable, while at the same time appearing sexy and interested in the males' advances. This is the sexual script that is common for our culture. In fact sexual scripts provide meaning for the internal sensations we feel during sexual desire and arousal (Else-Quest, Hyde, & DeLamater, 2005) and as a result, these scripts organise the order of our sexual acts and help us decode sexual situations and act on them if we desire. Without a script that is recognised so an individual can define the situation, name the actors, and plot the behaviour, nothing sexual is likely to happen (Gagnon & Simon, 1973; Laws & Schwartz, 1977). In other words sexual scripts are a way of anticipating how sexual behaviour comes to be enacted (Simon & Gagnon, 1984).

We learn scripts when we watch television, read books, and go to the movies, and according to Giddens (1992) the scripts have changed over time. If our traditional sexual scripts are that we see two individuals who meet, kiss, cuddle, touch each others, genitals, and eventually have intercourse, then this becomes our scripts for being sexual. While the script we learned growing up might have involved a man and a women having traditional intercourse with each other, by watching other more non-traditional movies and reading erotic books (Brown, 2002; Shortes, 1998) we find out that individuals are involved in all types of other sexual behaviours, such as, cross-dressing (Langstrom & Zucker, 2005; Wysocki, 1993), voluntary castration (Wassersug, Zelenietz, & Squire, 2004), an interest in feet and shoes (Weinberg, Williams, & Calhan, 1994), and S & M. Some of our knowledge about more non-traditional sexual scripts has happened because times have changed and the scripts that once were unacceptable are now more out in the open, and more attainable to those who want to view them. Some of the change is just a natural part of modernity (Giddens, 1992), and a result of the Internet that has increased our access to all kinds of sexual information for anyone with a computer (Ross, 2005; Wysocki, 1998).

It has been suggested in the mass media that the Internet, email, and chat mode is *the place* to go for online sexual relationships (Binik, Mah, & Kiesler, 1999; Elmer-Dewitt, 1995; Ross, 2005; Wysocki, 1998). Sex via the computer can develop through the interactive sharing of fantasies, looking at sexually explicit photographs, and/or sharing similar sexual interests (Bright, 1992; Rheingold, 1993; Ross, 2005). In 2004, ABC News Primetime Live conducted a sex survey to find out what Americans were doing behind closed doors and they found that as many as 40 million people admitted they have looked at porn websites (Langer, Arnedt, & Sussman, 2004). According to Survey.net, which began in October 2000 and currently has 69,435 respondents (InterCommerce Coporation, 2005), the Internet is a benign outlet for sexual frustration (38.6 per cent), makes the respondents more open-minded (36.8 per cent), improves their sex-life (24.9 per cent) and promotes more honest communication (21.5 per cent). Furthermore, the majority of respondents used the Internet to downloaded erotic pictures (56.1 per cent), read online sex stories (53.3 per cent), masturb-ated while online (40.5 per cent) or to the material they downloaded (34.6 per cent), talked dirty in IRC (25.5 per cent), exchanged erotic email (23.5 per cent), had sex with someone met online (15.0 per cent), placed or responded to an online personal ad (26.7 per cent), posted erotic pictures or sex stories (18.1 per cent), purchased a sex-related product advertised on the net (9.8 per cent), or watched or transmitted erotic CuSeeMe video (11.6 per cent).

People use the Internet to look for other people with similar interests and from those broader categories; people are able to locate more specific interests to satisfy whatever they desire. For instance, it is not difficult to find an Internet website that deals with sex and then from there, the individual can go to anything more specific, such as, transvestism, group sex, oral sex, or S & M. According to Wysocki (1998), people participate in online sex because they believe it offers them some sort of anonymity, they lack time in their personal life to find other people with similar sexual interests, the Internet provides them the ability to share sexual fantasies with others in the privacy of their own home, they can actually have online sexual activity (this includes mutual masturbation), and if they find someone they feel they are compatible with they can then meet this person offline.

It is through personal advertisements that people find each other on the Internet. With the increased availability of technological products, such as, computers, modems, and the Internet, social life as we have previously known it has changed forever. Personal ads, which used to be termed 'lonely hearts ads' (Strassberg & Holty, 2003), are an important source of gaining access to interpersonal relationships. Researchers have done experiments on the body types (Strassberg & Holty, 2003), linguistic behaviours (Groom & Pennebaker, 2005), and how the construction of gender takes place (Koch, Mueller, Kruse, & Zumbach, 2005) for people reading personal ads to see what they are looking for. Because it is too difficult for people who want to participate in S & M to find people who have similar desires in their day-to-day life (Sandnabba, Santtila, & Nordling, 1999), it makes sense that they would go to the Internet to find others who are also interested in S & M.

As a result, this study is a content analysis of adult personal advertisements of those who have placed ads for others to share their interest in sadomasochism on the Internet. The advertisements have not been manipulated; they are analysed as the author put them online. The goal of the study is to explore and describe the individuals who advertise online, while at the same time finding out what particular behaviours they are interested in and what type of person they want to find.

What is sadomasochism?

Sadism is a term that refers to the Marquis de Sade (1740–1814), a French author, philosopher, and a sadomasochist, who described in detail the pleasurable sexual experiences of people who dominated, humiliated, and hurt their sexual partners. In his writings he also described those people who enjoyed being dominated, humiliated, and hurt during sex known as masochists. While many researchers wrote on the topic of sadism and masochism (Ellis, 1926; Freud, 1920/1961; Krafft-Ebing, 1886/1965) over one hundred years ago, it was not until the 1980s that attempts have been made to identity more about this topic and the people involved in the activity (Weinberg, 1987). But even 20 years earlier Freud realised that those who participated in S & M were also 'normal individuals' (Freud, 1962).

Prior to this time it was thought that people who took part in bondage, being beaten, and humiliation for sexual pleasure, must have been mentally ill, violent, cruel, and crazy (Weinberg, 1987). Yet, what it really involves is the consensual power exchange between partners who are involved in acting where roles, such as, teacher–pupil, prison guard–inmate, or doctor–nurse are played out. S & M is very individualised and is sometimes used just to spice up sex lives of married people or for people who feel like they need sexuality to have a deeper meaning (LeMasters, 2002). Sometimes the submissive partner is physically bound and restrained, and while the goal is an orgasm, the act can be satisfying without an orgasm happening at all (Ernulf & Innalla, 1995). Furthermore, a sadomasochistic scene usually contains a relationship of dominance and submission, and the infliction of pain that is experienced as pleasurable by both partners. This is often times displayed as deliberate humiliation of the other party, where fetishistic elements, such as, toys and one or more ritualistic activities like bondage or chains are used (Sandnabba, Santtila, & Nordling, 1999).

There are a number of behaviours that those who participate in S & M can include in their sexual scene. According to Alison, Santtila, Sandnabba, & Nordling, (2001) while 'individuals emphasize a particular set of behaviors but also engage in other behaviors to a more limited extent ... suggest[s] that it makes sense to conceptualize sadomasochism as a distinct phenomenon' (p. 2). Therefore the sexual behaviours have been grouped by other researchers into four categories; *hypermasculinity, administration of pain, humiliation,* and *physical restriction* (Alison et al. 2001). This makes it much easier for researchers to categorise and analyse the data being investigated.

More current studies on sadomasochism have found that individuals are very interested in the subject and do participate in the behaviour (Alison et al. 2001; Apostolides, 1999; Donnelly & Fraser, 1998; Ernulf & Innalla, 1995; Santtila, Sandnabba, Alison, & Nordling, 2002). In one study of 320 college students in a large urban Southeast university, students were given a 220 closed ended survey that included questions on their current sexual practices and interests (Donnelly & Fraser, 1998). Results showed that males were aroused more often by both fantasising about and participating in a variety of sadomasochistic sexual behaviours than females. Another study was done to compare the S & M preferences between individuals obtained in two different S & M clubs in Finland (Sandnabba et al. 1999). One club was for heterosexual participants and the other was for homosexual participants. They found that between the ages of 21–25 years the majority of the respondents had their first S & M experience and then began to practice S & M on a regular basis. The emotional reactions after the first S & M experience were consistently positive and one-third of the respondents stated that only S & M sex could satisfy them. To distinguish if females would be more likely to engage in behaviours related to humiliation (i.e., receiving pain and gay males more likely to report behaviours related to hyper-masculinity (i.e., giving pain), women and men of S & M clubs were used for this study (Alison et al. 2001). They found that females engaged in more humiliation behaviours, while men engaged in hypermasculinity and administration of pain facets.

Method

In order to learn more about the sexual behaviours of sadomasochists on the Internet, permission was requested and granted from the University Institutional Review Board (IRB) prior to any data being collected. IRB approval is important in Internet research, even though individuals have publicly displayed their profiles on the Internet. Because they are human subjects, as researchers we are ethically bound to obtain permission from our institution as other researchers have suggested before collecting data (Jones, 1999; Schroer, 1999; Wysocki, 1999). It is noteworthy that we had no interaction with the people who put their profiles online. We only printed off their profiles and analysed what they had published publicly on the Internet. We have done our best to keep their identities hidden. Once permission was granted, a search for 'adult web personals' was conducted on the Internet and 'Alt.com' was discovered. Under 'alt.com' the 'World's Largest BDSM & Alternative Lifestyle Personals' was found and used to collect data for this project. The main page of the website stated it had '13,005 Members online NOW . . . 18,984 New Photos this week *ldots* and 3,462,337 Active Members [and had] 21, 036 listings in Nebraska!' where the study took place during the spring of 2002 (Alt.com, 2002).

On this website, individuals seek others to share in their alternative lifestyle. Locating someone with similar interests is pretty easy. When searching for others, one could choose who they were looking for, the role (S & M) they which to participate in, age range, state, country, and type of sexual behaviour they were interested in. Before any search could take place, one must first become a member. Jennifer Thalken, the second author of this article, went online and collected all the data for this project as part of her Women's Studies Senior Seminar Project.

It was agreed prior by Jennifer, Diane Wysocki (the first author of this chapter), and a research methods class that Jennifer was taking at the time she was designing this project, that Jennifer would put her own basic information onto the website (except anything that would identify her) to collect the profiles that were used for the analysis and that she would not give her credit card information. To become a member each person had to answer questions about who they were (man, woman, group, etc.), what they were looking for (man woman, group, etc.), what activities they were looking for (email, phone fantasies, etc.), the behaviour they wanted to explore (props, devices, and or scenes), their birthday, where they lived, the language they spoke, and their email address. The next step was to search specific behaviours that interested the viewer. Upon clicking the *Browse* button, Jennifer went to the page that gave the user the ability to search by state or by country.

For this study, the criteria used were both men and women seeking others, over the age of 19 years, for any role, any behaviour, and in the United States. The website gave a list of men and women seeking others. However, because the subscription was free, it limited the search to only ten profiles a day. Over a period of two weeks, 45 profiles for men and 35 profiles for women for a total of 80 profiles were collected. Jennifer Thalken had no interaction with anyone who placed an ad on the website. She only collected their profiles, printed them out, and filed them in a notebook under the category in which they belonged, such as, women looking for men, men looking for women, and men/women looking for groups. The profiles were randomly selected by the computer because of the free subscription. If we had decided to pay for a subscription we would have had more control over the random selection of the profiles, but since this was a student project, it was decided that no credit card information would be given. As a result only the free computer generated profiles were those that were coded and the data placed into SPSS. While we could have collected more, we made the decision to stop at 80 because there were so many variables that were going to be coded that it was decided that 80 members were enough to collect for the scope of this project.

The individuals whose personal ads were analysed ranged in age from 19–52 years for females and from 25–66 years for males. The mean age in this study was almost 40 years. This is similar to other studies that suggest that respondents are older individuals rather than those in their early 20s (Donnelly & Fraser, 1998). Therefore, they knew what they wanted. The majority of both males or females had higher than a college degree, were some other religion besides Christian or Catholic, and had a variety of occupations, as shown in Table 13.1.

Table 13.1 Demographic description of respondents

	Female	Male	Total
Sex	43.8%	56.3%	100%
Age (mean)	38.11	39.73	39.03
SD	8.0	8.68	8.37
Education			
High School graduate	5.3	1.3	6.7
Some College	12.0	8.0	20.0
Associates Degree	6.7	1.3	8.0
BA/BS	9.3	24.0	33.3
Some Graduate School	2.7	16.0	18.7
MA/MS/MBA	5.3	5.3	10.7
MD/PhD	1.3	1.3	2.7
Religion			
Christian	2.5	10.1	12.7
Catholic	6.3	6.3	12.7
Other	26.6	39.2	65.8
New Age/Pagan	7.6	1.3	8.9
Profession			
Prefer not to say	8.9	6.3	15.2
Engineer or technical	3.8	19.0	22.8
Medical (nursing or doctor)	3.8	0.0	3.8
	10.1	16.5	26.6
Business	2.5	0.0	2.5
Clerical (officer or shop)	.0	1.3	1.3
Design (architect or fashion)	2.5	2.5	5.1
	.0	1.3	1.3
Education	1.3	0.0	1.3
Government	10.1	10.0	20.3
Location of the advertiser			
Pacific	12.5	5.0	17.5
West Coast	2.5	3.8	6.3
Midwest	12.5	10.0	22.5
South and South East	3.8	22.5	26.3
East and New England	10.0	15.0	25.0
Did not answer	2.5	0.0	2.5
Sexual orientation			
Heterosexual	3.8	16.3	20.0
Bisexual	22.5	15.0	37.5
Homosexual	2.5	5.0	7.5
Prefer not to say	3.8	1.3	5.0
Open to anything	6.3	12.5	18.8
Curious	3.8	6.3	10.0
Transgender	1.3	.0	1.3

While the profiles were from all over the United States and individuals were able to find people in their own area, it was not necessary to meet someone in their own area because most people were willing to travel if they found someone they were interested in online. The profiles were divided into five regions using the state and regional atlas of the United States Environmental Protection Agency. Many people said they would travel if they found someone who interested them for further play. Furthermore, the Internet, chat rooms, video conference, and cameras make sexual play on the Internet very easy to do (Wysocki, 1998). Where someone lives is no barrier. The majority, 37.5 per cent of both males and females, stated they were bisexual, while 10 per cent said they were just curious. Other studies support this data and have found that S & M is popular among those who are educated, middle and upper classes, and both male and female (Alison et al., 2001; Apostolides, 1999; Sandnabba et al., 1999; Weinberg, 1987). That is not surprising considering the alternative lifestyle they are exploring. The cost of the travel and equipment and the time it takes would attract educated people with above average incomes.

Sex

The majority of advertisements displayed photographs in their ads. Surprisingly, many of the photos included face shots, and many included photos of their genitals. For men, they were often erect and stroking themselves or having themselves stroked by someone else in the picture. Most men mentioned the size of their penis. Women, on the other hand, were displayed in sexy lingerie and not-often-revealing shots. If they were revealing, their breasts were showing or they were bent over and their buttocks were showing. Rarely was there a picture of an exposed vagina.

As shown in Table 13.2, more females (19 per cent) than males (13.9 per cent) preferred the submissive role, and more men (21.5 per cent) were willing to switch between being dominant and submissive. Almost an equal number of males (30 per cent) and females (32.5 per cent) were looking for men to become involved with, while more males were looking for women (46.3 per cent), couples (36.3 per cent), gay couples (18.8 per cent), lesbian couples (20.0 per cent), and groups (25 per cent). Donnelly and Fraser (1998) suggest that there are gender differences and they might be due to the scripts that men and women learn when they are growing up. For instance, if women are socialised to be reluctant to express their sexual desires, they are then more hesitant about new sexual

Table 13.2 Percentages of sexual behaviours of the respondents

	Female	Male	Total
Preferred sexual role			
Dominant	11.4	12.7	24.1
Submissive	19.0	13.9	32.9
Switch between the two	8.9	21.5	30.4
Prefer not to say	5.1	7.6	12.7
Looking for men	32.5	30.0	62.5
Looking for women	26.3	46.3	72.5
Looking for a couple	15.0	36.3	51.3
Looking for a gay couple	3.8	18.8	22.5
Looking for a lesbian couple	8.8	20.0	28.8
Looking for groups	7.5	25.0	32.5
Interested in erotic email exchange	5.0	12.5	17.5
Interested in performing only with little or no contact	8.8	12.5	21.3
Interested in watching only with little or no contact	6.3	13.8	20.0
Interested in active participation	42.5	55.0	97.5

experiences such as S & M. This could be why women are more likely to want to be submissive than men.

Both males and females were looking for erotic email exchange (17.5 per cent), performing (21.3 per cent), and watching via video camera (20.0 per cent) with little or no actual contact. However, the majority of those who posted ads on the Internet (97.5 per cent) were interested in active participation. This means they wanted to meet each other. Wysocki (1998) found in her study of sex in an online chat line that 57 per cent of her respondents had already met someone face-to-face who they developed contact with initially online. It seems that the point of the Internet is to make the connection for the face-to-face meetings. But even Alt.com gives guidelines for 'going offline for a meeting' and warns 'don't head straight to the dungeon for your first meeting', but to always meet in a public place, stay in a public place and bring a cell phone. If all goes well, then set up another date.

Participants were looking for all different types of sexual behaviour as shown in Table 13.3. They had the option of checking boxes of the behaviours they were interested in. They could check as many as they wanted. As shown, the majority of those who placed ads were interested in bondage, ass play, dildos, and toys. After that the behaviours vary. While the individuals who placed ads were given many options, no one

188

Table 13.3 Percentage of sadomasochistic behaviours and role-plays

Behaviour *(http://alt.com/go/page/glossary.html?site=bdsm&trlid= mag_cover-1)*	% N = 80
Bondage – The generic term for practising tying or restraint. Bondage takes many forms, including elaborate rope bondage, chains, metal handcuffs, or leather restraints, as examples.	67.5
Ass play – Everything from drooling, spitting on, licking and eating around the asshole (rimming), to inserting dildos, beads, cocks, fists, and various other creative things (hopefully not food!) into the ass (arse).	66.3
Dildos – A dildo is inserted into the rectum. There are various sizes, from finger size to enormous.	55.0
Toys – Equipment used in an S & M scene; aka, tool, gear, equipment.	46.3
Domination – To be dominated by a Master/Mistress. This includes obeying instructions, carrying out tasks, humiliation, and being dominated generally. Domination, in its strictest definition, is largely psychological play and is distinct from 'topping' which refers to physical S & M.	38.8
Face slapping – Slapping someone's face with an open hand.	38.8
Spanking – Involves using the hand on someone's bare butt cheeks so they turn flaming red.	35.5
Whips – The sharp crack of a whip is a staple in BDSM games. Whips can be used gently and sensually or to turn someone's bare butt cheeks flaming red.	35.0
Oral fixation – Oral sex.	33.8
Vibrators – Sex toys that run on batteries and vibrate that can be inserted into the vagina or the rectum.	33.8
Clothespins – Clothespins, clips, often metal, sometimes clothes pegs, which are attached to the nipples, or genitals.	30.0
Masturbation – Giving oneself sexual relief or pleasure, whether male or female.	28.8
Gang banging – Usually one person getting fucked by many, but could also refer to orgies.	27.5
Leather outfits – Leather is not only the product, but also can be a keyword for a type of lifestyle. Leathermen are usually gay males who also are into BDSM. It can imply an 'old guard' sort of mentality where discipline is stricter and rules of interaction apply.	25.0
Blindfolds – From a make-shift scarf to custom leather eye covering, blindfolds are used in bondage and D/s situations or in vanilla sex to create helplessness, dependence, vulnerability, and/or to heighten other senses and intensify sensation play.	23.8

Breast torture – Erotic play that involves binding the breasts   23.8
tightly. *Generally it involves restraints (rope, rubber, etc.) that
encircle each breast tightly where it joins the chest. The breasts
and nipples become engorged with blood and exquisitely sensitive
to the slightest touch. Stroking, clamping, or whipping can cause
intense pain and/or pleasure.*

Exhibitionism – People getting off by exposing themselves, either   22.5
*alone or with a partner, in public places, or even in their homes if
they're aware they can be seen by neighbours, etc.*

Power exchange – A person who can 'switch' between being either   22.5
*a dominant or a submissive. Switching is quite common amongst
lifestyle Masters/Mistresses, but is rarely part of professional
sessions.*

Rimming – The act of licking the anal rim of another person in   21.3
order to gain and/or give sexual pleasure.

Voyeurism – For those who like to watch. *Broadly speaking, it   21.3
refers to being sexually aroused simply by watching other people
engage in sexual activity.*

Water sports – Practice where the dominant urinates on the   21.3
*submissive. Watersports includes 'golden showers' (q.v.) and may
also include 'toilet training' (q.v.). Also known as urolagnia.*

Cock binding – A ring made from metal, rubber or leather, worn   20.0
*round the base of the penis to control blood flow. A cock ring can
either help sustain an erection or prevent one if applied to a
flaccid penis.*

Fist fucking – A hand is inserted into the anus or vagina, usually   20.0
*one finger at a time. Getting the knuckle spread (the widest point
of the hand) through the opening is usually the most difficult part
of the process; after this point you are well and truly 'fisting'. The
process takes a lot of lubrication. It also takes patience on the part
of the dominant and openness and relaxation on the part of the
submissive.*

Handcuffs – Handcuffs are pre-made to bind hands to each other   20.0
*or to a stationary object – as opposed to rope or other bondage
methods. They have history and association – police, prison, etc. –
which makes them for fantasy play*

Wax – Hot candle wax dripped on the body is an effective means   20.0
of inflicting pain

24/7–24-hours, 7 days a week. *Where the sub lives with, and is   18.8
controlled by, the Master/Mistress on that basis.*

Collar and lead – Worn to denote submissiveness or slavery to a   17.5
particular Master/Mistress.

Table 13.3 (Continued)

Behaviour (http://alt.com/go/page/glossary.html?site=bdsm&trlid= mag_cover-1)	% N = 80
Cross dressing – To dress in the clothing of the opposite sex. Usually applies to men dressing as women, in heels, dresses, nylons, bras, women's underwear, and so forth, but may also apply to women.	13.8
Hair pulling – Usually part of rough play and brat play, like biting. Can also be used as a kind of bondage to incapacitate a person's head by holding tightly to the hair.	13.8
Shaving – Shaving hair anywhere on the body for excitement.	12.8
Enema – An enema is used to fill the colon with water or other liquid. Often used in medical scenes.	12.5
Chains – Erotic appeal drawn from chains, manifested in ornamentation (dog collars, etc.), in bondage activities (shackling legs together, etc.) or as leads and other symbols of 'ownership' (dog-leash).	11.3
Lace – Getting erotic pleasure from dressing in, viewing, or playing with silky/lacy items and fabrics	8.8
Body odours – Sexual stimulation from either good or bad body odour.	7.5
Electric shocks – Various devices delivering electric impulses or wave forms (e-stim) and applied to the skin for everything from sensation play to pain. It's often applied to genitalia and nipples and other sensitive areas, and as such can be part of great sexual arousal as well as heavy torture scenes – depending on the implement and the degree.	7.5
Latex – A type of rubber used in the fetish fashion world for a skin tight fit.	6.3
Tongue fetish – Someone who likes to use their tongue on another person for pleasure.	6.3
Chastity devices – Devices placed on both male and female genitalia to prevent sex. A dominant may put a chastity device on his/her submissive to show or exert control over the sub's sexual being.	5.0
Cupping (suction of the skin) – A process originating in traditional Chinese healing, but used as sensation play and for temporary marking. After creating a heat differential between the inside and outside of a glass cup, the skin is sucked up into the cup creating temporary circular mounds on the skin.	5.0

Mask, blindfold – Usually found at fetish balls, used by primitivists, and in-scene. Dominants may use them to create heightened sense of danger/arousal in a submissive or by submissives as a kind of sensory deprivation	5.0
Piercing – Either temporary or permanent. If temporary, needles are used and removed at the end of the scene. There are many kinds of body piercing which are permanent, including piercings to the genitalia and nipples.	5.0
Chinese balls – Inserted into the rectum and pulled out at the moment of orgasm. Chinese balls are said to increase the pleasure of the orgasm tremendously.	3.8
High heels – Having a thing for them or wearing them (esp. cross-dressing). In play, they can be worshipped and licked, or they can step on and crush.	3.8
Caging – A metal cage in which the submissive is locked as part of a scene. The related term 'cage of little ease' implies a cage which is so small that the submissive cannot rest in a comfortable position.	2.5
Feathers – A form of sensation play, used in warm-up to foreplay, massage, or sadistic pain, or to offer temporary relief from sadistic pain.	2.5
Slings, crosses – Being hung up, or suspended, by the tied wrists, wrists and ankles or even feet.	2.5
Knives, razor – Knife play can be any play involving a knife, for example using a knife erotically, especially around the genitals or nipples. The knife itself has erotic appeal and there's an appeal that comes from suggestions of danger to actual risk. Extreme knife play gets into cutting and scarification.	1.3
Rubber outfits – Worn or used in scenes. It is possible to acquire a massive wardrobe of clothing and toys.	1.3
Role Playing	26.3
Nurse/doctor	30.0
Rape scenes	27.5
Nun/Priest play	1.3

in this sample said they were interested in shit play, diapers, branding, or blood.

Almost one-third of the profiles stated they were interested in role playing. This makes sense given that S & M is really about acting out who is in charge and who is not. Some were interested in the roles of nurse/doctor, and a surprisingly large number were interested in rape scenes.

What the profiles say

Everyone who placed a profile on Alt.com was able to give a lot of detail about themselves and what they wanted besides being given the option of checking boxes about descriptions and behaviour information. The participants were very clear about what they want, and that makes posting online appealing (Ross, 2005; Wysocki, 1998). Participants can ask for what they want and another individual can read through the ads. If they see something that they are attracted to they can respond. If not, they go to the next ad. For instance, 'Love Grey' considers himself a gay novice. He has pierced nipples and would like other piercings, but says that he wants an older gray haired man to take over his body for his own pleasure. He says is also fascinated with electrotorture, but has never tried it.

Goffman (1963) believes that if an individual possesses attributes that discredits them in the eyes of others, it can greatly affect their self-concept of themselves and the way they interact with other people. The anonymity of the Internet allows the individuals to conceal themselves in a way to avoid receiving negative reactions from others and therefore provides a shield against stigma. Furthermore, the Internet is said to attract disproportionately those who might be stigmatised if their sexual interest should become known to others (Ross, 2005). Love Grey is not likely to ask someone in his face-to-face network of friends to electro-torture with him because the risk of stigma is just too large, but that risk is not so big online. As a result, asking for exactly what he wants and hoping he finds someone who has a similar interest is the perfect use of the Internet. In another example, 'Dog' might not be willing to say the following in a face-to-face group, but it is much easier behind the shield of his computer.

> I am looking for a LARGE COCK to fuck me HARD after I suck your cock to the brink...I don't play games, I just love to fuck hard and be fucked hard...One-timers are fine but it would also be nice to be able to rely on regular FUCK FESTS and I am MORE THAN WILLING to be USED & ABUSED. GANG BANGS or MULTIPLE FUCKS are welcomes; and quite honestly desired. NO PICTURES, NO RESPONSES!!! [Capitals are in the ad.]

Dog had four pictures that showed his naked shaved penis.

The Internet also provides room for individuals to express the 'unex-plored parts of themselves' (Turkle, 1995). Users can take on completely different identities and portray themselves as someone they might just be only in their fantasies. 'Stephanie' says she is a cross-dresser. She might not be able to be this in her real life, so she is able to explore this side of 'herself' online. She says she is bored with toys and 'needs to feel a warm dick in my ass and needs another cross dresser to fulfill me in every way'. She also says she wants her first encounter to be with a cross dresser who is passable because she is not just looking for a man to 'fuck me... I want a (wo)man who knows what it is like to be sexy!' It seems to be the same for 'Sub69' who is male, single, and looking for a dominant lady to serve and service. He goes on to say:

> I beg your forgiveness for my ignorance and inexperience about the proper terminology and protocol, but am willing to learn. I am looking for a local lady who would train me to meet all of your needs and who would find and push my limits. I beg that you please give a worthless sub a chance to prove his willingness to serve and please.

Since meeting the perfect sexual partner is not always easy (Wysocki, 1998), it makes sense that if someone finds another who can fulfil their sexual fantasies on the Internet, they are going to meet each other face-to-face. As we stated earlier, many of the profiles said they wanted to eventually meet the individuals in person. The Internet is just a vehicle to set up the meeting of those with similar sexual interests and a way of narrowing the field to find those with very specific sexual interests.

Discussion

In conclusion, this content analysis of advertisements on an S & M web site found that people used it for many different reasons. However, the most common reason was to meet people who had the same specific fantasies and desires so they could ultimately meet face-to-face to participate in S & M behaviours. The anonymity of this website and the ease in which one could get involved and place an ad made finding people with similar interests much easier than finding them in their face-to-face world. The Internet is the modern day vehicle for the older paper versions of the personal ads. Furthermore, the advancements of technology allow for the ease of matching those with similar interests. All the profiles need to do is check the boxes of the behaviours that interest them and the website plays matchmaker. The rest is up to them.

References

Alison, L., Santtila, P., Sandnabba, N. K., & Nordling, N. (2001). Sadomasochistically oriented behavior: Diversity in practice and meaning. *Archives of Sexual Behavior, 30* (1), 11–12.

Alt.com. (2002). *World's largest BDSM & alternative lifestyle personals.* Retrieved 3 October 2002, from: http://alt.com

Apostolides, M. (1999). The pleasure of the pain. *Psychology Today, 32* (6), 60–6.

Binik, Y. M., Mah, K., & Kiesler, S. (1999). Ethical issues in conducting sex research on the Internet. *Journal of Sex Research, 36* (1), 82–93.

Bright, S. (1992). *Susie Bright's sexual reality: A virtual sex world reader.* California: Cleis Press.

Brown, J. D. (2002). Mass media influences on sexuality. *Journal of Sex Research, 39* (1), 42–6.

Coveney, L., Jackson, M., Jeffreys, S., Kay, L., & Mahony, P. (1984). *The sexuality papers.* London: Hutchinson.

Doctor, R. (1988). *Transvestites and transsexuals: Toward a theory of cross-gender behavior.* New York: Plenum Press.

Donnelly, D., & Fraser, J. (1998). Gender differences in sado-masochistic arousal among college students. *Sex Roles: A Journal of Research, 39* (5–6), 391–408.

Ellis, H. (1926). *Studies in the psychology of sex: Analysis of the sexual impulses, love and pain and the sexual impulses in women* (Original work published in 1903) (2nd edn.). Philadelphia: F. A. Davis.

Elmer-Dewitt, P. (1995, 3 July). On a screen near you: Cyberporn. *Time Magazine,* 38–43.

Else-Quest, N. M., Hyde, J. S., & DeLamater, J. D. (2005). Context counts: long-term sequelae of premarital intercourse or abstinence. *Journal of Sex Research, 42* (2), 102–13.

Ernulf, K. E., & Innalla, S. M. (1995). Sexual bondage: A review and unobtrusive investigation. *Archives of Sexual Behavior, 24* (6), 631–55.

Fergunson, A. (1989). *Blood at the root: Motherhood, sexuality and male dominance.* London: Pandora.

Foucault, M. (1978). *History of sexuality (Vol. 1).* New York: Pantheon.

Freud, S. (1961). *Beyond the pleasure principle* (Original work published in 1920) (J. Strachey, trans.). New York: Liveright.

Freud, S. (1962). *Three essays on the theory of sexuality.* New York: Basic Books, Inc.

Gagnon, J., & Simon, W. (1973). *Sexual conduct: The social sources of human sexuality.* Chicago, IL: University of Chicago Press.

Giddens, A. (1992). *The transformation of intimacy: Sexuality, love and eroticism in modern societies.* London: Hutchinson.

Goffman, E. (1963). *Stigman: Notes on the management of spoiled identity.* Englewood Cliffs, NJ: Prentice-Hall.

Green, R. (1987). *The 'sissy boy syndrome' and the development of homosexuality.* London: Yale University Press.

Groom, C. J., & Pennebaker, J. W. (2005). The language of love: Sex, sexual orientation, and language use in online personal advertisements. *Sex Roles: A Journal of Research, 52* (7/8), 447–61.

Horney, K. (1967). *Feminine psychology.* New York: Norton.

InterCommerce Corporation. (2005). *Survey.Net sex survey.* Retrieved 16 December 2005, from: http://www.survey.net/sex1r.html

Jones, S. (1999). Ethics and Internet studies. *Iowa Journal of Communications, 31* (1), 1–7.

Kinsey, A. C. (1953). *Sexual behaviour in the human female.* Philadelphia, PA: Saunders Co.

Koch, S. C., Mueller, B., Kruse, L., & Zumbach, J. (2005). Constructing gender in chat groups. *Sex Roles: A Journal of Research, 53* (1/2), 29–41.

Krafft-Ebing, R. V. (1965). *Phychopathia sexualis* (Original work published in 1886) (F. S. T. Klaf, trans.). New York: Stein and Day.

Langer, G., Arnedt, C., & Sussman, D. (2004). *Primetime live poll: American sex survey. A peek beneath the sheets. ABC primetime.* Retrieved 8 February 2006, from: http://www.abcnews.go.com/Primetime/print?id=156921

Langstrom, N., & Zucker, K. J. (2005). Transvestic fetishism in the general population: prevalence and correlates update. *Canadian Journal of Human Sexuality, 13* (3–4), 193.

Laws, J., & Schwartz, P. (1977). *Sexual scripts: The social construction of female sexuality.* Washington, DC: United Press of America.

LeMasters, C. (2002, March/April). Confessions of an S/M leatherdyke. *Gay and Lesbian Review, March/April,* 15–17.

Masters, W. H., Johnson, V. E., & Kolodny, R. C. (1986). *Masters and Johnson on sex and human loving.* Boston: Little, Brown.

Michener, H. A., DeLamater, J. D., Schwartz, S. H., & Merton, R. K. (1990). *Social psychology 2nd Edition.* San Diego, CA: Harcourt Brace Jovanovich.

Rheingold, H. (1993). *The virtual community: Homesteading on the electronic frontier.* Reading, MA: Addison-Wesley.

Ross, M. W. (2005). Typing, doing and being: Sexuality and the Internet. *Journal of Sex Research, 42* (4), 342–53.

Sandnabba, N. K., Santtila, P., & Nordling, N. (1999). Sexual behavior and social adaptation among sadomasochistically-oriented males. *Journal of Sex Research, 36* (3), 273–82.

Santtila, P., Sandnabba, N. K., Alison, L., & Nordling, N. (2002). Investigating the underlying structure in sadomasochistically oriented behaviour. *Archives of Sexual Behaviour, 31,* 185–96.

Schroer, T. J. (1999). Studying your enemy: Ethical guidelines for online research. *Iowa Journal of Communications, 31* (1), 68–77.

Shortes, C. (1998). 'Cleaning up a sewer': The containment of S/M pornography. *Journal of Popular Film and Television, 26* (2), 72–80.

Simon, W., & Gagnon, J. (1984). Sexual scripts. *Society, November/December,* 53–60.

Simon, W. & Gagnon, J. (1998). Psychosexual development. *Society, 35* (2), 60–8.

Strassberg, D. S., & Holty, S. (2003). An experimental study of women's Internet personal ads. *Archives of Sexual Behavior, 32* (3), 253–60.

Turkle, S. (1995). *Life on the screen: Identity in the age of the Internet.* New York: Simon and Schuster.

Vance, C. (1993). *Pleasure and danger.* New York: New York University Press.

Wassersug, R. J., Zelenietz, S. A., & Squire, G. F. (2004). New age eunuchs: motivation and rationale for voluntary castration. *Archives of Sexual Behavior, 33* (5), 433–43.

Weeks, J. (1986). *The invention of sexuality.* New York: Tavistock.

Weinberg, M. S., Williams, C. J. & Calhan, C. (1994). Homosexual foot fetishism. *Archives of Sexual Behavior, 23* (6), 611–17.

Weinberg, T. S. (1987). Sadomasochism in the United States: A review of recent sociological literature. *Journal of Sex Research, 23* (1), 50–69.

Wysocki, D. K. (1993). Construction of masculinity: A look into the lives of heterosexual male transvestites. *Feminism and Psychology, 3* (2), 374–80.

Wysocki, D. K. (1998). Let your fingers do the talking: Sex on an adult chat-line. *Sexualities, 1* (4), 425–52.

Wysocki, D. K. (1999). Virtual sociology: Using computers in research. *Iowa Journal of Communication, 31*(1), 59–67.

14
Conclusion

Monica T. Whitty

The Internet has become a part of our everyday lives. The number of individuals using the Internet is continuing to grow, as well as the number of hours individuals spend online. In fact, the Internet has become so popular in the UK that the average Briton spends more time logged onto the Internet than watching television (Johnson, 2006). As reported in our tome, individuals are flocking to the Internet to find romantic partners (Madden & Lenhart, 2006). Yahoo.com claims almost 380 million visitors per month to their online dating site (Pasha, 2005), and FriendFinder.com say they have over 2.6 million active members (Dating Sites Reviews.com, n.d.). Social networking sites like Myspace, where romantic matches are often made, are also increasing in popularity. So much so, that the Nielsen 'netratings' report that Myspace has received 384 million unique visitors with a year-on-year growth of 367 per cent (Bausch & Han, 2006).

Our book has provided examples of the numerous ways individuals meet online. Some of these spaces were not set up with the intention to facilitate romance. For example, DeVoss (this volume) tells us how love blossomed in the early days of the bulletin board system. However, other spaces are set up for individuals to find a romantic match. Some of these online dating companies have attempted to take a scientific approach to matchmaking (see Whitty & Carr, 2006a). Whitty (this volume) and McKenna (this volume) describe how relationships initiate and develop on online dating sites. These authors concur that individuals can feel freer online to experiment with identity and explore presentations of self. Whitty and McKenna in their chapters also explain how the trajectory of relationships that initiate on online dating sites can be quite different to how relationships progress in other spaces online.

Pop psychology books abound that provide the online dater with advice on how to best go about winning over a mate. Topics include what information they should place on their profile, how they should initially communicate with a potential date, how quickly they should respond to emails from others from the site, and how to go about that first face-to-face meeting. Paasonen (this volume) points out that these books are mostly written for women. Earlier researchers envisaged the Internet as a utopian space where one might be liberated from traditional gender roles (Turkle, 1995). Paasonen demonstrates that cyberspace has not lived up to this utopian dream. These advice books instruct women to take on their traditional passive roles.

It is perhaps no wonder that so many advice books on online dating exist. As a number of the chapters in our book demonstrate, online dating is no 'easy street'. Whitty (this volume) presents her BAR approach theory, which contends that successful online daters need to construct a profile with a balance between an 'attractive' and a 'real' self. Baker (this volume) suggests that individuals need to be skilled at displaying their emotions and feelings online. Given that the traditional face-to-face expressions and body movements that convey emotions are typically absent online, individuals need to find new ways to express themselves. Baker suggests that this can be done through the use of emoticons and acronyms. Displaying emotions through text is obviously an important skill to have if love is to grow in cyberspace.

Meeting and developing romantic relationships via online dating sites are very different to meeting in other spaces online. McKenna, Green, and Gleason (2002) have found that individuals communicating in newsgroups gradually self-disclose details about themselves to potential romantic partners. Whitty and Gavin (2001) found this was the case in chat rooms. On online dating sites, however, self-disclosure is not gradual (McKenna, this volume; Whitty, this volume; Whitty & Carr, 2006a). Unlike in many other online spaces individuals are presented with a plethora of information prior to communicating with a potential date. Although this is less conventional than other forms of dating, there are parallels between online and other forms of dating that have been around prior to the advent of the Internet. For example, Horning (this volume) and Whitty (this volume) compare online dating with newspaper personal ads. Both types of dating, as well as video dating (Whitty, this volume) provide descriptions of the advertiser as well as what characteristics the advertiser is looking for in a potential date. Interestingly, similar strategies that men and women use to find a suitable date are used in each of these dating arenas.

Online dating is perhaps a little like selling and shopping (Whitty & Carr, 2006a). One might even say that it is shares much in common with eBay. For instance, on online dating sites individuals need to present themselves as a valued commodity (Whitty & Carr, 2006a). Moreover, they employ strategies to test out whether they are getting the genuine product. Horning (this volume) compares personal ads and job ads. Quite rightly, she believes that a personal profile is similar to a résumé. Individuals need to present their positive qualities in both personal ads and résumés and are unlikely to point out their negative points. Perhaps for online daters that first date is akin to a job interview where individuals use it as a screening process – more than an actual date (Whitty, 2006).

Sexual partners are also sought out online. Sometimes people seek out others to have casual flings with offline, and at other times people seek out individuals with similar sexual interests. Mathy (this volume) provides descriptive statistics on how homosexuals, heterosexuals, and bi-sexuals use the Internet to arrange offline sexual meetings. Wysocki and Thalken (this volume) examine less traditional personal ads – those looking for others with particular sadomasochistic fetishes. We find here that cyberspace is a safe space to self-disclose about one's sexual desires. However, it does not remain there. As Wysocki and Thalken demonstrate, individuals use the Internet to seek out individuals with similar sexual interests so that they can live out their fantasies face-to-face.

Of course some individuals do not hope to meet up with their cyberspace play-mates. Some hope to remain friends in this space, while others hope to live out their sexual fantasies within cyberspace. Hamman (this volume) provides some interesting examples of his observations of sexual encounters in the early days of the Internet. Mathy (this volume) considers who is more likely to engage in sexual activities in cyberspace. There still remains the contentious argument of whether it is healthy to live out one's sexual experiences online (Cooper, Delmonico, & Burg, 2000).

Many of the chapters in our book suggest that cyberspace provides some wonderful new opportunities for individuals to seek out friends and romantic partners. People often feel more comfortable to self-disclose to others in this space. Cyberspace makes it easy for individuals to seek out like-minded others. Those who might have given up hope for love have renewed hope now that we have the Internet. However, cyberspace is not a bed of roses. New skills are required to attract others (Whitty, this volume) and to express oneself in this space (Baker, this volume). More than this, as with the offline world, not everyone who inhabits the cyberworld is a savoury character.

People lie online, and sometimes more so than they would offline (Whitty, 2002). This is perhaps because of the lack of social presence online – where people might feel less accountable. Albright (this volume) provides evidence that individuals can be quite deceptive in cyberspace. One way that they are deceptive is by maintaining multiple relationships in cyberspace. Albright suggests this is easy, not just because of the lack of social presence, but also because the exact same romantic email can be sent to many online lovers simultaneously. Moreover, individuals can be engaging in romantic chat with a number of lovers at the same time via chat rooms or by using Instant Messenger.

Spitzberg and Cupach (this volume) and Jerin and Dolinsky (this volume) explain how online dating is not always a safe experience. Cyber-harassment and cyberstalking are evident online – between strangers, work colleagues, and online daters (Whitty and Carr, 2006a, 2006b). Spitzberg and Cupach discuss that often the stalker is someone known to the victim. They may be an ex-partner of the victim or an individual who unrealistically believed they had a chance with the victim and is not able to let go of their hope for a happy ending. Jerin and Dolinsky report their results from a survey of women who had used an online dating service. They provide details of an array of cyber-harassing experiences. Given these experiences, it comes as no surprise that online dating sites often provide safety tips for their clients.

The authors in this book, in the main, suggest that in the future many individuals will continue to find their romantic and sexual partners in cyberspace. How they do so, however, will probably change. As Whitty and Carr (2006a) state: 'how we develop online relationships and engage in cyberspace will modify as technology is developed and as people discover new ways to utilise this space' (p. 190). They also predict that online dating sites will work more at developing scientific tools for more successful matchmaking. Moreover, less formal online dating will probably take place on sites such as Myspace. Lovers will also continue to meet via blogs and mobile phones. Specialised sites for individuals with less traditional sexual fetishes will continue to sprout online. So what does the future hold for online matchmaking? The authors here suggest that cyberspace promises to offer more ways and opportunities for individuals to initiate and engage in online relationships and sex. Moreover, in the future individuals will become more skilled and savvy at developing relationships and engaging in sexual activities in this space.

References

Bausch, S., & Han, L. (2006, May). Successful sites drive high visitor retention rates. (Nielsen/netratings). Retrieved 14 May 2006 from: http://www.nielsen-netratings.com/pr/pr_060511.pdf

Cooper, A., Delmonico, D. L., & Burg, R. (2000). Cybersex users, abusers, and compulsives: New findings and implications. *Sexual addiction and compulsivity*, 7(2), 5–29.

Dating Sites Reviews.com (n.d.). Retrieved 13 April 2006, from: http://www.datingsitesreviews.com/staticpages/index.php?page=2010000100-FriendFinder

Johnson, B. (2006, March). Britain turns off – and logs on. *Guardian*, 8 March 2006, Retrieved 25 March 2006 from: http://technology.guardian.co.uk/news/story/0,,1726018,00.html

Madden, M., & Lenhart, A. (2006, March). *Online dating*. (Pew Internet & American Life Project). Retrieved 22 March 2006, from: http://www.pewinternet.org/pdfs/PIP_Online_Dating.pdf

McKenna, K. Y. A., Green, A. S., & Gleason, M. E. J. (2002). Relationship formation on the Internet: What's the big attraction? *Journal of Social Issues, 58*, 9–31.

Pasha, S. (2005, August). Online dating feeling less attractive. *CNN/Money*, 18 August 2005, Retrieved 13 April 2006 from: http://money.cnn.com/2005/08/18/technology/online_dating/index.htm

Turkle, S. (1995). *Life on the screen: Identity in the age of the Internet*. London: Weidenfeld & Nicolson.

Whitty, M. T. (2002). Liar, Liar! An examination of how open, supportive and honest people are in Chat Rooms. *Computers in Human Behavior, 18* (4), 343–52.

Whitty, M. T. (2006, May). Online dating strategies: Balancing an 'attractive' self with an 'actual self'. *Nottingham Trent University*, 10 May 2006.

Whitty, M. T. & Carr, A. N. (2006a). *Cyberspace romance: The psychology of online relationships*. Basingstoke: Palgrave Macmillan.

Whitty, M. T. & Carr, A. N. (2006b). New Rules in the workplace: Applying object-relations theory to explain problem Internet and email behavior in the workplace. *Computers in Human Behavior, 22* (2), 235–50.

Whitty, M. & Gavin, J. (2001). Age/sex/location: Uncovering the social cues in the development of online relationships. *CyberPsychology and Behaviour, 4* (5), 623–30.

Author Index

Subject Index